MIZPAH.
Christmas 1996

To Mam,
Have a great
Christmas and
New Year.
With all our love
always.
Katherine &
xx   Peter

HALF THE RACE

Crowds of more than 20 000 watched the Manly women's surf lifesaving team at their 1912 surf carnival. Percy Spence, *Women Lifesavers, Manly Beach*, 1910.

MANLY MUSEUM AND ART GALLERY

HALF THE
RACE

MARION K. STELL

A History
of Australian Women in Sport

An imprint of HarperCollins*Publishers*

FOR MY GRANDMOTHER
M. MAUDE COLLESS 1900–1973

AN ANGUS & ROBERTSON BOOK
An imprint of HarperCollinsPublishers

First published in Australia in 1991 by
CollinsAngus&Robertson Publishers Pty Limited (ACN 009 913 517)
A division of HarperCollinsPublishers (Australia) Pty Limited
4 Eden Park, 31 Waterloo Road, North Ryde, NSW 2113, Australia

HarperCollinsPublishers (New Zealand) Limited
31 View Road, Glenfield, Auckland 10, New Zealand

HarperCollinsPublishers Limited
77–85 Fulham Palace Road, London W6 8JB, United Kingdom

National Library of Australia
Cataloguing-in-Publication data:

Stell, Marion K.
   Half the race : a history of Australian women in sport
   Bibliography
   Includes index.

   ISBN 0 207 16971 3

   1. Women athletes — Australia — History.2. Sports —
   Australia — History. 3 Sports for women — Australia —
   History. 4. Women — Australia — Social conditions.
   I. Title.

796.082

Cover: Top *Photograph by Graham Monro, Stockshots.*
Left *Kathy Saxby. Photograph by Julie Howard, Stockshots.*
Right *Photograph by Clifford White, Stockshots.*
Printed in Australia by Griffin Press, Adelaide

 5   4   3   2   1
95 94 93 92 91

CONTENTS

ACKNOWLEDGMENTS

Thanks are due to Megan Mitchell . To Mary Johnston and Carolyn Walsh for reading parts of the manuscript and to Sue Hardisty.
To two groups who are light years apart at the Australian National University — members of the ANU Women's Cricket Club for their tolerance and conviviality, and members of the Division of Historical Studies, Research School of Social Sciences for their encouragement and interest.
To staff at the National Library of Australia; Jan Brazier at the ABC Archives; Jenny Ensbey at the Overseas Information Branch; Sally Penson, Women's Weightlifting; and Annie Quadroy, Executive Director, YWCA of Canberra.
To the women of the 1934/1935 and 1937 Australian cricket teams who were a delight to meet, an inspiration and a rich source of history.
And to my publisher Collins/Angus & Robertson. To Claire Craig, Liz Seymour and Melanie Feddersen and especially to Kim Anderson.

INTRODUCTION

Australian women's success in international sport has been nothing short of astonishing when you consider the encouragement, resources, facilities and sponsorship directed elsewhere. Women have won the most prestigious titles in the world, including Wimbledon, the USA Open Golf Championship and the British Squash Championship. Women's teams have been the world champions in netball, hockey, cricket, softball, lacrosse and waterpolo. Australian women's names have been etched in the record books of sport throughout the world. At the Commonwealth and Olympic Games generations of Australian women have crowded the victory dais. Over the years 940 women have represented their country at all the Games, winning an incredible 425 medals — 163 of them gold medals. But after the golden girl hype has died down and the gold dust has settled, women's sport is ultimately awarded a bronze medal in our national identity, a cultural third place behind sportsmen and racehorses.

What has caused this to happen? Although much of our sporting heritage, as well as the actual types of sport played, has been directly imported from Britain, the cultural exclusion of women's sport in Australia has occurred deliberately and independently of other countries. Such a situation, although worthy of investigation, would not be so important if sport could be dismissed as a mere pastime. But an understanding of the rules of the game is intrinsic to our society. It is needed in every situation where two adversaries meet — whether in business, in the law courts or in the playground. Sport provides discipline, leadership, co-operation, confidence, self-esteem and relaxation not readily available through any other medium.

The exclusion of women from the traditions of sport does not mean that they have actually been absent from the sporting fields. Women of all ages and classes have embraced the enjoyment, thrills and satisfaction derived from playing sport. By 1940 over one million women belonged to a registered sporting association. In 1990 it was estimated that one in seven Australian women played netball, with millions more regularly playing a multitude of other sports.

For women sport is a challenge. Having the leisure time to indulge in sport does not necessarily require money or the benefits of class, but it does involve a certain degree of selfishness and choice. From the weekend netballer to the professional athlete, a very deliberate decision has to be made to set aside some (or most) of their time for sport. This is contrary to many women's pre-assigned roles in life as the carers and nurturers of others.

Individual women must dare to challenge elements of the prevailing male-dominated culture just to walk onto the sportsfield. Those who do have faced a gamut of social hurdles in their sporting lives. Each has overcome these hurdles in her own way. At the beginning of this century sportswomen carried their hockey sticks in public when dressed in their ankle-length hockey skirts so that their 'daring' costumes would be excused. Australia's first Olympic athlete Edie Robinson used her time during her sea voyage to the 1928 Olympic Games in Amsterdam to convert her cumbersome official knee-length running bloomers into a more practical pair of shorts. Champion hurdler Shirley Strickland competed at the 1956 Olympic Games, ignoring the taunts by some sections of the Melbourne crowd to retire from sport and give someone younger a go. A woman from Newcastle in New South Wales entered and won her district's A-grade squash championship in 1975 despite being eight months pregnant.

For two centuries Australian women have struggled against forthright opposition to their participation in sport. They have been trivialised, banned, excluded, ignored, oppressed, degraded, unsung, discouraged—yet still they played on. After decades of medical argument, exclusive clubs and lower levels of funding, what is surprising is the enormous number of women who actually play sport.

To reconstruct the traditions of women's sport in Australia is also a challenge. The sources for the history of women in sport are scarce. Sometimes all that is left from another era is a faded photograph to prove that women played. Little attention has been accorded sportswomen in colonial or modern newspapers. Few memoirs exist and local histories give but a glimpse of their lives. But ordinary women as well as champions have their own strong sporting traditions.

To understand the place of Australian women in sport is to understand their position in society. This book is not only about which women in Australian history have been able to run the swiftest, swim the fastest, throw the furthest or hit the hardest, but which women have had access to sport, what types of sport have been played, what obstacles have been put in women's way and how they have overcome them. It is a story full of dedication, perseverance, persistence and courage.

COLONIAL
PLAYERS

1788–1900

IT IS NO ACCIDENT THAT
AUSTRALIA'S MOST FAMOUS SPORTSWOMEN ARE ALL FROM THE
TWENTIETH CENTURY. A conspiracy of silence has enshrouded the deeds of
colonial sportswomen — a cultural exclusion which was started by their male
contemporaries and relayed by generations of male sports commentators.
The literature on colonial women's participation in recreation, leisure and
sport is riddled with myth. From ill-informed and patronising articles to
token comments in general sporting histories, writers have hidden and
downplayed both the nature and the extent of women's physical activity.
Colonial women have been relegated historically to few sporting activities —
tennis and cycling in some publications, golf and archery, or croquet and
riding in others. But colonial women of all classes, in the cities as well as in
the country, were drawn in ever increasing numbers to the pleasures and fun
of a wide range of physical activity.

THE FUN BEGINS

In the early years of the colonies women inhabited three separate social
spheres — convict, free and Aboriginal. Each group had different ways of
spending what recreational time was available to them. Gambling was a

1

major component in most leisure activities. The colonists were prepared to stake a wager on horses in a race, on a hand of cards or on any sort of contest imaginable. White women participated in all the public diversions of the day, the most common being foot races, regattas, picnics, festive sports and horse races. The *Sydney Gazette* of 1810 recorded a day of 'humour and fun' held in Parramatta. Three women competitors who entered the sack race event managed to stay upright, the paper reported, but as such competence was not 'altogether answerable to the wishes of the spectators, the sacks were soon disburdened of their fair contents, and the prize was given to the lucky fair one'. Walking matches, known as pedestrianism, were popular among women and some of the more unusual ones were noticed by the colonial press. In 1817 a 68-year-old Hobart woman was challenged to walk up and down a steep hill 50 times in 12 hours for a wager of five shillings. The *Hobart Town Gazette* reported that the elderly woman was confident of success. She needed to be optimistic, she had been walking with the aid of crutches for seven years.

Skiing was well established at Kiandra, NSW by the early 1860s. Photograph by Charles Kerry, c. 1900.
NATIONAL LIBRARY OF AUSTRALIA.

The women who accompanied their marine corps husbands had more time and freedom for outdoor recreational pursuits. These consisted of formal occasions as well as picnics, outings and camping expeditions. Occasionally they embarked upon walking excursions. One group set out in 1809 on a four day excursion to Cow Pasture Plains, outside Sydney. Annie Baxter of Hobart recorded that she went on a picnic-type expedition which lasted several days, in the course of which she climbed Ben Lomond Mountain. As the country was opened up in the second half of the century, women's expeditions reached as far as snowfields like Kiandra, New South Wales, where women indulged in skiing, tobogganing and cross-country skiing.

The simplest recreational diversions in every social sphere were games. The merchant Sarah Packer advertised cards for sale from her Sydney shop in 1810. Many forms of card games became popular in the colonies with all classes of women, especially in the more remote areas. Ann Dixon absconded from her employment as a housemaid and was later apprehended enjoying a game of cards and a drink. Jane Eliza, who sat in on a card game at the Governor's Ball in Perth in 1832, first lost heavily, then regained her finances during the course of the night. Various forms of table and parlour games were common among more well-to-do women and their daughters. Margaret May played blind man's buff, hunt the slipper, chess and backgammon in South Australia in 1844. The parlour game 'table-turning' was played by Lady Caroline Denison and her guests at an evening at Government House in Hobart in 1853. The publication *Australian Etiquette* listed a great variety of indoor amusements played in the colonies by the upper classes in 1885 including dancing, private theatricals, twirl the platter, forfeits, schoolmaster and cotton flies.

Aboriginal women and girls also amused themselves with a number of games. 'Warru warru' involved manipulating string on the fingers to form different figures — a game known to Europeans as cat's cradle. Although both sexes enjoyed this pastime, it was said that women could remember a greater number of designs and make more elaborate manipulations. One Aboriginal woman could reputedly create more than two hundred designs. Aborigines used the words 'warru warru' for the European fences newly built in the colonies as these resembled the patterns created by the string. Young Aboriginal women also skipped with vines, climbed trees and played 'purru purru', a ball game based on the principle of keepings-off. The ball was made from kangaroo skin stuffed with grass.

For those whose parents could afford to indulge them, young white women in the colonies had access to a surprising (though thoroughly British in origin) range of games and pastimes. An 1837 notice in the *Sydney Gazette* advertised for sale musical fruit, improved musical walking sticks, fishing rods, billiard balls, mosaic games, dissected puzzles, magic ducks, fishes and swans, sets of bats and balls, polished marbles, skipping ropes, wax dolls, mouth organs, rocking horses, battledores and shuttlecocks and kites.

LIKE A DUCK TO WATER

One of the most common forms of physical recreation for women was swimming, although few colonists and even fewer convicts were adept at it. Some learnt the skill, as well as the obvious pleasures derived from swimming, by watching the original inhabitants of the country enjoying themselves in the water. Early observers of coastal and river-dwelling Aborigines noted the proficiency of Aboriginal women in the water. This was also reflected in the portrayal of Aboriginal women by European artists. Francois Peron, who accompanied a French expedition to Tasmania in 1792, was so impressed that he drew the Tasmanian Aboriginal women, who were actually quite small in stature, as Amazonian giants. An observer in Queensland noted that Aboriginal women had the habit of jumping into the water feet foremost, 'bending up both legs and holding with their hands to each ankle'; what we would now call playful bombing. Such harmless amusements were soon turned to the invader's profit. Aboriginal women in Western Australia were kidnapped and used as divers for pearl shell in Broome's pearling industry. The pearlers chose them in preference to men because of their proficient swimming and superior underwater lung capacity. By 1871 the use of Aboriginal women on the pearling boats was prohibited by legislation following the death of many and the continued rape and sexual exploitation of the women by the pearlers.

Sea bathing for white women was difficult in the towns because of the need to maintain privacy from males. Segregated bathing was stipulated by law and bathing machines were stationed at many beaches to afford even greater privacy. A bathing machine, built in Hobart in 1827, quickly became one of that town's most fashionable amusements for women. The *Sydney Gazette* reported that 'the ladies are provided for by Mrs Bigge's accommodations in bathing', a pastime they described as 'the favourite recreation in Sydney'. In Adelaide the Marine Baths were established in 1839 and had in attendance 'a respectable married female, previously accustomed to Baths in England'. At Glenelg, South Australia, a bathing machine in 1845 replaced the need for improvised strips of canvas attached to posts near the waters edge to provide women bathers with privacy. Such baths throughout the colonies cost money to visit and women of lesser means were more likely to be subjected to the unwelcome gaze of male observers. The Newcastle Council employed a woman as caretaker of the Ladies' Bathing Place in 1884 and charged women up to sixpence per visit.

Bathing boxes afforded some privacy from prying male eyes.
MUSEUM OF VICTORIA.

Women in rural areas also campaigned to have private swimming areas. A bathing house was built in Deniliquin, New South Wales, in 1859 after women swimming in the Edward River were harassed by men. At Glenelg, it was reported that males 'discomfited' and 'annoyed ladies' and 'stationed themselves in groups . . . to watch'. The answer was often to legislate to segregate the beaches and prohibit all males from being in the vicinity of women bathers. Above the baths at Brighton beach in Victoria there flew a white flag to signify women bathing or a red flag to signify men bathing. A campaign for private, safe swimming areas for women was waged in virtually every inhabited coastal and river area of Australia throughout the nineteenth century.

This campaign was intensified after the building of many municipal swimming pools and the increasing interest shown by women in taking swimming lessons. Sea baths were not suitable places to learn to swim, usually being rocky and dangerous. Each municipality allocated different swimming hours for women and men at the local baths. Women did not receive equal access, invariably being relegated to one or two mid-week days. Such restriction bore no relation to the number of women wishing to use the facility. When open, women of all classes flocked to enjoy the baths. At the first Ladies' Day at the Rockhampton baths in Queensland, 60 women and girls attended and formed a Ladies' Swimming Club. In 1894 Newcastle's wealthier women petitioned on behalf of the local tradeswomen to have their hours extended from one day to two days a week. But their application was unsuccessful. Gradually even the hours previously allocated to Newcastle women were whittled away when men, with the backing of local aldermen, decided to use the baths from 6 am to 9 am on 'Ladies' Day'. The women's grievance was taken up by the editor of the *Newcastle Herald* who thought it unreasonable for women to have to bathe in water just vacated by dirty men. The newspaper drew the attention of the town's aldermen to the number of female ratepayers wishing to use the baths and the proximity of the next polling day, but his arguments fell on deaf ears. In Albury, New South Wales, the municipal baths were only open to women between 3 pm and 5 pm daily. Such regulations prohibited women of all classes learning to swim and restricted the development of organised competition swimming for women.

From the 1870s, swimming instruction for women became common. The 'Ladies' Own Column' of the *Illustrated Sydney News* published a detailed lesson entitled 'Swimming Made Easy for Ladies' in 1876. The lesson recommended an appropriate bathing costume — a long-sleeved jacket and drawers cut in one piece with a peplum and belt, plenty of room across the chest and shoulders, a waist four inches larger than in an ordinary dress and no cap. The first step, accompanied by a reassurance that seawater seldom injured the hair, was to wet the head thoroughly to prevent headache. The lesson progressed from the art of floating through to breaststroke. It warned against reliance on the arms which would 'strain the chest and hurry the breathing' and recommended at least ten minutes practice each day. For the more advanced skills of diving and side-swimming the paper recommended personal instruction.

The personal instruction of women swimmers received a boost in 1876 with the arrival in Melbourne of Harriett Elphinstone Dick and her partner Alice Moon. Harriett Elphinstone Dick (her professional name, her real name was Harriett Rowell) was born in Sussex in 1853. She was well known in Australia after she had publicly demonstrated her swimming prowess in England by swimming in a heavy sea from Shoreham to Brighton, a distance of nearly 10 kilometres, in 2 hours 43 minutes in September 1875. She spent two seasons at St Kilda giving exhibitions of fancy swimming at Captain Kenney's Bathing Ship and taught over three hundred women to swim at the Victoria Ladies' Baths. She also organised two series of swimming matches for women at the baths. She was held in high esteem by the women of Melbourne and the governor's wife, Lady Roma Bowen, whose daughters she had taught to swim, publicly presented her with a gold bracelet bearing the testimonial:

Presented to Miss Elphinstone Dick by her Melbourne pupils in recognition of her successful efforts to promote the art of swimming among the ladies of Victoria, and in admiration of her skill as a swimmer and her efficiency as a teacher, April 16, 1878.

As more and more women throughout Australia learnt to swim races were organised. The 1881 Queen's Birthday festivities in Sydney included a women's swimming tournament. Sydney women had learnt to swim at the Lavender Bay Baths in Sydney Harbour where Professor Cavill ran a course of instruction. Cavill attached a piece of rope around his pupil's waist, the other end of which he held while walking up and down a long jetty extending into the baths. The swimming 'instructress' at the Adelaide City Baths, a Miss Bastard, organised swimming races for women from the mid 1870s.

The main obstacle to both efficient and competitive swimming, however, remained the restrictive bathing costumes worn by women. While upper class women continued to import their bathing costumes, middle class women were encouraged to make their own from the new paper patterns published by the Melbourne-based *Madame Weigel's Journal of Fashions*. The journal recommended the use of cotton twill or serge, materials that did not cling when wet. Although advertised as simple to make, the costumes were far from simple to swim in. One newspaper in 1881 lamented the use of a garment that,

seemingly holds each fair nymph in bondage, when her limbs should be free . . . it remains for some one of enterprise and inventive powers to design and introduce . . . some novel and effective bathing-dress, which may enable the art of swimming to be more generally practised.

Eight-oar crew training on the Mitchell River, Bairnsdale, Victoria, April 1895.
STATE LIBRARY OF NEW SOUTH WALES.

The recreational activities of boating and rowing thrived on the waterways of Australia. Lady Jane Franklin in Tasmania actively promoted water sports and was instrumental in establishing the annual Hobart regatta. Women with access to boats ventured onto the water whenever possible. In 1885 *Australian Etiquette* recommended rowing as a healthy and delightful recreation for women, many of whom, it noted, had become expert and skilful at it. Rowing also required an adaptation of women's clothing — a dress which gave perfect freedom to the arm, a short skirt, stout boots and large hat were suggested as suitable. Women's rowing clubs were organised throughout Australia and women's boat sheds were built on many rivers and lakes. At first rowing was usually reserved for the daughters of wealthy families. Young women from four of Perth's leading families rowed together on the Swan River. In Adelaide women from the Torrens River boating club combined rowing with their activities to promote the federation of the Australian colonies. As well as rowing for pleasure and recreation, women trained and competed in single sculls, fours and eights. The sculler Cassie

Single-sculler Cassie McRichie, founder of the Albert Park Lake women's rowing club, c. 1900.
MARY-LOU JOHNSTON COLLECTION.

McRichie was a founding member of women's rowing in Victoria and a regular competitor on Albert Park Lake. Sailing was also enjoyed by women of some means although all colonists may not have exhibited the bravery and physical endurance of Mrs Boldt, the captain's wife, on the German cargo ship *Moorburg* bound for Melbourne in 1880. After the captain and all six crew members became ill, Mrs Boldt took the helm, steered the ship through perilous seas, and 'as well as doing work as a sailor, nursed the sick and cheered them', and cared for her baby. On her arrival in Melbourne with the cargo of tea intact, Mrs Boldt received the proceeds of a public subscription in her honour from the Mayor of Melbourne, as well as a 'handsome donation' from the insurance offices.

As women acquired boating prowess they could also regularly indulge in the popular recreation of fishing. Fishing was another skill already practised in Australia by Aboriginal women. In 1821 the Governor's wife Elizabeth Macquarie set the standard by throwing in a fishing line (appropriately) at Watson's Bay in Sydney and catching more fish than either her husband or her son. It was common for women to participate in fishing expeditions in the colonies and they fished either from a boat with hand lines or from the shore with a rod.

RIDING TALL IN THE SIDE-SADDLE

As stock in the colonies increased, women used horses both as a means of transport to cover the vast outback distances and for sport. The upper classes quickly established hunting clubs in Australia and the Sydney Hunt Hurdle Races of 1837 offered a 'Ladies' Purse' of £25. Hunts were often held mid-week, days on which only upper class women could free themselves for sport. Women's riding habits were advertised extensively in the colonial press. They consisted of a jacket and skirt covering breeches, which were cut in a manner to accommodate the knee as the woman sat side-saddle. They were usually made in black or dark blue cloth, which distinguished them from the traditional pink jackets worn by men. Many women rode to hounds and during a hunt in Melbourne the visitor Anthony Trollope was requested to observe them 'as they would assuredly ride well'. Describing himself as one of the 'second-bar men', he noted that women rode at the top bar of the hurdles with spirit and in gallant style. Not an easy feat side-saddle.

In the absence of a native fox the colonists looked to other animals for their blood sports. Both 'ladies and gentlemen' in the country districts regularly indulged in kangaroo hunting, or kangarooing as it was called. At the conclusion of the hunt women claimed for themselves the kangaroo tail which 'most ladies well-know how to convert into kangaroo tail soup — a dish greatly esteemed by epicures.'

The first coursing meeting in the colonies was held in Melbourne in 1873 with vice-regal patronage. The Victorian governor's wife, Lady Roma Bowen, followed the judge fearlessly on horseback and by the conclusion of the meeting was covered in mud. In 1876 a Ladies' Coursing Meeting was held in Melbourne.

Women also competed at annual shows throughout the country. At the jumping trials of the 1886 National Agricultural Society's Show in Melbourne, Mrs Ambrose riding *Innisfail* was placed first as well as earning a special prize as best 'equestrienne'.

Women regularly attended horse races in the colonies as spectators, horse owners and gamblers. Mary Spencer who went to the three-day-long Wangaratta Race Meeting in Victoria in 1854 noticed that there were several young women who rode competently and were attired in well-fitting habits. One horse owner, a Miss Dixon, became infamous in the Goulburn area after perpetrating a Fine Cotton style substitution with two of her race horses in 1863. At the city races some women participated in sweeps, while in the rural areas women often placed bets with their friends. Katie Hume attended the Toowoomba Races in Queensland in 1867 together with 'all the elite . . . besides a good muster of the common herd — perhaps 2000'. Riding to the meeting took half a day and once there she cantered round the course between races visiting her friends: 'Walter & I were both fortunate in the single bets we made. I won a pair of gloves from Mr Ramsay & Walter half a crown from Mrs R.'

Side-saddle jumping required greater skill and competency from colonial horsewomen. Ensay, Victoria, c. 1900.
MUSEUM OF VICTORIA

TARGET PRACTICE

Archery clubs in the cities maintained only a small elite membership and meetings were usually held under vice-regal patronage. Unlike other sports, archery did not require a change of costume except to ensure no flowing ribbons, lace frilling or loose jewellery got in the way. The amount of physical exertion required also meant that women of all ages could participate. Lady Roma Bowen, an enthusiastic archer, gave archery parties at Government House in Victoria. The lawns of 'Rippon Lea' in Melbourne were given over to mixed bow parties of private friends from the 1870s. Miss Daly, daughter of the South Australian governor, was the Adelaide women's champion in the 1860s. In country areas, targets were occasionally set up in a paddock during a picnic for the amusement of visiting friends.

Women, especially those in the country, were also familiar with the use of guns and joined shooting expeditions. In Queensland many women claimed the scalp hunters bounty of eightpence for kangaroos and fourpence for wallabies paid by the government under the Queensland Marsupials Act of 1877 and 1881. It was with some surprise, therefore, that observers at the opening of the Victoria Rifle Range in 1878 regarded the elaborate stand prepared for Lady Roma Bowen to fire the first shot. The spectators were under the impression that Bowen, a competent markswoman, was to put the rifle to her shoulder and fire in the usual manner. Instead the organisers had rigged up a stand to which the rifle was attached and aimed at number 24 target on the new range. Bowen was even saved the physical effort of touching the rifle, instead she pulled a ribbon attached to the trigger!

Spectators were surprised in 1878 when they saw the elaborate stand for Roma Bowen to open the Victoria Rifle Ranges. Bowen was accomplished with a rifle, and enjoyed hunting, coursing, archery and skating. *Australasian Sketcher*, 31 August 1878. NATIONAL LIBRARY OF AUSTRALIA.

Another target sport played by women was ringoal. Using two nets about 2.5 metres high and 3 metres wide, placed 24 metres apart, the object of the game was to propel a hoop into the opponent's goal, and reach a score of eleven. The hoop was caught and thrown on one or two sticks. It afforded 'good exercise for the muscles of the shoulders, arms and wrists' with some champion women able to throw the ringoal hoops more than 90 metres in a straight line.

GAME, SET AND MATCH

The French game of croquet became popular with the upper classes in England in the 1860s and was soon a favourite pastime in the colonies. Croquet is a very precise game, described as a mixture of snooker and chess, requiring complex mathematical judgments. By 1869 the *Illustrated Sydney News* offered sets for sale manufactured by Jaques's Croquet of London. It was the wealthier members of Australian society who could both afford the 'Finest Turkey Boxwood' sets and the expanse of lawn needed to play on, although some colonists played croquet in their back gardens. The rules of croquet actually specified the feminine form of the personal pronoun, but extant photographs of colonial croquet matches typically show groups of both women and men playing the game. The first croquet club was formed in Kapunda, South Australia, in 1868, the same year that private lawns were laid at Government House in Brisbane. In the following years public croquet lawns were established throughout Australia and were usually located in the botanical gardens, such as the ones laid in the Launceston Public Gardens in 1871 and the Brisbane Botanical Gardens in 1879. Public lawns were also laid in country areas, Ballarat in Victoria having two at the recreation reserve in 1871. Dressed in restrictive crinolines, women competed against men and were often successful, even though the latter possessed the advantage of being able to effect a more comfortable strike with the mallet. Women were forced to hold their mallets at their side until the shorter skirts of later eras allowed them the freedom to swing their mallet vertically.

In 1877 the Wimbledon All England Croquet Club was renamed the All England Lawn Tennis and Croquet Club and the first tennis championships were played. The game of lawn tennis soon spread to the colonies and swept across Australia. The same lawn was often used to accommodate both games, the absence of a wire netting enclosure giving some indication of the pace at which lawn tennis was played. The game was first played by the upper classes on private courts, but it soon spread to the middle classes with the building of public tennis courts and church courts. It was a pastime played increasingly by the daughters and sons of professional town people. Intercolonial matches, contested between New South Wales and Victoria, and New South Wales and Queensland were held from the late 1880s, and usually consisted of women's and men's singles and doubles, and mixed doubles. The women's games were widely reported in the colonial press and were usually the most popular with spectators.

Although *Australian Etiquette* in 1885 affirmed that lawn tennis 'affords ladies a training in graceful and charming movements', a great deal more exertion was needed to win the women's intercolonial championships. The first intercolonial lawn tennis match between Victoria and New South Wales was played from 30

April to 7 May 1885 on courts marked out on a cricket ground at Moore Park in Sydney. The *Illustrated Sydney News* reported that many women, probably players themselves, were present in the grandstand as spectators, and that the greatest crowd attendance was on days featuring rounds of ladies' matches. The championships were played as the best of three sets and Miss Lamb, whose volleying and placement were 'quite too much' for her opponent, defeated Miss Gordon in the final. The intercolonial matches of 1890, which were held in Melbourne, saw Miss Shaw who possessed a 'fine, fast overhand service' defeat Miss Mackenzie, despite the latter being a reknowned hard-hitter with a 'thoroughly masculine style of play'. Miss Mackenzie combined with Miss A. Chenery who had a 'slashing style and hits very hard from the back of the court' to win the doubles. In Queensland in 1890 May Quinnell successfully defended her ladies' singles championship title, exploiting her strong backhand stroke.

Although it was the women's intercolonial matches that received the most press coverage, many women took up lawn tennis as a social as well as a competitive sport. Makeshift tennis courts were fashioned on ships as amusement for the voyage. Women passengers stranded at the Sydney Quarantine Ground after an outbreak of smallpox on the steamer *Garonne* in 1882 whiled away the days on the tennis courts there. Social tennis parties in country areas were taken seriously enough for Sophie Clark of Goulburn to write to the 'Sports and Pastimes' editor of the *Illustrated Sydney News* in 1890 requesting advice on how to improve her backhand. Lawn tennis was a game that women and men could compete against each other on a social

Women took every opportunity for social 'lawn' tennis, as well as contesting regular inter-colonial championships. *Illustrated Australian News*, 1 October 1890.
NATIONAL LIBRARY OF AUSTRALIA.

level and women reportedly had their share of success. Women did not compete with men in football, but they did form their own Australian rules teams in both Melbourne and Perth from the 1890s.

The billiard table manufacturer and promoter Henry Alcock considered that women were suited to billiards as the game combined science with pleasure and exacted judgment, knowledge and precision. A game of an hour's duration resulted in the player walking a distance of nearly five kilometres, 'and this to him or her almost imperceptible'. Alcock wrote that women could participate in the 'true home of billiards . . . the quiet table, whether in familiar hostelry, or club, or private apartment'. Billiard parlours still retained unsavoury elements and therefore restrictions for the single woman. An act of the New South Wales parliament in 1881 legislated that 'no unmarried woman not being a widow shall be capable of holding a billiard or bagatelle license'.

WICKET WOMEN

Historically women have had an enormous influence on the game of cricket. Their full dresses caused them to adopt the overarm rather than underarm style of bowling, a method which later spread to the men's game. The first reference to a women's cricket match in Australia was a game played between the women of the goldmining towns Sofala and Hill End, New South Wales, in 1855. The batswomen earned a sovereign for each run scored.

Cricket became a favourite sport in Australia after a visit in 1874 by the English men's eleven who toured many country centres. The passion for cricket reached the goldmining town of Bendigo in Victoria whose citizens decided to organise their annual Easter fair around the theme of cricket. Thirty-five Bendigo women attended a meeting in March 1874 called to express interest in a women's cricket match. Practice was organised, sides chosen, and 22 white calico dresses were ordered from Messrs Buick & Co. The game was played on the 7 April 1874, mostly between miner's daughters although some married women also played. The *Bendigo Evening News* reported that 'the batswomen unquestionably showed excellent play, and drew forth the repeated plaudits of the spectators.' Proceeds from the match were donated to the Hospital and Benevolent Asylum, as were the calico dresses. As news of the game spread throughout the Australian colonies, other women formed teams and played matches. Women in the Steiglitz district in Victoria played a match as part of the Queen's Birthday celebrations in June 1874. A game was played in Yass, New South Wales, in December 1878, and a match played at the Association Cricket Ground in Sydney in April 1886 witnessed the emergence of Australia's first cricket star, Rosalie Deane. The match, between the Siroccos and the Fernleas, was dominated by Deane and the three Gregory sisters. These teams included no married women. The women practised every morning from 6 am to 8 am and every evening from 6 pm to 7 pm. They played in long striped dresses and wore functional cricket caps, rather than the more common but cumbersome cabbage tree hats. Trophies included a diamond and pearl brooch, gold rings and other jewellery, with Deane and Nelly Gregory receiving gold watches for the highest batting scores. The match raised more than £215 for charity and was a great success 'both regards the play and the attendance'. More than 3500 spectators attended and the *Illustrated Sydney News* described the game as being, 'played with great vigour and energy, some of the combatants evidencing a keen appreciation for, and a long acquaintance with, the finer points of the game.' Rosalie Deane, a Sydney musician, continued her cricket career, and scored 139 runs in a game in Maitland, New South Wales, followed by 195 runs and a century in each innings at the Association Cricket Ground in February 1891. Deane was the first woman cricketer to be recorded in *Wisden* and received front-page honours as one of the four record scorers of 1895 alongside batsmen W.G. Grace, A.E. Stoddart and A.C. McLaren in R.J. Ironside's *The World of Cricket 1856-1895*.

Cricket continued both as a competitive and a social sport for women. In the 1890s several clubs in the Warrnambool district of Victoria played a series of regular competitive matches, the players travelling to the games on horseback. Some matches were played for a cause other than charity. In 1892 women in Rockhampton, Queensland, played cricket to raise money for their recently

Cricketers from the England versus Australia match played at East Melbourne Cricket Ground, 13 March 1895. Sides were composed entirely of players resident in Australia. *Illustrated Australian News*, 1 April 1895.
NATIONAL LIBRARY OF AUSTRALIA.

formed Women's Separation League. A wide cross section of women played cricket throughout the colonies, with the upper classes tending to be represented in the more social matches. In March 1895 two sides composed entirely of members of prominent cricketing families resident in Australia participated in an 'Australia' versus 'England' match at the East Melbourne Cricket Ground. Although the women wore 'short' skirts these revealed only the ankle and proved much too cumbersome. More than 2000 spectators attended and £200 was raised for charity. The newspapers reported a fairly ordinary standard of play, mostly attributed to the players reluctance to adopt 'rational dress'. May McDonnell proved the star of the match. She 'played forward, cut, drove and hit to leg in a manner which aroused the enthusiasm of the spectators'. Between the fall of wickets she played the bowling of the umpires (and cricketers) Percy Lewis and Albert Trott for practice, one leg-hit far beyond the boundary off Lewis 'fairly bringing down the house'. McDonnell scored 62 not out and led 'England' to victory.

Women in New South Wales were drawn to a new game in great numbers. Called rockley, it was a cross between cricket and rounders and was played with a rubber ball. Each boundary hit counted for two runs. It was invented in 1895 by an inspector of lands, John O'Hara, from the village of Rockley, near Bathurst. In his travels around the district villages O'Hara provided all the necessary costumes and materials for the games. It proved extraordinarily popular and thrived for about ten years, with 100 teams of young women playing regularly in the district competition, which included Wattle Flat, Hill End, Sofala and O'Connell, Gundaroo and Queanbeyan.

CITY SPORTS

Australian women joined the American inspired roller skating craze of the 1870s. Because of the need for special rinks, roller skating was usually located in the cities and larger towns. The rinks were commercial ventures and membership was usually required. One month's subscription of ten shillings and sixpence was required to join the 'select' roller skating club in Newcastle in 1877, although the rink was open a couple of evenings a week to the general public on payment of admission. The rink on the corner of Bedford and Elizabeth Streets, Sydney, was titled the 'Elite Skating Rink'. For women unable to afford high membership fees some city stores set up their own clubs, such as the one at Sydney's Farmer & Co. In Melbourne Lady Roma Bowen was a regular winter patron of the Lowe rink in Stephen Street where as many as 200 members took part in the 'sliding evolutions on the broad floor'.

Another sport to spread rapidly with Australia's increased industrialisation was gymnastics. Devised to offset the sedentary nature of urban living it was introduced with gusto in Victoria by the entrepreneurs and former swimming instructors Harriett Elphinstone Dick and Alice Moon. They opened a women's gymnasium in Collins Street in 1879 and by 1881 had 190 pupils. They had trained in London in the Swedish Ling Method, a system which used little or no fixed apparatus. For 29 shillings a quarter they taught Indian clubs, ring-resistance, dumbbell exercises, free-exercises and marching to the young women, society and business women of Melbourne. The pair secured upper-class patronage including that of Mary Moorhouse, the wife of the bishop of Melbourne, in support of their physical education ideals. They held regular massed displays of their 'rational gymnastics' at the Melbourne Town Hall and offered medals and prizes each year to the best of their pupils. At these displays the pupils were usually dressed in special costumes. In the privacy of the gymnasium the women dressed in rational gymnastic clothes, consisting of knickerbockers worn under a short tunic jacket.

Aware of opposition to gymnastics, they were careful to exploit public opinion which regarded the neglect of physical education for women as a 'national injury, since the race depends

Harriet Elphinstone Dick demonstrating club work at her Melbourne gymnasium which she opened in 1879 with her partner Alice Moon (right). *Australasian Sketcher*, 23 July 1881.
NATIONAL LIBRARY OF AUSTRALIA

largely for its stamina on the mothers'. After one of their massed displays the *Australasian Sketcher* expressed the hope that in future 'Victoria's daughters as well as her sons, will have reason to be proud of their physique'. In Tasmania Marie Bjelke-Petersen taught gymnastics to women at the family-owned Bjelke-Petersen Physical Culture School in Hobart from 1891. In Sydney Miss Foster opened a Ladies' Gymnasium in Hyde Park with several suburban branches. Her pupils gave annual displays at the Exhibition Building. These included not only muscular exercise, but 'marching evolution, wheeling round, counter-march, turning in and out, quick step and slow step'.

GO AS YOU PLEASE

Outdoor physical exercise in the form of athletics continued to flourish, especially among working class women. Participation required little financial outlay. Picnic races were commonly held on the numerous public holidays, and usually contained at least one women's race. Divisions were not always according to age. The picnic held at Flemington racecourse and sponsored by the *Argus* newspaper in 1882 contained a race for young women '3 feet 6 and over'. Women's foot races and skipping races were held at the Queen's Birthday celebrations in Sydney in 1880 and on board ships during long sea voyages.

Among the women who earned their living from sport were professional foot racers, c. 1900.
MITCHELL LIBRARY, STATE LIBRARY OF NEW SOUTH WALES.

Women also competed for financial reward in the organised walking or 'go as you please' races. The *Bulletin* reported a women's tournament in 1881 which offered prizes of £50, £25 and £10, with a gold locket to 'neatest and best dressed'. Twelve women entered the race, their ages ranging up to fifty. One woman was recognised by the paper as being a barmaid. The contestants walked round and round a large tent over six days, with patrons paying to enter and gambling on the outcome. The women were attended by personal trainers who kept them supplied with plates of food and 'something in a soda-water bottle'. The winner Mrs Wallace completed 396 kilometres during the six-day tournament, compared with the second placegetter Miss Phillips who managed 391 kilometres. The following year Miss Phillips strode ahead of Mrs Wallace to win the colonial walking championship and £200 by completing 452 kilometres in six days. Later in the year Miss Phillips raced against a male competitor. After receiving a 48 kilometre start she completed 516 kilometres in six days, finishing six laps behind her opponent. Some women made walking a profession. Miss Azella not only competed in Sydney, but travelled to Goulburn to compete in the women's walking matches held in the Goulburn Mechanics Hall. Goulburn patrons were charged two shillings entry fee and were encouraged to come early to avoid the rush.

PUGILISTS

Women also boxed for financial reward. In April 1874 the *Bendigo Advertiser* gave an account of a prize fight at the Grassy Flat reservoir between two women named Clark and Williams. In June of the same year a prize fight for £5 was held between two women at Castlemaine, Victoria. In 1890 a public women's kickboxing match was held in Sydney. Local champion Kit Carter met Jessica Maloney from Adelaide who claimed to be undefeated by either women or men at the sport. Maloney lost several teeth in the second round but came good to corner Carter after the sixth round and, according to one report, 'rolled her off her chair, filling her ears full of dirt and kicking her around the body'.

ASSOCIATING WITH GOLF

One woman participated in a golf match played in Sydney at Moore Park in July 1884, among the earliest matches on record. Like most of the other players, she had learnt the game in Scotland. By 1892 a women's club was established in Melbourne and by 1894 it had 106 women players who could be seen, on days other than Saturday, wearing their distinctive scarlet blouses on the course. Twenty women formed a club at Geelong in 1893. They played on any day except Wednesday and Saturday for five shillings a year.

Golfers at the Royal Melbourne Golf Club, Caulfield, 1892. Although males did not permit them to play golf on Wednesdays or Saturdays or to use all the clubhouse facilities, women organised the first inter-colonial matches played in Australia.
NATIONAL LIBRARY OF AUSTRALIA.

By 1895 golf clubs in every colony had begun to accept women as 'associate members', requesting a membership fee of between five and ten shillings a year. All clubs limited the days on which women could play and usually excluded them from the clubhouse. In 1894 the first Australian women's championship was held in Geelong. It was won by Evelyn MacKenzie, who also took out the championship in 1895, 1896 and 1898, playing with hickory shafted clubs.

MacKenzie was unable to play in the first intercolonial tournament held at Bondi in Sydney in August 1897. This match, between Victoria and New South Wales, preceded the first intercolonial men's golf match by several months. The Victorian women were far too strong and were easy winners over New South Wales.

WOMEN'S CYCLES

One of the most challenging forms of recreation for women was cycling. Like the majority of Australian sports, it was an English import. The bicycle brought many changes to Australian society in the latter part of the nineteenth century, the most

Annie Dawson Wallace wearing knickerbockers, Sydney 1899. The controversial cycling suits challenged the notion of how women should dress in public.
STATE LIBRARY OF NEW SOUTH WALES.

significant of them for women. To women, bicycles represented transport, independence, rational clothing, travel, exercise, competition and fun. They provided the city woman with advantages previously only enjoyed by her horse-owning country sisters. Women readily joined the cycling craze, influenced both by visiting women cyclists, and advertising directed specifically at the female market. An English bicycle performer, Madame Franzina, had visited Adelaide in 1876 and given demonstrations on a boneshaker bicycle. Wearing tights she was able to ride the machine astride. Some boneshakers were designed side-saddle, a function that only permitted the rider to coast downhill. In 1885, a 4800 metres women's tricycle race was included in a championship meeting held in Adelaide under the auspices of the South Australian Bicycle Club. The winner Miss Wills covered the distance in 9 minutes 43 seconds off a handicap of 361 metres.

From 1887 the Safety bicycle became commercially available throughout Australia. Unlike its predecessors it had two wheels of equal size, making it both easier and safer to ride. The bicycle proved extremely popular and women jumped aboard enthusiastically. Cycling schools were established for women and some bicycle shops provided retiring rooms for women who cycled into the cities. In 1888 the Sydney suburb of Auburn became the site of the first women's bicycle race, not only in Australia, but the first in the world. The 3200 metres race was won by Dot Morrell. In the 1890s two cyclists, Barbara Whitcher of Newcastle and Margaret McLachlan of Dulwich Hill, Sydney, were barred from racing against male cyclists in their clubs after winning several events.

Women's bicycle clubs were soon established throughout Australia. The rapid drop in the price of a bicycle, from an average of £30 in the early 1890s to £6 in 1897, opened up the membership of the clubs to middle class and business women. The sport still enjoyed upper class patronage. When Lady Sybil Brassey at Government House in Melbourne and Lady Mary Lamington in Brisbane took to wheels the fashionable women of those cities quickly followed suit. Australia's first long-distance woman cyclist, Mrs E.A. Maddock, started her riding career in Sydney in 1893, two years before the inaugural meeting of the Sydney Ladies Bicycle Club. She cycled to Bega, a distance of 500 kilometres, averaging 100 kilometres a day. She followed this in 1894 with a record nine day journey from Sydney to Melbourne. In 1895 she set out from Sydney and cycled 2600 kilometres on a round trip to Brisbane. She made these journeys wearing a skirt, rather than bloomers, and a high-necked blouse. She travelled on a step-through (and therefore weaker-framed) bicycle. The challenge of lowering women's long distance touring records took off. In 1897 the Sydney-Melbourne record was lowered to six days and thirteen hours, and then cut to six days and seven hours by Mrs H.P. Nicolls in 1898. In 1899 Mrs D. McDonald completed the 925 kilometres journey in seven days four hours, riding completely alone when her partner Mrs C. Birkin was forced to abandon the race after an accident on the first day. It was no accident, however, that long distance cyclists were usually married. Providing a suitable female chaperon for a single woman travelling by bicycle hindered the aspirations of many. Despite the restriction, ever increasing numbers of both single and married women participated in the day touring organised by their clubs.

The most serious challenges to society's mores came not with women owning, touring or racing bicycles, but with what they wore while so doing. Cycling suits were widely advertised and featured knickerbockers or split skirts. Despite controversy, these 'rational' and potentially liberating costumes could now be worn in public for the first time by respectable women.

THE MADDING CROWD

Women were also present in vast numbers as spectators at all kinds of sporting events in the colonies. In 1890 Australia was visited by the celebrated American aeronautical family the Van Tassells. The troupe toured New South Wales and Victoria with their hot-air balloon. Thousands of women and men turned out in Newcastle to witness the daring ascents by the Van Tassell sisters in February 1890. The sisters entertained the crowd with 'daring trapeze feats' on the ground before Val Van Tassell, attired in a blue costume, climbed onto a trapeze attached to the balloon. The balloon ascended with its 'plucky occupant' who eventually parachuted to earth. The *Newcastle Herald* congratulated her on being the 'first of the fair sex who has gone so far up into the air in the land of the Southern Cross.' The balloon was recovered and a week later the elder, and more daring, Van Tassell sister made an ascent during which she performed her trapeze acts beneath the balloon. At a height of 90 metres she hung by her toes before jumping out at 600 metres and parachuting back to earth. The Van Tassell's brother married a Ballarat woman who joined the act and performed the mid-air trapeze acts with the two sisters.

UNSPORTING BARRIERS

The participation of women in all forms of vigorous social and athletic activities was not achieved without some concerted opposition from men in the Australian colonies. There were many lines of argument put forward against their participation — aesthetic, social, temperamental, medical — but one factor was common to all excuses and that was to keep sport a male domain.

The colonial newspapers were at the forefront of the vanguard against women's sport being seen in public, a cause which was taken up with enthusiasm by individual men. The public abuse of women bathers by men and the subsequent need to segregate bathing set back the development of women's competitive swimming until the next century. Despite the fact that women had justly earned their spurs on horseback, public furore was created by the proposal of the Gawler Racing Committee to include a women's race at their 1859 meeting. An editorial in the *South Australian Register* stated 'most earnestly do we entreat our spirited young country ladies — splendid horsewomen as many of them are — to reflect before they give their sanction to this indelicate proposal'. Although he appealed to their 'feminine sense of propriety', it was in fact the presence of the crowd, 'the hoi polloi who would wish nothing better than to witness the unhorsing of some

THE EMANCIPATED FEMALE.—SEVERAL QUERIES ADDRESSED TO HER.

O Emancipated Female,
In the days that are to come,
Will you get upon your muscle
And make all creation hum?

Will you cultivate the morals
Of the tardy evening lark;
And "do" the "masher toddle"
"On the block," or in Hyde Park?

Will you spend the evening gaily,
Till the early sunshine winks,
In the palace of Gambrinus
Playing vulgar "pool for drinks"?

In the days emancipated
Will you squirt tobacco-juice,
A-loafing on the corners
Like a Venus on the loose?

Will you come home in the morning
When the air is damp and chill,
And go fumbling for a key-hole
That refuses to stay still?

O Emancipated Female,
You may do these things, indeed;
But we fear it isn't sewing
That has planted such a seed.

As women gained more independence through sport, attempts to satirise and ridicule their efforts increased in the conservative, male-owned colonial press. *The Bulletin*, 28 June 1884.
NATIONAL LIBRARY OF AUSTRALIA.

of these unblushing damsels' that the editor seemed to fear the most. Bowing to public pressure the gentlemen of the racing committee cancelled the race. After a tricycle race in Adelaide in 1885, *Australian Cycling News* lamented, 'Where we would ask is the man who would care to see his sister, or maybe his mother-in-law, straining her muscular energy tricycle racing before an assemblage of people?'

A journalist responding to the 1898 Australian tour by the French racing cyclist Mlle Serpolette reported 'the morbid curiosity attracted by these exhibitions is one not likely to influence the pastime for its good.' As in swimming and horse racing, it was the gaze of males that prohibited 'unblushing' women from physical activity.

One effective way to limit women's participation was to direct satire and ridicule at them and belittle their sports. After the first women's cricket match in 1874 the *Australasian Sketcher* prophesised with doom, 'matches between eleven unmarried girls and eleven matrons, eleven governesses versus eleven telegraph operators, or eleven mothers-in-law against eleven maiden aunts.' When all other arguments failed there was always the standby mother-in-law jokes.

The *Bulletin* addressed several queries to the physically emancipated female in 1884 — would she take on the masculine pursuits of promenading, smoking and staying out late as well as billiards and gymnastics to the neglect of her sewing? The *Melbourne Punch* in 1884 visualised an alarming result from athletics for ladies — physical power for women over their husbands, power with the potential to restrict his private life. In this era newspapers adopted a supposedly feminine form for sporting terms when none was needed — cricketress, equestrienne, cycliste make the sports sound more gentle and less serious.

Just before the first Australian women's golf championship in Melbourne in 1894 a male commentator wrote, 'Women will never go through one championship with credit. . . Constitutionally and physically women are unfitted for golf. They will never stand the strain of a 26-hole final. . . The first ladies' championship will be the last'.

After the Wimbledon tennis final in 1877 another male commented, 'I do not think that any lady can or ever will, be able to play this game . . . Furthermore, no lady would ever be able to understand the system of scoring.' Frequent bicycling for young women was said to cause 'trouble for their womanhood'. In response to these arguments the exponents of gymnastics for women were anxious to establish that their exercises were based on scientific principles and emphasised good deportment, grace, flexibility and co-ordination. The *Illustrated Sydney News* stated that 'every woman who helps on the physical culture of her sex is thereby helping the cause of national progress and the happiness of the race.' Only when physical activity could be seen to keep women within their 'natural' roles as mothers and wives was it to be allowed.

Opposition to women's sport was not, of course, exclusive to this period. Many commentators have since under-represented the numbers of colonial women participating in sport, recreation and leisure. Although impossible to count, the fact remains that all classes and all ages of women played a variety of sports in significant numbers throughout the nineteenth century. Women had learnt to swim, dive, row, fish, cycle, swing clubs, exercise, lift weights, march, walk, run, skip, hike, roller skate, ski, toboggan, shoot, box and kickbox. They played tennis, cricket, golf, archery, croquet, billiards, cards and football as well as several variations of these games. They hunted, owned, raced, rode, jumped and bet on horses, they went mountain climbing, they parachuted and they ascended in balloons. And that was only the beginning.

LESSONS
IN SPORT

WHILE ADULT WOMEN WERE ENJOYING THE NEW ADVANTAGES OF SPORT, RECREATION AND LEISURE IN AUSTRALIA, THEIR DAUGHTERS WERE BEGINNING TO GROW UP WITH REGULAR PHYSICAL ACTIVITY SOUNDLY INCORPORATED INTO THEIR LIVES. The formalisation of education for young women throughout Australia in the 1870s provided the most significant stimulus to the growth of sport, games and physical culture for all women. The benefits of sport eventually filtered through to both the Catholic and government schools, but it was within the independent girls schools that the cult of physical activity first took root. In particular it was from the schools owned and run by the Wesleyans that the passion for sport developed and was most enthusiastically encouraged. The Methodists saw a need to compensate for omitting dancing from the education of young women by placing a stronger emphasis on gymnastics, sport and games.

Many of the independent girls schools were started as commercial ventures by women. As such the school prospectus needed to entice clientele and the syllabus needed to offer more than the basic education provided in government schools. A specialisation in physical education was one means by which the schools could attract paying clients. In return parents expected and received more for their money than the tedious military drill offered in government schools. Most of the independent schools were founded by women trained in England. These educators brought to Australia a new commitment to physical activity as a way to counteract the effects of study and to enhance the lives of young women. At a speech day in Melbourne in 1901 a headmistress affirmed,

The great importance of sport in schoolgirl life should be at once recognised. Our girls need open-air exercise just as boys do, especially if they are doing good mental work. More especially they need the discipline of the playground which boys get, and which enables them to understand the value of co-operative effort in later life.

The schools adopted a logical balance between intellectual and physical development at a time when many considered both to be detrimental to young women's health.

The new independent schools had many advantages for young women of the middle and upper classes who could afford to attend them. They provided the grounds and facilities necessary for physical development — from gymnasiums, swimming pools and tennis courts to playgrounds and even just open spaces. As well they offered a wide range of extra-curricular sporting activities. But above all they were owned, staffed and run by people who believed in the benefits of physical exercise for women. Once firmly established in the private schools, the practice of more strenuous physical activity for women was accepted in the community at large.

Private schools offered physical education to attract clientele. *The Home*, 1940.
NATIONAL LIBRARY OF AUSTRALIA.

For a long time the only physical exercise taught to girls in government schools was military drill. It was introduced into the schools as a defence measure in response to the Crimean and Franco-Prussian Wars. The role of Australia's daughters during an international crisis was not to be neglected. The 1871 annual report of the New South Wales Inspector of Schools extolled the need for universal military drill,

> *Whilst providing so useful a physical training to the male pupils of our schools, the claims of the girls to the like advantages have not been overlooked . . . the exercises they are put through are conducive to health . . . and they are deriving lifelong benefits.*

Instructors, usually retired military men, were appointed by the defence department to visit schools and teach the drill on a regular basis. Students at Sydney Girls High School were taught a combination of physical jerks and Swedish drill once a fortnight by a visiting 'ferocious red-bearded sergeant'. By the 1880s female government teachers were being trained in calisthenics in the teacher training colleges and by the 1890s drill and calisthenics were compulsory for girls in high schools.

Pupils at Fort Street Public School, Sydney, 1896.
NSW DEPARTMENT OF EDUCATION.

Nevertheless opportunites for sport remained much wider in the independent schools. There were several levels of physical activity which young women were encouraged to pursue. These included regular physical activities like brisk walks, swimming and rowing, physical culture and gymnastics and organised team games such as croquet, tennis, rounders, cricket, hockey, lacrosse, baseball, basketball as well as organised athletics.

Pupils, usually boarders, were encouraged to participate in regular, daily exercise. At the signal 'If you please, young ladies' boarders of the Methodist Ladies College (MLC) Burwood commenced a daily march two by two through the paddocks of Strathfield and Concord in Sydney. At MLC Claremont in Western Australia the headmistress led her crocodile formation of boarders at a brisk pace through the school gates every winter morning at 7.15 am on a walk to Cottesloe. The mistress on duty led the same walk every afternoon. In summer the line of girls wound down a steep cliff to the school's own bathing box at the end of a private jetty where they changed into their black flannel costumes and caps. Young women at Kambala in Sydney were encouraged to ramble in the sandhills and scrub adjacent to the school at Rose Bay. Here in summer they may have met the young women from Kincoppal convent on their climb down to the pool and long dressing shed at the water's edge. Inside the shed their blue and white striped neck-to-knee bathing costumes hung neatly on hooks.

This individual commitment to a salutary form of regular exercise was backed by a firm belief in the principles of organised physical education for women. At first the independent schools utilised the services provided by various visiting physical culture instructors from the commercial gymnasiums that had been established in the cities. The gymnasium owners and businesswomen Harriett Elphinstone Dick and Alice Moon created for themselves something of a monopoly among girls schools in Victoria. They taught at most of the independent girls schools, as well as travelling each Wednesday by train to schools in Ballarat. Harriett Elphinstone Dick's Swedish gymnastics were based on the curative and therapeutic effect of regulated exercise on the body and her advertisements in 1880 promised schoolgirls, 'gradual gymnastic development of the whole body by exercises carefully adapted to each individual, calculated to counter-act the effects of constant study, and ensuring good health, ease of movement and graceful carriage.' To her private school clientele she taught free exercises, jumping, club swinging, wand work, dumbbells, rings as well as rope and apparatus work. At MLC Kew, in Victoria, Miss McMillan who had 'made a special study of physical drill for girls during her travels' took classes every Tuesday afternoon. Her classes were based on the ideas in her book *Swedish Games and Recreative Exercises*. In Adelaide Adolf Leschen and his son Hugo taught calisthenics at the Advanced School for Girls, Dryburgh House and

Tormore. Parents paid about a guinea a term for their daughters to be taught calisthenics as an extra-curricular subject.

This strand of physical exercise was aided by the fact that many of the Protestant and independent schools built gymnasiums where young women could be put through their paces indoors, in privacy and seclusion, and where they could dress in gym clothes appropriate to the exercises they performed. In Melbourne, the Presbyterian Ladies College (PLC) opened in 1875 with a gymnasium as did MLC Kew in 1882. Melbourne Church of England Girls Grammar School (Merton Hall) built their gym in 1902. MLC Burwood had a fully equipped gymnasium within four years of the school opening in 1886. Catholic and government schools were not so fortunate. Kincoppal convent pupils had to perform their calisthenics on an open-air verandah, where climbing equipment and chest expanders had been installed.

MLC Burwood's school gymnasium opened in 1890 and offered climbing ropes and poles as well as club work. Specialist instructors were employed and the era of the sportsmistress began. Photograph by Charles Kerry.
MITCHELL LIBRARY, STATE LIBRARY OF NEW SOUTH WALES

The biggest changes occurred, however, when the independent schools no longer employed visiting instructors, but appointed teachers on permanent staff to take physical education. Because physical education was then provided at no additional cost to pupils, it became compulsory for all young women. The turn of the century saw the era of the sportsmistress begin. The first headmistress of MLC

Burwood Minnie Wearne, who, according to the school's historian, had 'quite a fixation about exercise' appointed a specialist teacher to take the girls through their physical drill. The headmistress of Tormore in Adelaide dispensed with the services of the Leschen family and appointed an English physical education mistress, Miss Loxdale, when the school gymnasium opened in 1909. In 1903 Mary and Edith Morris, the co-principals of Merton Hall, travelled to England and were inspired by the prominence given to a physical education syllabus. The following year they sent their younger sister Gwynneth Morris to study at Madame Osterberg's Physical Training College at Dartford, England. She brought back to Australia not only the system of Swedish gymnastics, but a revolutionary box-pleated tunic. Morris immediately undertook the management of gymnastics and games throughout the school. A special exhibition gymnastics class was founded to perform before visiting educationalists, doctors and others. At the 1907 Australian Exhibition of Women's Work, pupils of Merton Hall gave a demonstration of free-standing and living-support movements wearing the new navy blue tunic, white blouse, stockings and black sandshoes. This was the first time the tunic had been seen outside the school gymnasium. Despite the extra expense for parents, the new uniform became popular and was soon adopted by nearly all girls private schools in Melbourne. The boundaries of women's physical culture expanded rapidly. By 1910 the Merton Hall gymnastics team gave the first exhibition of vaulting by girls in Australia.

Physical culture was promoted within the private girls schools not only in the cause of improved health, posture and vitality, but as a pre-requisite to strenuous outdoor games and sport. It was the introduction of organised sport that popularised physical activity among the girls themselves. Sport contained elements of fun which were not necessarily present in massed Swedish gymnastic exercises and daily drill.

Early games present in all independent girls schools closely imitated those offered in English middle class schools. They included croquet, quoits, archery, rounders and, after the first Wimbledon tennis championship in 1877, tennis. In addition, the school gymnasium was often put to a variety of uses other than physical culture. At MLC Kew in 1887, boarders were allowed two afternoons a week for what were described as 'romps' in the school gymnasium. Boarders at PLC in Melbourne used the gym for roller skating practice in 1876, the same year one girl called for the formation of a school football team.

Boarders were the most frequent users of each school's sporting facilities, suggesting that day girls had access to their own tennis and croquet courts. Matches with day girls were the first form of competition incorporated into the sporting life of the schools. After the turn of the century the house system was adopted and trophies for school championships were awarded. Schools within the same geographical area or of the same religious denomination organised themselves into regular competitions. As pride in the school developed interschool championships were contested. Schools vied for the kudos associated with sporting victories and the added clientele. Some schools joined the state associations of each specialty sport that were then being organised and established. Interstate matches between schools run by the same religious denomination were also held.

In the 1890s sport in girls schools was still an extra-curricular activity. The new century heralded a time of more highly organised and more competitive sport. The success of the independent school's sporting teams came to be seen as a reflection of the school's own success. Participation in team sport was widely regarded as character building, promoting co-operation, team spirit and self discipline. Some form of sport or games was made compulsory for all young women, day girls or boarders, and the school magazines were filled with the sporting prowess of the teams. Sometimes even the school song had a number of verses devoted to the glories of sport. Sports captains were appointed and prizes and school colours were awarded for excellence on the playing fields as well as in the class room.

The success of the private school sporting teams came to be seen as a reflection of the school's own success. The competitive spirit beat strongly in young women's hearts and sports leaders were idolised. Church of England Girls School Sports Team, Warwick, Qld.

Tennis clubs were one of the most common form of sporting teams at independent schools. Once courts were marked out they were rarely vacated by the students. By 1885 PLC and MLC in Melbourne were playing regular inter-school matches, and the formation of the Kia-Ora Club in 1902 brought six independent girls schools in Melbourne into regular competition for a pennant and silver cup. By 1906 Merton Hall had replaced their croquet field permanently with an asphalt tennis court and by 1913 the school had three tennis courts, already an inadequate number. The tennis team played in blouses and long navy blue skirts, until a breakthrough in 1914 when they were permitted to play in public in the sports tunics that were still generally reserved for the seclusion of the gymnasium. In 1910 a team from MLC Adelaide travelled to MLC Kew to play 'the first inter-State girls public school tennis match'. In Sydney Kambala initiated tennis matches on a hired court with Ascham in 1888, the same year MLC Burwood played PLC Croydon. The colour white was still reserved for church, and most girls wore their school uniform of blouses, long skirt and ties for tennis. By 1900 MLC Burwood boasted 46 members in their tennis club. In 1914 all the private schools in Sydney joined the Schools Tennis Association. Tennis took longer to become a competitive sport in Catholic schools. Matches were played within each convent until the formation of the Catholic Girls Schools Tennis Association in 1918.

Another game played regularly between boarders and day girls was rounders, an early form of baseball. At MLC Kew students played hildegarde, a glorified and hybrid form of rounders, until they abandoned it in favour of the less complicated game in the 1890s. In 1908 Merton Hall made baseball compulsory for all who did not play other games. Weekly practices were held for each form and the school regularly competed with PLC and Lauriston. Unlike other team sports, baseball was played year round, and helped to improve cricket skills as well as provide training for winter games. Long dresses did, however, make rapid movement on the rounders field impractical in the 1880s. At one school two masters, captaining opposing teams of boarders and day girls, did all the running.

Rowing was offered for senior girls and boarders at schools with ready access to the water. Crews of fours and eights from Tormore in Adelaide regularly rowed on the River Torrens from 1900 to 1915. In 1906 MLC Burwood had a rowing club, organised by the science teacher, Miss Knight, which practised on the Parramatta River every Thursday afternoon. Students at Sydney Church of England Girls Grammar School (SCEGGS) Redlands, where rowing was the most popular sport from 1895, were more enthusiastic, practising for a couple of hours each morning on Elizabeth Bay.

One game that brought the independent schools into more contact with girls from government schools was cricket. Games were also played against private teams. Cricket was introduced and actively encouraged in the late 1880s. It quickly became one of the principal games, and Merton Hall even gave cricket bats as prizes on speech day. Regular interschool competitions were held but these ended when cricket was discontinued during the First World War. Cricket needed a level, large playing field and many schools were forced to improvise and adapt to games of 'hillside cricket'.

Cricket was also the main game among Catholic schools, with matches often used as entertainment for distinguished visitors. Cardinal Moran, together with a party of ten bishops and 20 clergy, witnessed a game between the school colours Reds and Whites at the Kincoppal convent in 1895. Many boarders from country areas brought the skills of cricket with them. A group of clergy who had kindly consented to coach the girls at MLC Kew were quickly outplayed by them. Cricket also flourished in government girls schools when coaching was available. Mrs Donnan, sister of the cricket playing Gregory brothers, had herself played in several early matches in Sydney. She taught and coached the cricket team of Sydney Girls' High School. Under her influence the school adopted peaked caps rather than the more common and cumbersome large straw hats. When she left the school in 1913 cricket vanished from the sports list.

One game for schoolgirls that came to stay, and caused a great deal of controversy because of its vigorous and supposedly dangerous nature, was hockey. Two letters to the editor of the *Argus* in 1910 deplored the 'rough and boyish game of hockey' as an 'objectionable and unmaidenly pastime', and called for the replacement of the field by a tennis or croquet lawn. Again it was the presence of men that was the dangerous element, the game attracting 'the noisy attention of loafers'. Correspondents, including one signing herself 'Ardent Hockeyite', defended hockey as making girls strong, healthy and robust.

An early form of hockey called 'shinty' was played at the Cambridge School in Hunter's Hill, Sydney in 1903, on the asphalt tennis court between sides consisting of a row of forwards and a row of goalkeepers. After the tennis court proved impossibly small (and the Maths mistress sported a shiner), a nearby level cow paddock was used once the girls had coaxed its occupant to greener pastures. At this time there was not 'a hockey-stick or ball, or book of rules to be had in Sydney' so the headmistress and two women teachers lent the sticks they had brought with them from Britain. Two dozen sapling sticks with slightly curved root ends were fashioned for use by the others.

Because many women teachers chose hockey as their own form of sport, acceptance and organisation of the game quickly spread. Staff teams were formed in schools, and competition with girls proved popular. Hockey was introduced into most schools in the early part of the new century, and within a couple of years girls school hockey associations had been formed and teams from country as well as city schools affiliated. Winifred West, headmistress of Frensham Mittagong, New South Wales, from 1913, had convened the first meeting of the New South Wales Women's Hockey Association in 1908. West played left-inner for New South Wales in the first interstate match against Victoria in 1909. Not surprisingly hockey became a popular sport with young women at Frensham. When Sydney Girls High applied to join the New South Wales hockey association in 1909 it registered 66 players.

Another game from England that was tried in girls schools was lacrosse. It too was fast and strenuous, and recommended for the posture because it required no bending over the ball.   Gywnneth Morris introduced lacrosse at Merton Hall in 1908 but it survived only two years, mainly hampered by the fact that interschool competition was not available.

Basketball (renamed netball in 1970) was first played with five-a-side teams and shots for goal were taken underarm.
MLC Burwood, c. 1910. Photograph by Charles Kerry.
MITCHELL LIBRARY, STATE LIBRARY OF NEW SOUTH WALES.

The new game of basketball was introduced as an alternative to hockey, but not all schools possessed sportsmistresses or teachers with knowledge of the game. In 1904 MLC Burwood sent prospective captains and umpires to PLC Croydon to observe the game there and report back to the school. When interschool games were played the umpires had to ensure that they determined the rules at the beginning of each match as all the schools played according to their own variation of official rules. Five-a-side games were usually played and participants shot for goal underarm with both hands on the ball, a very imprecise angle. By the second decade of the twentieth century basketball courts had been constructed in most girls schools. The problem of rules dogged the game for many years, preventing interschool, interstate and international matches.

All was not fun and games, however. The passion for sport once unleashed among young women sometimes became a monster. The leaders in sport were idolised in schools. Although sport was introduced to foster school spirit, ill-feeling reportedly grew among the schools as 'arrogance' developed in the winners and charges of unfairness were raised by the losers. The competitive spirit was as much alive in young women's hearts as it was in those attending the contemporary boys schools. As early as 1907 Gywnneth Morris deplored the attitude of 'win at all costs' creeping into the games at Merton Hall, 'we need to cultivate the spirit for which fair play comes first — defeat or victory afterwards' she said. Not all schools shared the problem, however. The headmistress of Cromarty in Melbourne reflected that although it was correct to be good losers, her school was just too good at losing.

At state schools young women had to make do with the equipment and sporting facilities available. Some exercise was rigid and lacked fun. Deniliquin, NSW, 1914.
STATE LIBRARY OF NEW SOUTH WALES.

The formalisation of major sports and games occurred much later in Catholic and government schools. Young women at these schools were forced to improvise many of their playground activities as they lacked both the space and the necessary equipment for sport. Games like handball, requiring only a brick wall and a tennis ball, were more common although pupils at an inner city girls high school were still forced to keep the compulsory school hat nearby to venture into the street and retrieve a lost ball. When Sydney Girls High School opened in 1883 it was 'bleak and cramped', there were no playing grounds, certainly no gymnasium and no physical culture teachers, trained or untrained on the staff. Improvisation was needed in the playground. Nellie Heuston who attended Maitland Girls High School in 1890 recalled:

> *Playing grounds were nil. There was a kind of backyard in which the flood had ripped a large hole. To organize a game of rounders would have been impossible, but some of the energetic juniors invented a game involving one of our brother's hockey sticks and a tennis ball. The idea was to mashie the ball over the hole. Not very exciting, but I can remember quite a lot of fun, especially in recovering the ball from the bottom of the hole.*

The game of vigoro was first introduced into government schools by its English inventor J.J. Grant in 1919. He reportedly visited each school for a period of some weeks to teach the girls the fundamentals of the game during their lunch hours. He also held lessons and organised games in the Sydney Domain. Vigoro combined elements of cricket and baseball and attracted a large following in New South Wales, Queensland and Tasmania. The game was faster than cricket, involved more players and was played on a smaller sized field.

Physical education and sport played almost no role in the curriculum of many convent schools. Dancing was promoted in preference to physical culture as it was thought to aid the 'social graces'. Indeed the Catholic church was the least well-disposed of the major denominations towards the serious education of young women. Girls at Kincoppal played tennis, rounders and flags, the latter a war-like game with each side out to capture the enemy flags. Kathleen Fitzpatrick, who attended both a Catholic and later a Protestant school in Melbourne (Presentation Convent and Lauriston), later observed that 'the mania for sports which swept the Protestant girls' schools in the second decade of the twentieth century hardly touched our school. The convent had a tennis-court and one for basket-ball but no one taught us how to play games'. In contrast she found Lauriston,

> *a crack sporting school, famous for the tougher types of games, such as hockey and baseball. Tennis was the only game I knew how to play, but that did not count at Lauriston because it lacked the 'team spirit' said to be so character-forming. Team games were compulsory and I was ordered to play baseball and did so.*

Skipping races, sack races and tug-of-war were contested as keenly as sprint events at
athletic carnivals. Ballarat, c. 1930.
MUSEUM OF VICTORIA.

In addition to organised games, the independent girls schools accelerated the growth and acceptance of competitive athletics and swimming for women. By the early 1900s most of the schools had acquired the grounds on which to hold athletic meetings or were committed to levelling their playing fields where necessary. Members of the MLC Burwood basketball team mooted the possiblity of the school holding a full sports day in 1907. It was a bold proposal as it would involve a considerable number of parents and friends as spectators. The headmistress enthusiastically consented but senior male clergy hesitated until reassured that all high jumps and hurdles could take place before the carnival in the seclusion of the school's grounds. The athletics programme catered to a wide range of talents from the more serious sprint and middle distance championships to sack races, tug of war, skipping races, fancy dress races, egg and spoon, old girls' races and nail driving competitions (dominated by the country girls). The meeting was a great success and quickly became the highlight of the school year. It also set a respectable precedent for other girls schools. Competition at sports days was always intense, especially following the universal adoption of the English house system within the schools. Athletics standards were high among the young women. At the sports day held to mark the opening of the new games field at Merton Hall in 1913 one girl set a school high jump record that stood for more than 40 years. Her box-pleated tunic sailed with her over the bar set at 1.409 metres. According to the school magazine 'the gymnastic costume worn by all the competitors greatly assisted speed and motion'. Young women in the swimming pool, however, were still weighed down by the neck-to-knee garment.

Some of the wealthier girls schools had constructed indoor swimming baths as well as gymnasiums in the 1890s. This enabled students to be taught both swimming and lifesaving in privacy. Those not so fortunate attended nearby swimming pools, still segregated, where women's swimming clubs were flourishing by

Jess Browne and Joyce Lovering vie for honours in the sack race at the school athletics carnival, Cootamundra, NSW, 1933.
STATE LIBRARY OF NEW SOUTH WALES.

the turn of the century. Annual swimming carnivals were not open to males. When Merton Hall entered a team at the Brighton Ladies Swimming Carnival, only 'lady members of council and mothers' could watch the competition. Swimming received a tremendous boost in 1912 when the Sydney swimmers Fanny Durack and Mina Wylie took out the quinella of gold and silver in the 100 metres at Stockholm in the first swimming event open to women at the Olympic Games. Young women now had not only female role models, they had world and Olympic records against which they could compare their own times. When MLC Burwood first joined an interschool swimming carnival at Drummoyne Baths in 1913 they sent five pupils to compete. In 1916 they sent fifty. Swimming was one of the few sports promoted for young women in government schools, largely because of the safety factor involved in learn-to-swim and lifesaving classes. In 1907 Miss Kilminster and the 'outstanding swimmer' Ella Gormley were appointed by the New South Wales Education Department to teach swimming, rescue and resuscitation techniques to women teachers. In the same year that women first swam at the Olympics, more than 7500 girls at government schools across New South Wales were receiving regular swimming instruction.

By the First World War, competitive sport had obtained an unshakeable place in

From the early 1900s trainee teachers were instructed in swimming when learn-to-swim and lifesaving classes were made compulsory for all pupils at government schools. A chance to let their hair down, Torquay, Vic, c. 1915.
MUSEUM OF VICTORIA.

the lives of the middle and upper class young women at independent girls schools across Australia. The organisation of sport in Catholic and government schools soon followed the path set by the private schools, but they still had some way to go, especially in overcoming prejudices inherent in the community. In Maitland where there were separate girls and boys government high schools, a special school prize was inaugurated in 1916. The boys school voted for the best sportsboy and the girls school voted for the most popular girl! The irony was that at a private independent girls school in 1916 the most popular girl would have been the girl who was best at sport.

UNIVERSITY WOMEN GET THE BLUES

THE FEMINIST MOVEMENT OF THE 1890S INFLUENCED THE PROMOTION AND ADOPTION OF SPORT AMONG AUSTRALIAN WOMEN. A group the press liked to call the 'new women' first appeared outside the gates of Australia's oldest universities, clamouring to get in. More than likely they had bicycled from a suffrage meeting. According to the *Adelaide Observer* of 1896, 'The sensible new woman can ride, and swim, and run, and row, and her nobly developed limbs are clad in garments of becoming looseness and shortness when she takes her exercise'. When women were admitted to degree courses at the universities they faced a great deal of public criticism and hostility. They were on trial. The new women needed to be better than the male students academically and they had to be seen as not overstepping the bounds of femininity, of not becoming masculine as many predicted. The new women had been satirised and ridiculed in the colonial press. They were anxious to share in the recreational possibilities of university life, but were mindful that public displays of rugged sportswomen would do their cause no good.

Most of the 'new women' had come from the private independent schools where they had already experienced the liberation of physical activity. Some returned to the school system after university thereby nurturing and perpetuating the sporting traditions among young women. Along the way they gained valuable experience in lobbying for sporting facilities and in administration. They also developed personal networks which were to link the administrators of women's sports, especially hockey, through their formative years.

Many 'new women' chose to continue some form of exercise while at university, a tennis court being regarded as the minimum requirement for women's colleges. Some were more daring, and also conscious of the new choices opening up to them. In 1892 Louisa Macdonald was appointed principal of the Women's College at the University of Sydney. When it opened its temporary accommodation in a house at Glebe, it had a solitary recreational facility, a billiard table. For the first week there was only one student and Macdonald remembers, 'She and I amused ourselves at intervals by trying to play billiards, at which neither of us was an adept.' The plans for the new college included one asphalt and two grass tennis courts, and tennis parties and games soon became the major form of relaxation for foundation members. Tennis tournaments were inaugurated and in 1897 members of the University Women's Boat Club subscribed to purchase a boat, the *Vaka*:

> *an unconventional, but light and lovely little craft, with three pairs of oars arranged as sculls, and a few seats to spare for tired oarswomen; her build would never have made it possible to compete in races, but only to enjoy ourselves pottering and picnicking about the harbour.*

Four law students at the University of Adelaide also started a rowing club and not only had to find a boat but had to invent something to wear: 'we concocted a uniform. It was a top with short sleeves and the old fashioned bloomers right down to your knees'. By 1919 they had nine women's crews on the water.

But the tradition of rowing for university women was not to continue uninterrupted. When the first English women's four-oar team (which included one doctor) visited Australia in 1938 they were surprised to find no university based teams, unlike their own country where universities 'were the nurseries of women's rowing'. Rowing had opened up to a wider class of women in Australia than was the case in England.

The independent new women at the universities often had a family or educational background inspired by physical exercise. They had been brought up believing that education and exercise were appropriate for girls. A young woman who believed sport inappropriate for herself was hardly likely to aspire to a medical or legal degree. The Adelaide medical student Helen Mayo had 'read the

Boys Own Annual' and 'played games, cricket, tennis, rounders and so on'. From the age of five Phyllis Cilento had learnt to row, swim, shoot, ride and play cricket. Her family pursued a strict exercise regime. She exercised every morning, doing skipping, club work and dumbbells. Every Wednesday after school at Tormore she attended the Leschen Gymnasium, to exercise with 'climbing poles and rings and trapeze and parallel bars and horizontal bars'. While studying for her medical degree Cilento won a blue in tennis.

Jessie Street grew up in the Clarence River district of New South Wales where she had learnt to swim, ride and row a boat. For her schooling she had been sent to Wycombe Abbey in England where sport was compulsory. Wycombe's three terms were devoted

Jessie Street received her schooling at Wycombe Abbey, England, where sport — lacrosse, hockey and cricket — was compulsory. In Australia, Street founded the hockey club and women's sports union at the University of Sydney.
NATIONAL LIBRARY OF AUSTRALIA.

to lacrosse, hockey and cricket, with tennis and golf played year round. When she returned to Australia she remained keen on exercise: 'I became quite a strong young woman and was very proud of my muscles'. When Street arrived at the University of Sydney as an undergraduate in 1908 there were tennis courts but no other sporting facilities. At the university she met other women who were Australian-educated but just as keen on sport as she was, including Nellie Meares from Mudgee Grammar, Janet Beith from Sydney Church of England Girls Grammar School and Kittie Prescott from MLC Burwood. Each had the experience of interschool tennis, swimming carnivals, football, Swedish drill and walking competitions. Together they joined the women's tennis club and lobbied to improve the standard of the courts which had irregular surfaces and lacked surrounding nets.

Jessie Street also suggested the formation of a hockey club. Fifteen women joined the club, an insufficient number to hold a game. Finding time to play sport was difficult for many women at university who were still required to perform domestic duties at home as well as study. Many had to return home immediately lectures ended. Street solved the problem by forming a mixed hockey club, as no men's hockey club then existed at the university. Street coached the team on a

Generations of women continued their sporting careers at universities across Australia. The 'square' at the University
of Sydney was levelled for hockey, cricket, baseball and other sports in 1910.
NATIONAL LIBRARY OF AUSTRALIA.

hired oval after the men's sports union refused her and the other women (whom
they derisively called 'Newtown tarts', as the women's college bordered the
working class suburb of Newtown) permission to practise on a university oval.
The University Women's Hockey Club affiliated with the recently formed New
South Wales Women's Hockey Association in 1909 and Street became both a state
selector and honorary treasurer. Street had captained the university hockey team
since 1908 and she was selected to play centre forward in the first New South
Wales women's hockey team to tour to Melbourne in September 1909. The
university hockey team played regular interclub as well as intervarsity matches.
Street's hockey protogees wore skirts about six inches shorter than their coach to
enable them to move more freely about the oval.

Before the First World War, University of Adelaide students raised a storm of
criticism by appearing in the street in their hockey costume. Their ankle length
skirts, high necked white blouse with long sleeves, stiff collars and a high waist
earned them the title 'hussies'. An infinitesimal glimpse of their thickly
stockinged ankles resulted in a rule insisting that, when in costume, hockey
players should always carry their hockey sticks. Only with this precaution could

they hope to have their short skirts pardoned and outraged propriety mollified.

Although other sports were offered at universities, hockey became the most popular and performed something of a networking role among women undergraduates and graduates, many retaining their connection with the sport long after leaving university. The scientist Freda Bage had been a hockey enthusiast at the University of Melbourne and in 1908 managed the first Victorian women's hockey team to travel interstate, from Melbourne to Adelaide. After accepting a lectureship at the University of Queensland she was president of the Queensland Women's Hockey Association from 1925–1931. The zoologist Dr Gwynneth Buchanan held office as president of the University of Melbourne hockey club before becoming Victorian president in 1927. At the University of Adelaide, Millicent Proud won first class honours in classical languages as well as a blue in hockey. Dr Phyllis Cilento recalled, 'when we went to play interstate tennis or hockey teams, Millicent, the captain, made us get out at every station and run up and down the platform to keep fit'.

At the University of Melbourne in 1907 one of the initial requests made by the newly formed women's club was the construction of a hockey stick rack in their club rooms. The first blues for hockey were awarded in the same year, with inter-faculty and intervarsity matches being keenly contested. Turnouts of more than 50 women to hockey practice were not uncommon.

In 1913 an archetypal new woman arrived at the University of Sydney. The medical student Evelyn Dickinson wore her hair short, had written a number of novels containing 'advanced ideas', and rumours abounded that she smoked in private. She was a particular friend of the principal Louisa Macdonald whom she encouraged to join her in her craze for bicycle excursions. She was fond of all sports and had a room at the Women's College fitted out as a gymnasium where she instructed other students in the processes of keeping fit. She presented a silver cup as a trophy for the annual tennis tournament.

Bicycling was popular among the students as it emphasised and promoted independence. Dorothea Proud embarked on cycling tours around the University of Adelaide, sometimes travelling more than 500 kilometres. As they needed greater mobility, medical students were commonly found on bicycles often cycling to patients with their medical bags strapped to the handlebars. Many later became keen motorists, an innovation too late for Dr Mary Page Stone who was killed in a collision between her bicycle and a waggon in 1910.

By the second decade of the twentieth century most universities had women's clubs for hockey, tennis, swimming and athletics. Women at the University of Sydney formed their four clubs into a central Women's Sports Union which was incorporated on 5 August 1910, with Jessie Street as honorary secretary. They lobbied the university senate for grounds for their hockey and tennis clubs, finally

Of all the changes the bicycle brought to Australia, the most significant were for women. The bicycle provided freedom, transport and independence for an emerging group of professional women, from teachers to doctors, in both city and country areas. School teacher Ms Marley, 1898.

STATE LIBRARY OF NEW SOUTH WALES.

having the 'square' levelled for that purpose, and changing sheds and showers built. They adopted a sports blazer in university colours. They resisted all attempts by the men's sports union to strip them of their oval or amalgamate. Affiliation was proposed the year after the Women's Sports Union was founded but rejected as the men proposed to give the women one vote, rather than one each for their four clubs. Full time administrative positions were created at the sports union and sport was promoted to generations of women students. At the University of Melbourne the women's clubs also flourished and they held an annual women's sports day which combined conventional athletic pursuits with novelty events. As other universities were founded across Australia later in the century, they adopted the sporting traditions pioneered by women in the early universities.

Universities continued their role as promoters of women's sport. Many touring state and international teams resided at the Women's College while playing in Sydney, including the English Women's Cricket Team in 1934–35, captained by Betty Archdale who returned as Principal of the Women's College in 1946. Archdale was a close friend of the architect Barbara Peden and her sister Margaret Peden, both cricketers and graduates of the University of Sydney. Finding it difficult to work as an architect in Australia, Barbara Peden travelled to England and met Archdale through local cricket games. This connection was helpful when negotiations were commenced to invite the English women's cricket team to tour Australia in 1934.

Barbara Peden's elder sister Margaret had learnt to play cricket at Abbotsleigh School in Sydney and while attending the University of Sydney had founded the university cricket team. Margaret captained the Australian women's cricket team from 1934 until 1937, after winning blues in both hockey and cricket at university. Margaret had also been sportsmistress at Sydney Church of England Girls Grammar School (SCEGGS) Redlands in the 1920s.

Many outstanding women athletes emerged from the universities in these early years. The historian of the women graduates at the University of Melbourne commented, 'many of the best athletes were — seemingly unfairly — those who also took academic honours.' One of the most outstanding was Alison Hattersley who had won every sporting championship at SCEGGS Redlands as well as being dux. She topped this by winning blues at the University of Sydney for tennis, swimming and basketball.

But more important than the athletes themselves were the new crop of administrators who were instrumental in forming separate associations for women's team sports in every state of Australia in the first half of the twentieth century. Although not all who helped form these sporting associations were university educated, the 'new women' provided some of the backbone, connections and dedication needed. When the new women set their sights, they set them high.

A Sports Association of One's Own,

1901-1939

O N 1 JANUARY 1901, 20 CRACK
SHOTS FROM AUSTRALIA'S FIRST WOMEN'S RIFLE CLUB, THE MULGRAVE
LADIES' RIFLE CLUB, ASSEMBLED AT GLEN WAVERLEY PRIMARY SCHOOL
OUTSIDE MELBOURNE AND FIRED A VOLLEY IN CELEBRATION OF
AUSTRALIA'S NATIONHOOD. Their action heralded not only a new era in
Australian history but represented the first shots fired in the battle for
women to establish control in their own sporting organisations and clubs.
Skirmishes occurred on many fronts throughout the next couple of decades
as groups of determined administrators and players worked to establish
women's sport throughout Australia. By 1939 there were well over one
million amateur sportswomen, together with a sprinkling of professional
sportswomen, who belonged to these sports associations across Australia.

The one million women were members of a broad range of sporting
associations. These included team-based as well as individual sports. At the
start of the new century males still retained various levels of control in some
of the non-team women's sports. As a consequence these sports faced greater

obstacles in their expansion. When women began organising team sports they were mindful of the hard lessons learnt and took care to establish them solely under the control of women.

The 40-year period between the turn of the century and the start of the Second World War saw rapid growth and expansion in women's sport in general. A number of major sports were placed on a sound footing as rules were codified, state and national associations inaugurated, interstate competitions organised, national teams formed, overseas players invited to visit, and finally international tours embarked upon. Australia's geographic isolation was a major stumbling block to the development of sport. The administrators and promoters of women's sport were quick to recognise that each sport needed strong competition from overseas. They knew Australian women possessed the potential to become world champions but to bring this out commitment, foresight and dedication were required from administrators.

The logistics of organising even a national competition of amateur sportswomen, to bring them together from as far away as Western Australia, Tasmania, Queensland, South Australia, New South Wales and Victoria, were mind boggling. Women possessed neither the economic independence nor the generous patronage that helped the formation of men's sport. Married women had family responsibilities that prevented easy travel, and social conventions dictated that single women could not travel without the attendance of suitable chaperons. In addition, women had to fight prejudice from individual men, male-controlled sporting organisations, and a hostile male-dominated press that deemed their efforts trivial and second rate. Women's sport was financed on a shoestring, administered by armies of unpaid volunteers without political clout, played at considerable personal cost to the sportswomen involved but produced nevertheless crop after crop of world champions. Like so many other aspects of women's lives, when they took to sport women needed to be better than men to be given the same opportunities.

Before the First World War most sporting associations were termed 'ladies' associations. During the war the 'ladies' of the sporting fields became the women who kept things going on the home front while the men were away. After the war the word 'ladies' disappeared from many sports. Administrators, anxious to reflect the broadening social base of sport and the expansion in women's lives and opportunities, began instead to use the term 'women'.

FOR THE SAKE OF THE TEAM

A combination of events in the 1920s and 1930s caused a boom in women's team sport. These were the consolidation and control of sport by women competent in administration, the formation of the Amateur Sports Associations which brought all the women administrators into close contact and co-operation, and the successful staging of national sporting events. Also, for the first time women could read about their own and other women's sporting achievements in the national press.

CRICKET AND HOCKEY

Many women combined the pleasures of two games — hockey in winter and cricket in summer. From their inception both sports were administered by women. The first interstate competition in any team sport was cricket. Victoria, the state that had pioneered women's cricket during the gold rushes, formed a women's cricket association in 1904. Within two years a Victorian eleven had been selected from the association's 19 affiliated clubs to play a visiting Tasmanian team. This represented a divergence in women's cricket, for it was the first time that the 'gate' was not donated to a charity or cause. Instead the proceeds were used to promote women's cricket in Victoria. The Islanders, as the Tasmanians were called, were drawn from clubs in Devonport and other north-west districts and contained one married woman. Two matches were played, with the home state successful on both occasions. A series of return matches was played in Tasmania in 1907.

A strong women's cricket competition existed in NSW, Victoria and Tasmania before the First World War. The captain of the Bega women's cricket team, Mrs Evershed, exerted her authority dressed in black. Bega, NSW, 1910.
STATE LIBRARY OF NEW SOUTH WALES.

The cricket associations were disbanded during the First World War as women spent their time in wartime occupations, but not all women put away their bats. Interest in the game was sustained and opportunities for social matches were relished. Australian nurses serving in England even played cricket against their convalescing Australian patients. When the Victorian Womens Cricket Association was re-formed in 1923, players acknowledged the debt they owed to the pioneers of the game. Retired players formed the Pioneer Victorian Ladies Cricket Association to assist with the continued development of the game. They were prominent in the many fundraising ventures needed to finance international cricket visits and tours in the 1930s. Their annual reunion drew many women together and as late as 1940 were attended by more than 100 players from the 1904-1914 era.

The administrators of hockey were even more ambitious. When the New South Wales Association was formed in 1908, followed by the Australian Association in 1910, the game was already strong in the schools and universities due to the enthusiasm of English-trained sportsmistresses. Within five years an invitation to play in Australia had been accepted by an English women's hockey team. The team arrived in New South Wales during the first months of 1914. This bold and enterprising invitation had been extended by an association that comprised only seven teams.

Hockey flourished in both the country and city, especially after a visit by the English women's team in 1914. Albury, Goulburn and Cootamundra hockey teams at Cootamundra, NSW, 28 June 1915.
STATE LIBRARY OF NEW SOUTH WALES.

However, it was the tour to Australia by the English Women's Hockey Team in 1927 that proved a great impetus to the game (second only to the crowning of the Australian team as Olympic champions in Seoul 61 years later). The 1927 tour marked an era in which women's hockey came to be seen as a more scientific game. The English visitors not only demonstrated tactics unfamiliar to local players, they employed new stickwork including the drive, flick and push strokes. Moreover the English women extended their influence beyond the cities. The team toured the country areas of Australia where hundreds of teams were by now affiliated with their state bodies. Tenterfield, New South Wales, declared a public holiday for the whole town to watch England defeat the local girls, despite 'a very hectic thirty-five minutes each way on a field which ran into hollows every now and again'. Patricia Bryant, England's left-wing, enjoyed her stay at Frensham Mittagong, New South Wales, so much that three years later she left her job as games mistress at a Leeds school to become sportsmistress at Frensham. Women in the Australian associations quickly emulated the new skills, tactics and stickwork. The game was taken more seriously, especially after the publication of a book on hockey by English player-author Marjorie Pollard. Young women throughout Australia stood in front of their mirrors and carried out in every detail the exact grip, correct stance and action recommended by Pollard.

The impetus within the hockey associations propelled the game so quickly that by May 1930, in the depths of an economic depression, the first Australian women's hockey team embarked on an overseas tour of Great Britain, Africa, Germany, Belgium and Holland. As most women were unable to contemplate financial contributions, the entire tour was financed by the All-Australia Women's Hockey Association. According to the New South Wales and Australian centre-forward Ena McRae, the team was sent away, 'to learn all we could from the various countries in which we played. Winning did not matter. The idea was to absorb every detail as to technique and tactics.' The bold financial commitment by the association paid rich dividends. The team spent nearly nine months abroad and on their return they were able to offer their services as coaches to players of every grade.

Following the lead of Victoria, cricketers in New South Wales founded their state association in 1928, followed by Queensland, South Australia and Western Australia in 1930. Interstate matches were re-started and in 1931 these were staged under the auspices of the newly formed Australian Women's Cricket Council. In the summer of 1932–1933 Australia had been rocked by the controversial men's bodyline cricket tour. It was a bold move, therefore, for the newly formed women's council to issue an invitation to the English Women's Cricket Association to send a team to Australia for a series of test matches in 1934–1935, especially considering the council's own finances stood at about five shillings. England accepted and the team led by Betty Archdale toured all states before playing test matches in Brisbane, Sydney and Melbourne. Crowds thronged to the tests, and public holidays were declared wherever the English played country matches. Although the local team was comprehensively beaten, the Australians made a handsome profit from the tour. To prepare for the matches the women's association, with advice from cricketer and architect Barbara Peden, constructed the first indoor practice nets in Australia in the YWCA building in Elizabeth Street, Sydney.

But it was the overseas tours by hockey and cricket teams in the late 1930s that really consolidated the position of both sports. Lack of funds prevented the hockey association paying for the 1936 hockey tour to America. Each woman contributed £160 for three months in the United States and Canada, the highlight of which was the International Federation of Women's Hockey Associations' Tournament in Philadelphia. The teams present included England, Ireland, Scotland, South Africa and the United States.

When the 15 cricketers set sail for England and Holland in 1937 one significant change had occurred in the rules of cricket which enabled women to play it to the best of their ability. In 1936 the English and Australian associations proposed the adoption of a smaller cricket ball for use in all matches. The five ounce ball (rather than the five-and-a-half ounce) also had a smaller circumference which permitted women to grasp the ball and the seam more comfortably. To the extent that each player had to be able to contribute or raise £120 towards her expenses, it was a representative team, but it also included at least one player from each state. The idea was that each woman would help promote the game on her return and all players signed a contract promising to continue playing cricket after the tour. The games of cricket and hockey duly improved following the overseas tours and both the cricket and hockey associations were set to host 1939 tours by England when the Second World War intervened.

BASKETBALL

Basketball (renamed netball in 1970) was an American game that had been introduced to England in the 1890s. It too spread to the colonies and grew in popularity among Australian women as a winter sport and rival game to hockey. As basketball was a game not played by men it needed considerable capital investment before it could be universally adopted in Australia — grounds needed to be levelled and marked out, goal posts bought, and umpires, captains and coaches trained. It took longer to acquire such resources than it did to walk on to hockey or cricket pitches already constructed by the local councils, although even in those two sports many teams had to acquire new ovals. Priorities of aldermen were more likely to favour the allocation of money for grounds for the football codes than for basketball.

The development of basketball was also hampered for many years by two rival codes within the one sport — one a seven-a-side and the other a nine-a-side competition. The first interstate seven-a-side competition was played in 1926 for the Prouds Cup between New South Wales, Victoria, South Australia and Queensland. In 1927 the All-Australian Women's Basketball Association was formed which entered into negotiations for many years with New Zealand basketball authorities whose country followed the nine-a-side format. Proposed tours in 1936 by two New Zealand teams had to be cancelled for financial reasons. No competition was possible until 1938 when New Zealand agreed to tour under the Australian (and English) seven-a-side format. Queensland remained a basketball anomaly in Australia for many years. Basketball was controlled in that state by two associations, one titled the Queensland Womens and the other the Queensland Ladies Basketball Association. The names, however, bore no relation to the class of women playing the game. The former controlled the seven-a-side game in Brisbane, the latter the nine-a-side game, more popular in the country areas of Queensland.

The popularity of basketball was such that in 1933 the Victorian association started a separate night basketball competition expressly for those who had daytime industry or office commitments. Games between 46 teams were played at the indoor courts of the Melbourne Exhibition Building.

VIGORO

Other team sports, including vigoro and cricko, were established and prospered in this period but their popularity did not survive past the Second World War. By 1933, vigoro, another women-only game, had more than 300 teams in New South Wales alone, making it the largest women's sport in that state, with hockey a close second. The rules, formerly owned by an Englishman, had been willed to Mrs Dodge of the Sydney sports firm L.W. Dodge & Co. She had them copyrighted and published in the late 1920s and set about organising teams and instructing players. Vigoro games held in Sydney's Domain on Saturday afternoons drew large crowds of spectators. To encourage the bowlers it was common for spectators to place silver coins on the stumps — from two shillings to threepence — with the bowler taking all.

At the first interstate test matches, played between New South Wales and Queensland at Randwick Racecourse, the players followed a tradition started by English sportswomen and spectators by burning the bails and stumps and placing the ashes in a silver casket to be competed for at future interstate vigoro championships. The game never truly became a national one, but the existence of a three-way interstate competition (Tasmania joining in the mid 1930s) provided some stimulus for the game to thrive. Demonstration vigoro matches were staged in Victoria but the game failed to attract the interest shown in the other eastern states and waned after the introduction of softball during the Second World War.

Another derivation of cricket, cricko, was started up in New South Wales and Queensland in 1935. As in vigoro, the game was played with bats shaped like canoe paddles and two hard balls of a different colour bowled alternately but there were slight rule differences, and a cricko team consisted of 12 not 11 players.

BASEBALL AND LACROSSE

Baseball also enjoyed a brief appearance among Australian sportswomen, although rule variations made interstate competition impossible until 1934. In 1933 each state elected representatives to attend a special meeting the following year to draft a national constitution and to formulate rules. In New South Wales and Queensland players pitched overarm while Victorians pitched underarm. The delegates decided to favour the overarm method, unanimously agreeing that it was faster, more accurate and more difficult to hit. A slightly smaller junior professional ball was adopted as well as a smaller diamond. The meeting concluded with the formation of the Australian Women's Baseball Association. Western Australia joined the association in 1936.

By April 1934 the square at the University of Sydney had been turned into a 'maze of queer markings' and the first national baseball championships were contested. At the conclusion an Australian team was selected. This was a common practice among sports with no international competition, as it enabled players to still strive for the highest honour. Negotiations were commenced in 1936 with Canada, the United States and Japan with a view to possible international matches. Not all sections of the community favoured women's baseball. Members of the Kelvin Grove club in Brisbane had their equipment sold from under them in 1934 when the athletic club to which they were affiliated suddenly decreed 'baseball is not a woman's game'.

Attempts were made to expand and popularise lacrosse, the first all-women's club being formed in Melbourne in 1935. The game was played on a hockey size field and a solid rubber ball was passed between players via a long stick to which a net was attached. Women in England played the game with special short lightweight lacrosse sticks but as these sticks could not be procured in any number in Australia the game languished.

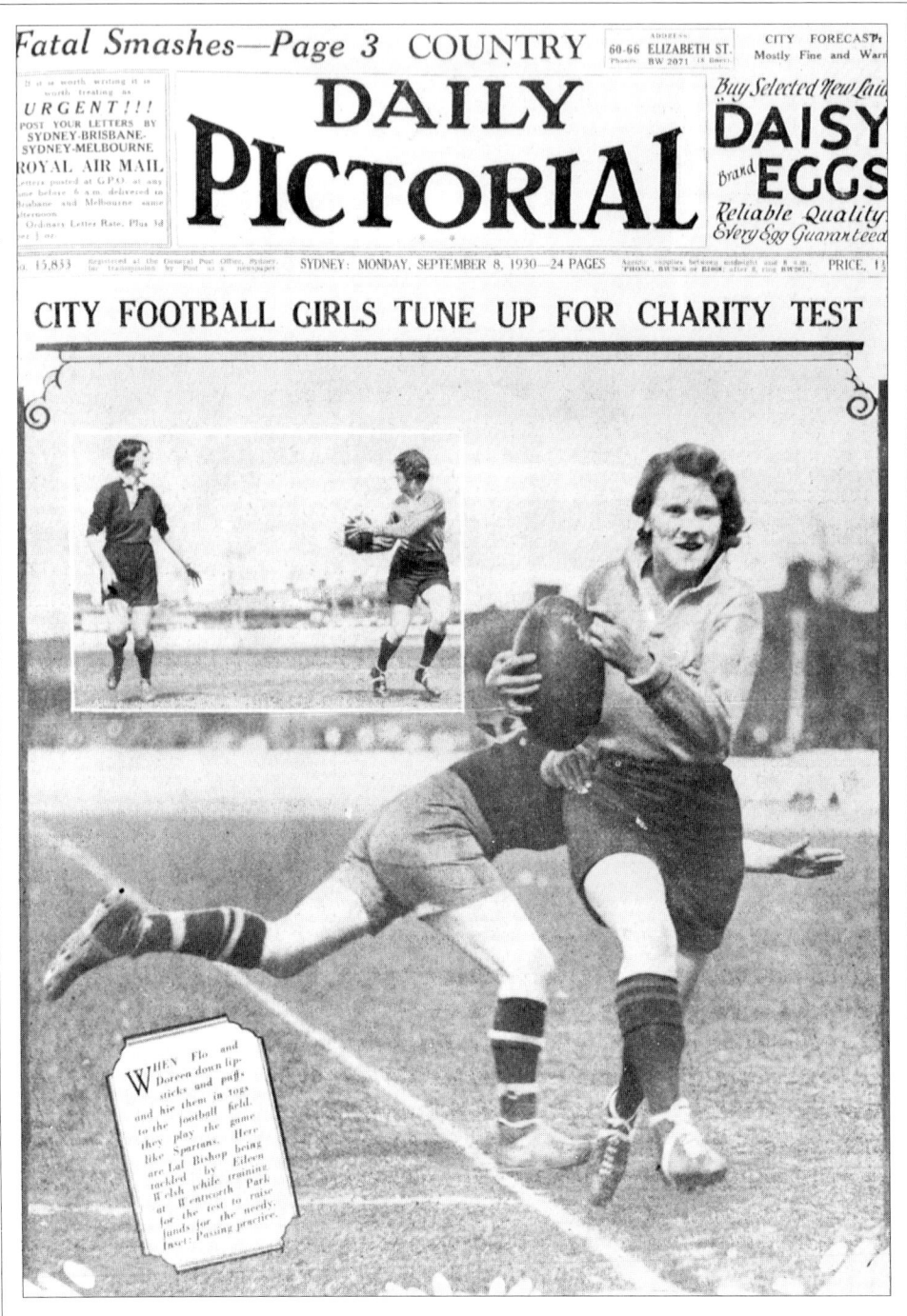

A full women's rugby league competition existed in Sydney from 1921. More than 2500 spectators watched the players contest a charity test in 1930 to benefit Sydney's unemployed women. *Sydney Telegraph*, 8 September 1930.
NATIONAL LIBRARY OF AUSTRALIA.

FOOTBALL

Football was another team sport that attracted women in the first half of the twentieth century. Just as rugby league enthusiast Annette Kellermann kicked off in Frank Burge's testimonial match in 1923, Dally Messenger kicked off in a women's match at the Royal Agricultural Society's Showground in 1930. The two sides, New South Wales and Metropolitan, played before 2500 spectators to raise funds for Sydney's unemployed women.

A full women's football competition had existed in Sydney in 1921 when five women's teams were formed. A meeting of more than 200 women players in 1921 established the Ladies' Rugby Football League. The women played in the same attire — shorts, jumpers and boots — as that worn by male footballers. Numerous country teams were also formed in New South Wales, including the West Wyalong Canaries Football Team, the name an ironic comment on football's supposedly manly traditions.

The West Wyalong Canaries Football Team, c. 1920. Their name belied their commitment to the game of rugby league.
NATIONAL LIBRARY OF AUSTRALIA.

ROWING

Women rowers faced a great deal more criticism than other sportswomen. Numerous articles appeared in the press asking 'Is rowing a harmful sport?' or 'Is rowing too strenuous?' Rowing had the frightening potential to produce women who did not quite fit the feminine mould. Under the headline 'Strong but dainty' the *Australian Women's Weekly* in 1936 told its readers that in the state crews,

Most of the rowers are nearer six feet than five feet in height, and their weights average well over ten stone . . . Some of them ate steak three times a day, which is not surprising as they practised twice daily.

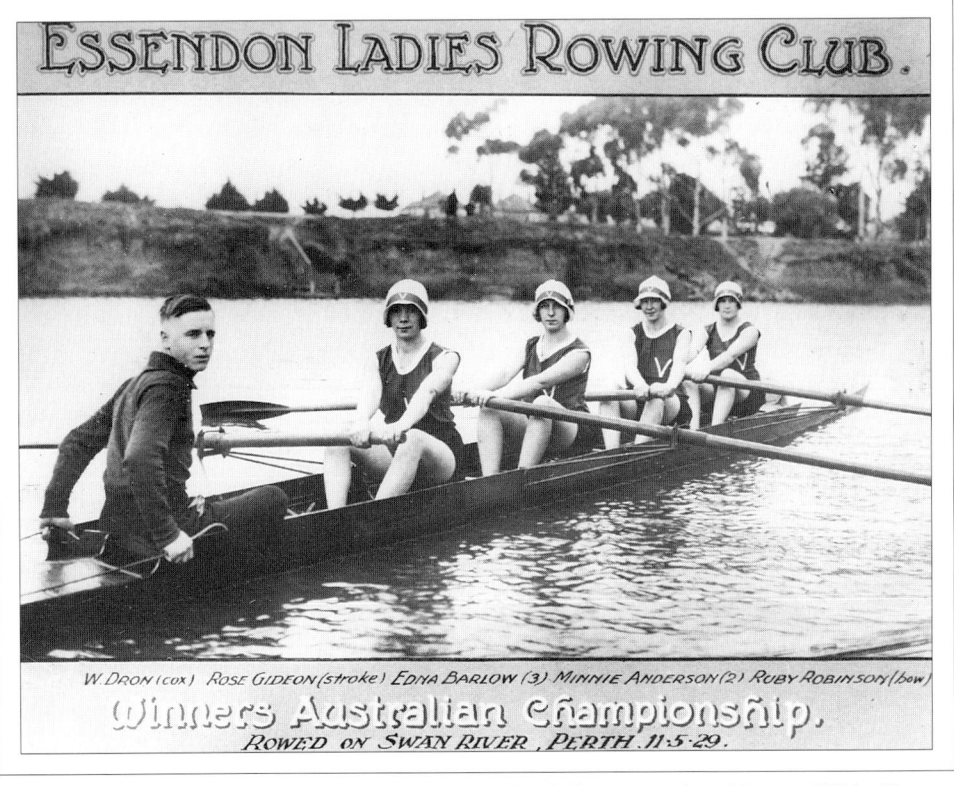

ESSENDON LADIES ROWING CLUB.

W. DRON (cox) ROSE GIDEON (stroke) EDNA BARLOW (3) MINNIE ANDERSON (2) RUBY ROBINSON (bow)

Winners Australian Championship.

ROWED ON SWAN RIVER, PERTH. 11·5·29.

Because rowing required daily practise, it had the potential to challenge women's social responsibilities. The Australian four-oar championship was first contested in 1920. Essendon Rowing club, 1929 winners of the Australian championship, Perth.
MARY-LOU JOHNSTON COLLECTION.

In fact rowing was probably the first sport played by women in Australia that required them to practise every day. Most other sportswomen (and men) would never have dreamed of practising more than once or twice a week — the era of scientific training had not yet arrived. If a rower worked, her training schedule would probably have cut into the time she was expected to perform family domestic duties. The rowing Amazons — 'heathly, sun-tanned, bright-eyed and muscular' — could be seen as threatening the very basis of the social order.

The Australian women's four-oar championship was first contested in 1920, the same year the Australian Women's Rowing Council was formed. State championships were held regularly and the Australian titles were staged in a different state every year. South Australia dominated the four-oar championship for many years, until challenged by New South Wales and Victoria in the late 1920s. From 1934 women also formed crews of eight for competitive races. In 1936 Rose Gideon of Melbourne was the first woman to cox a state team.

In 1939 the women's championship was cancelled at short notice when the gentlemen of the Victorian (Men's) Rowing Council dug deep into their rule book to resurrect an 'almost forgotten' rule that prevented women rowing on the same programme as men in that state. 'Besides', the gentlemen added, 'apart from the rules, the Henley committee was faced with a long programme, and it would have enough to handle without additional women's races'.

SPORTS COUNCILS

As sportswomen formed themselves into state and national associations, many women also foresaw the benefits that a combined association of all women's sports would bring. In 1931 the Victorian Women's Amateur Sports Council was formed. It was made up of representatives of all women's sports in that state and acted in an advisory capacity to their associations. The New South Wales Amateur Women's Sports Council was formed in 1933 and, under the patronage of Lady Gwendolen Game, affiliated hockey, cricket, basketball, baseball, rowing and vigoro. Similar moves were made in Queensland, Western Australia and South Australia, but the problems of distance proved insurmountable for women in these states. The Councils were active in lobbying for the interests of sportwomen — including the allocation and building of grounds and playing fields, running coaching and umpiring courses and co-ordinating tours, carnivals and overseas visitors. Ambitions went even further, and sportswomen continued to clamour for the formation of an All-Australia Women's Sport Federation throughout the 1930s.

The Victorian Women's Amateur Sports Council organised the Victorian Women's Centennial Sports Carnival, a large-scale event held in 1934 to commemorate Victoria's foundation. The highlight of the celebration was a combined sports day and pageant held on the Melbourne Cricket Ground with more than 3000 young women participating in cricket, hockey, basketball, bowls, rowing, swimming, athletics, rifle shooting, baseball and badminton. In addition there was a series of individual fixtures for women arranged by the different sections of women's sport. Victorian basketballers played a challenge match against the Australian team, bowlers held a competition week for more than 1000 bowlers in Victoria, the Victorian cricket team played a match against the visiting English eleven, swimmers and rowers held a combined water sports day, a centenary tennis tournament was staged, visiting British golfers competed in the Victorian championships, a Pacific hockey tournament was held with competitors from Fiji and New Zealand and a massed physical culture display by more than 4000 young women was staged.

PLAYING FIELDS

One of the most important and urgent roles of the Sports Councils and women's sports associations was to lobby for more women's sports grounds. In 1928 the City Girls Amateur Sports Association persuaded the New South Wales minister for lands to make available 11 acres of land in Maroubra for their playing fields. The site was to be financed by the subdivision and sale of surrounding crown land. Deputations of sportswomen lobbied metropolitan racing clubs to use their grounds and dressing room accommodation on non-racing days.

The Amateur Sports Councils also recognised the need and advantages of women owning and controlling large grounds similar to the Sydney Cricket Ground and Sports Ground. Here national and international fixtures could be staged and women's sport would reap the benefit of entrance fees. In turn, this money could be used to send more teams overseas. Despite being ratepayers, women were forced to rely on the benevolence of men's sporting associations to use major sports grounds.

Individual associations, and in fact individual teams, physically cleared, levelled and prepared their own sports grounds across the country. The Women's Hockey Association levelled Woollahra Park for their own use. Cricketers, led by Margaret Peden, acquired a former market garden in Kuring-gai which they cleared and turned into a suitable cricket ground. (Despite their efforts former players still remember fielding among potatoes.) Sportswomen needed to utilise whatever influence they had in the community. During the Depression, women cricketers in the Sydney suburb of Annandale lobbied the council to put down a concrete wicket on the local park for the use of the women's team captained by Amy Hudson. The council did this, but as soon as the pitch was down men took it over. Fortunately, Hudson's mother had some interest in the allocation of food coupons and she threatened to withdraw the Depression benefit from the male cricketers concerned. The women got their wicket back.

FOR THE SAKE OF THE INDIVIDUAL AND THE CLUB

Women organised and administered their own team sports in Australia because these were the least acceptable sports for women to play and would not have prospered (let alone existed) under male control. Funds would certainly not have been made available in 1930 by a hockey association administering both women's and men's hockey for an international tour by a women's team intent on learning rather than winning. Individual women were less threatening as sporting entities and the attentions of male administrators were directed at women who participated in non-team sports like tennis, golf, swimming and athletics. In contrast the more acceptable sports for men were deemed to be those that built team spirit and co-operation such as football and cricket. Individual sportswomen may have been more acceptable, but they too were involved in a constant struggle for recognition, facilities and funding for their clubs.

GOLF

From the introduction of golf in Australia women were deemed as 'associates' while men were 'members'. Some clubs even restricted associate membership to the wives of club members — single women and women whose husbands did not play therefore could not join. It took until 1921 for the Australian (Men's) Golf Union to finally relinquish control of women's tournaments to the Australian Ladies Golf Union (ALGU). Autonomy was achieved largely through the efforts of the New South Wales president Lady Halse Rogers who had won the Australian amateur championships in 1904. Under the direction of the ALGU the interstate matches, which had been played since 1897, were scheduled immediately prior to the Australian championships. This saved costs by gathering all women together at once. It also increased the number of women who could participate by reducing the number of interstate trips needed by the top women golfers. Because national tournaments were based in three states — New South Wales, Victoria and South Australia — the annual player affiliation fee of five guineas was used to subsidise the travel expenses of Queensland, Western Australian and Tasmanian players.

In 1931 the ALGU affiliated with the English LGU making international competition possible. To finance this, the ALGU devised a series of new annual state tournaments. The entry fees provided a reliable cash flow to finance women's international trips and visitors. A regular competition with New Zealand, for the Tasman Cup, was inaugurated in 1933. In

Jo Allan at the Hume Country Golf Club, Albury, NSW, 1920, the year before women administrators wrested control of their golf championships from men.
STATE LIBRARY OF NEW SOUTH WALES.

1935 a British team played their way round Australia and filled the top four places in the Australian championships. The star attraction, however, was the visit to Melbourne in 1939 of Olympic gold medallist and professional golfer Babe Didrikson from Texas. Male golfers backed by the Melbourne *Argus* refused to believe the claims of 25-year-old Didrikson that she averaged 290 yards on the drive. The paper scoffed,

> *she could not have been speaking seriously . . . recently Sam Snead — the longest hitter in first class golf — won a long-driving competition with a shot of a few yards more than the 300. But not even Snead would claim an average of 290 yards.*

The next day, in a much smaller article, the *Argus* blandly reported, 'From the first tee she hit a drive 301 yards . . . At the second hole her drive exceeded 300 yards'. Didrikson also claimed a card of 85 playing only with her right hand and 81 playing left-handed. The standards of women's and men's golf in Australia would never be the same again.

TENNIS

Throughout this period women tennis players needed the approval of male administrators before touring overseas. This approval was never automatic and money was only granted if it could be spared by male players, or if the claims of women champions proved impossible to ignore. Women were caught in the classic catch-22 situation where they were deemed too inexperienced in international competition to warrant overseas tours. No international competition existed akin to the Davis Cup for women (the Federation Cup was first held in 1963), although women proposed such a competition as early as 1935. New Zealand women's teams visited Australia every 13 years (1909, 1922, 1935), hardly a regular competition.

In 1919 the singles champion of Australia Lily Addison became the first Australian woman to play at Wimbledon. In 1928 one of the first women's teams to tour abroad included Daphne Akhurst. That year she became the first Australian woman to reach the Wimbledon semi-finals. She won the Australian title a record five times. In 1934, following a strong appeal by Australian champion Joan Hartigan, three crack English women toured Australia and drew record crowds at their White City matches in Sydney. The decision to finance their tour had been through the New South Wales tennis administration, the only state to allow women representation as councillors. The control of tennis by men seriously hampered the development of women's tennis and the women knew it. A woman sports journalist noted,

The Walker family dressed for tennis at Tenterfield station, NSW, 1900. Women who wanted to play at a competition level were denied the opportunity and experience of overseas travel for many years. Photograph by D.M. Cameron.
STATE LIBRARY OF NEW SOUTH WALES.

Here in Australia we have a wealth of tennis talent which could with proper handling be built into teams capable of competing with the best women players in the world. But all the say in matters of policy, and of representation abroad, is with the men.

But the power was not relinquished, and the Australian Lawn Tennis Association (ALTA) continued to act to the detriment of the women's game withholding their sanction for a 1937 women's team to tour the Continent and the United States. To contravene the decisions of the ALTA the women would have needed to forfeit their amateur status by accepting expenses and travelling allowances. The crop of potential Australian women champions had to wait until after the Second World War to emerge onto the world scene, many under the guidance of the 'Mrs Pankhurst of Australian tennis', Nell Hopman.   In 1939 the Queenslander Malla Molesworth, who had won the Australian title in 1923, became Australia's first woman professional tennis coach.

SWIMMING

The fact that swimming and athletics were sports in which women enjoyed Olympic status proved to have both advantages and disadvantages. As with tennis, amateur women swimmers and athletes still needed approval from male administrators before overseas competition could be sought. This was the case even after women formed their own associations as international organisers of

Brisbane City Swimming Club Team, 1907.
JOHN OXLEY LIBRARY, BRISBANE.

both the Olympic and Empire Games recognised only one controlling body (male) in each country.

When Annette Kellermann won the inaugural New South Wales women's championship in 1902 no higher level of competitive swimming was open to her. She turned professional and made a living from long distance, exhibition swimming and movie appearances. At that first 1902 competition an 11-year-old competitor was entered in the schoolgirl race. She was Fanny Durack. Ten years later, as Australian champion, she was nominated by the New South Wales Ladies Amateur Swimming Association (NSWLASA) to contest the first Olympic swimming races for women at Stockholm, along with Mina Wylie. But nomination never guaranteed travel. The Australasian Olympic Council lacked the necessary funds to send all its nominated athletes overseas and were

Australian champion Beatrice Kerr at Blackpool, England, c. 1906, where she gave many displays of diving and swimming. In 1906 she swam a new record of 82 seconds for the 100 yards.
STATE LIBRARY OF NEW SOUTH WALES.

not over-keen to spend what funds they had on women competitors. No funds were forthcoming from the all-male Amateur Swimming Association who channelled their finances into sending male swimmers. Funds from a public subscription organised by the NSWLASA permitted Durack to sail for Stockholm, followed by Wylie soon after. They won gold and silver medals respectively.

The NSWLASA was formed in 1906 with five clubs and 349 affiliated members. In 1925, with only £35 in club funds, they invited American Olympic champion Etheldra Bleibtrey to Australia for exhibitions at the Domain Baths to demonstrate the American crawl stroke. Two years later they changed their name from Ladies to Womens to reflect a broader base of members. The efforts of the women's associations enabled women to achieve success right from the first Olympics, and it was a tradition that continued. In 1932, 16-year-old Sydney swimmer Clare Dennis captured Olympic gold in the breaststroke, with Philomena Mealing winning silver in backstroke. International success also meant that international tours continued. In 1934 the English champion Joyce Cooper toured Australia and Clare Dennis and Frances Bult toured New Zealand.

Australian swimming clubs, including this one in Brisbane, sponsored championship meetings from the early 1900s.
Australian women achieved immediate success when swimming was first included as an
Olympic women's sport in 1912.
JOHN OXLEY LIBRARY, BRISBANE.

ATHLETICS

With the decision in 1924 to include athletic events for women in the next Olympics, the 1926 New South Wales athletics championships contained three events for women — the 75 yards, 100 yards and 4 x 110 yards relay. These races, held at Manly Oval, were open to women who were members of existing sports clubs, combined women's sports organisations, schools and independent athletes from all states. New South Wales athlete Edith Robinson won both sprint distances and after further success in 1927 and 1928 was nominated to compete at the 1928 Olympics in Amsterdam. Robinson contested the 100 metres and 800 metres races, although she had no previous experience in the latter event. She secured third place in her 100 metres semi-final.

Women's athletics associations were first formed in Victoria and Queensland in 1929, South Australia in 1931, followed by New South Wales in 1932, Western Australia in 1936 and Tasmania in 1937. In 1932 the Australian Women's Amateur Athletic Union was founded. It was not until 1936, however, that women took full control of their meetings. That year the Australian meeting, which was held once every two years, was for the first time organised solely by women and staffed by women judges, timekeepers and starters. This at last brought athletics into line with the majority of women's sports which were under the control of women administrators.

The 90 yards hurdles at the Sydney Sports Ground, 1931. The first athletic championship events for women were staged in 1926. Hurdlers recall obtaining permission from the local police station to compete in shorts.
NATIONAL LIBRARY OF AUSTRALIA

But disadvantages and prejudice against women athletes remained. The women's union still had to rely on the men's association to submit names for Olympic representation to the international body. In preparation for the 1936 Olympics, the names of high jumper Doris Carter and the 80 metres hurdles champion (and world record holder) Clarice Kennedy were both submitted to the men's union. Only Doris Carter's name was put forward, the men's union inexplicably 'losing' the second name. The *Truth* newspaper offered to pay Kennedy's expenses to Berlin and questions were asked in parliament but the men's union remained firm that they had never received the name. Before the war only three women athletes represented Australia at the Olympic Games, and the only Empire Games team to include women athletes was the 1938 Sydney Games.

Professional foot racing for women had been staged in Australia until it was banned in 1922, 'because of the undesirable mixing of women with men trainers and the methods of betting on the appearances of women in sprint events'. After an agreement to bar male trainers from attending professional women runners the ban was lifted in 1936. The newly formed Victorian Women's Athletic League held its first series of races at Castlemaine in December 1936. Professional women runners competed at the White City meeting in Sydney for the first time in March 1938. The women's amateur athletic associations, however, remained numerically superior to the professionals as prize money for women's events could be as low as £5 per race. Clarice Kennedy noted a further difference between amateur and professional women runners in this period. Professionals used starting blocks, an innovation not used by amateurs until after the war.

RIFLE SHOOTING

Expert riflewomen could display their skills in their own hunting or rifle clubs, c. 1914.
JOHN OXLEY LIBRARY, BRISBANE

Another women's sport fighting to overcome bans in this period was rifle shooting. Rifle clubs for women were established earlier in Australia than any other part of the British Empire. One of the oldest surviving clubs was the Commonwealth Ladies Rifle Club, which had been formed in 1901. Women regularly competed at the prestigious Kings and Anzac rifle meetings. In 1934 the gentlemen of the Victorian (Men's) Rifle Association, which controlled all shooting in that state, hastily forecast a national emergency. Claiming that all ammunition should be saved for male-only practice, they issued an edict barring women from competition. They were to be restricted to canteen duties and wifely encouragement in what even the press regarded as an illogical move,

Women have been competitors in rifle shooting events for many years past, and to debar them now under the guise that a Rifle Association must be of an entirely military nature seems a very feeble excuse.

Following Victoria's lead the National Rifle Association also banned women in 1938, but not without some criticism. The *Sydney Morning Herald* reported,

Many riflemen disagree with the official view. They believe that if the question of home defence becomes a realistic problem in Australia, then the women would be called upon to play a part no less important than the men.

LIFESAVING

In January 1908 women in Newcastle formed the Newcastle Ladies Surf Club. Two months later they gave an exhibition of the line and reel method of surf rescue at the first surf carnival held in Newcastle. The women's team was so impressive they were invited to give a demonstration at the Bondi carnival. The team of six — four single and two married women — travelled to Sydney with their chaperon and were given 'a long and wholehearted ovation' after performing a rescue. Membership in the club quickly expanded to 620 women. The Manly women's team competed at the 1912 surf carnival before a crowd of 20 000, having already been immortalised in Percy Spence's 1910 painting 'Women Lifesavers, Manly Beach'. The Surf Life Saving Association, however, stepped in and banned women from gaining the bronze medallion, which was necessary to qualify them as lifesavers.

Women practised full lifesaving procedures. Coffs Harbour Jetty Surf Club Team, NSW, 1924.
STATE LIBRARY OF NEW SOUTH WALES

When women's surf clubs were formed throughout Australia women were restricted in competition to march pasts, drill, surf races, beach relays and novelty events. But this did not prevent them from practising full lifesaving procedures, and many clubs formed in association with swimming clubs. The first women's club in South Australia was formed in 1931 and in 1933 the premier Sydney and Melbourne clubs, coincidently from Brighton, Victoria, and Brighton, New South Wales, challenged each other to an interstate competition.

CYCLING

The ownership of bicycles among women rapidly increased in this period as women in Sydney and Melbourne caught up with the sport already popular in the other capital cities. Cycling clubs were established in the country as well as city areas. Women of all ages raced each other over short distances and continued the long distance endurance challenges. Mrs M. Price, 'a prominent woman cyclist in Southern Tasmania and the mother of four children' set the inaugural Hobart to Launceston and return cycling record of 20 hours, 25 minutes and 35 seconds in May 1932. The following month she bettered Madge Steward's one-way record producing a time of 7 hours, 26 minutes and 34 seconds. Other champion distance riders were Elsa Barbour, Billie Samuels, Lillian Thorpe and Valda Unthank, the latter setting a record for seven days and nights of continuous cycling in 1939 to earn herself the title 'woman endurance cyclist of the world'. Unthank was a prominent official of the Victorian Amateur Cycling Association and organised weekly handicap races and distance events for members.

Ollie Adams playing croquet at Carinya guest house, Lorne, Vic, 1925. The adoption of shorter skirts enabled the new generation of women players to swing the mallet from a more precise angle. Photograph by Elma Adams.

STATE LIBRARY OF NEW SOUTH WALES

CLUBS, CLUBS AND MORE CLUBS

The first women's bowling association was founded in Victoria in 1907 by Mrs G. Bleazby the daughter of the Premier, Sir Thomas Bent. The first New South Wales club was formed in Hamilton, Newcastle in 1915. In 1936 more than 8000 women bowlers thoughout Australia affiliated to form the Australian Women's Bowling Council. Like women golfers and tennis players, their main concerns for many years centred on battles for equal access to the greens on weekends. Squash, originally called squash racquets, was first played by women in Victoria in 1928. In 1936 the first public squash court was built in New South Wales giving women greater access to the game. The major courts in that state had been located at the exclusive Royal Sydney Golf Club. In 1935, despite the fact that the majority of Australia's 16 000 croquet players were women, only one woman was chosen in the national team to contest the three way internationals with England and New Zealand.

Despite unfavourable economic conditions, and sometimes because of them, a host of new women's clubs were formed. With a reduction in the number of men in polo clubs during the Depression, women were invited to take up the game. In 1932 the first women's polo clubs were founded in Melbourne and Adelaide, and those two states held an interstate match in 1934. In times of greater affluence, however, women's presence on the fields was not quite so welcome.

Shaping up, Queensland, c. 1915.
JOHN OXLEY LIBRARY, BRISBANE

The club boom extended far and wide. Women formed their own clubs or auxiliary clubs in such recreations and sports as fencing, chess, cars, speedway, motor boats, sailing, badminton, jiu-jitsu, angling, kennel-owners, horse owners, skittles, skating, billiards and skiing. Women belonging to club sports in in Australia fought battle after battle to establish their associations and retain ground already won amid a generally hostile environment. One newspaper commented in October 1938,

Sportswomen have come to regard it as inevitable that after any meeting they hold in any sport they will be immediately subjected to a series of denunciations from a section of the community. Their performances are compared unfavourably with those of men in similar sports, their dress and uniform are criticised, their appearance bewailed. Indeed, sportswomen are considered fair targets because they do not live up to some individuals' idea of what women should do — principally stop at home. This attitude is quite in keeping with the supreme ego of the male. The idea that a woman might do something for her own enjoyment is incredible to him.

ONE MILLION SPORTSWOMEN

Who were the one million women who made up the membership in these teams and clubs in the late 1930s? The answer is that they were drawn from no particular class or age group. Some were factory workers, domestic servants, business women and professional women and some were single, married with children, perhaps surviving on the breadline or with servants themselves. For some women the time spent playing competitive sport was the most enjoyable of their lives while others regarded it as a fleeting interest. Young women of the 1930s had been born in the new century, they had lived through a world war and the resulting technological expansion that had seen rapid growth in their employment. As well they were caught in the middle of an economic depression. Some commentators believe a boom in women's sport occurred during the Depression because it was a cheaper form of entertainment than going to the cinema or dances. This was not the case. Women took up sport in the 1930s in addition to their other leisure activities. There were simply more choices available for women. The First World War had broadened women's horizons, and playing sport was a further expression of this.

While the administrators and those prominent in the public promotion of the sports were most likely university educated, many of the players were from the working classes. But very few women's sports can be categorised as exclusive to one class. The composition of teams differed from sport to sport and from state to state. Similarly, while economic constraints would have prohibited some women from fulfilling their sporting ambitions at a national or international level, representative teams were never the exclusive preserve of the wealthy. In a way, women's general lack of economic clout brought them together into a united group constantly required to raise funds by whatever resourceful means imaginable.

The newest and biggest employers of women in this period were retail and industrial concerns. Women worked an average of 45 hours per week at their paid employment. Many of the larger institutions employed welfare superintendents to look after the interests of their women workers. These welfare superintendents organised them into sporting teams and the companies provided all necessary equipment. This both attracted women to work for the companies and increased productivity.

One of the first women to promote sport in industry was Eleanor Hinder who was appointed welfare superintendent at Farmer & Co in Sydney in 1919. While promoting loyalty to the company she encouraged young women employees to use their leisure constructively and keep fit. With Jean Stevenson of the YWCA she established the City Girls Amateur Sports Association. Young women from all over Sydney joined the association including workers from Farmer's, David Jones, Anthony Horderns, Harrington's and the Will's Tobacco Factory. By 1926 the association sponsored 30 basketball teams, nine hockey teams, 21 tennis clubs, a swimming school and physical culture classes. In 1926 they organised three camps, numerous weekend walking tours and bought a holiday house at Narrabeen. They also gave members individual advice on diet, exercise and general health care.

Once public opinion accepted that sport was not detrimental to women's health, it could be used to exert a moralising influence on young women. During this period the YWCA was one of the major promoters and sponsors of women's sport throughout Australia. In 1926 large groups of single women were recruited to work in the Commonwealth public service in Canberra. The YWCA took a particular interest in their welfare. In what was then no bigger than a country town, they provided a fully equipped gymnasium and employed a physical culture teacher to run fitness and fencing classes for women during hours compatible with their working or domestic commitments. They started the Blue Triangle Association which ran women's cricket in the territory, and hosted the tour to Canberra by the visiting English women's cricket team in 1935. Hockey, basketball, baseball, volleyball, vigoro, tennis and badminton teams were formed in the late 1920s and early 1930s and hikes around Canberra both on foot and by bicycle were regularly sponsored. Older or married women were also catered for (it was compulsory for women to resign from the public service on marriage) with various sports teams as well as bridge lessons.

The National Council of the YWCA held an annual meeting of all their sports councils to determine the types of sport their members preferred and the value of 'sportsmanship' in women's lives. In 1932 the Adelaide branch responded to the national questionnaire by unanimously voting hockey, basketball, volleyball, tennis, vigoro, archery, badminton, ping pong, 'team games' and swimming as their preferred sports. These, they said, taught them loyalty to the team and umpire, fair play, co-operation, friendliness, unselfishness, self-control and doggedness.

Sports that had previously been the preserve of middle class women were opening up to all. Many churches and local councils constructed asphalt tennis courts. Compared to lawn, these courts were low cost and needed minimum maintenance. Local councils also constructed many more public golf links. These did not charge the large membership fees required by private courses and country clubs. By 1935 golf had become the most popular pastime for Australian women.

Women at the top of various sports were drawn from a variety of occupations. Sports such as rowing were not composed solely of women from the middle and upper classes as was the case for men. The women who contested the 1936 four-oar national rowing championship were from a broad range of society. The Adelaide crew contained a retail worker, mannequin and two dressmakers; New South Wales: two clerks, a textile worker and a machinist; Queensland: a Burroughs machine operator, office worker, machinist and tailoress; Tasmania: a pianoforte teacher, photographer, typist and farmer; Victoria: two munitions workers, a tyre factory pattern maker and a domestic worker.

Employment profiles can also be constructed for the 1937 Australian women's cricket team that toured England and Holland. Players included an architect, a Girl Guide commissioner, an art photographer, a factory packer, a buyer and assistant manager of a jewellery business, a superintendent and director of a kindergarten, a boot machinist turned forewoman, a machinist of cardboard boxes, a typist, a supervisor in a needlework factory, two clothing machinists, a companion, and a merchandise forewoman at a drapery firm. Clearly the only link between some of the players was cricket. Another feature of this team was that every woman played at least a couple of other sports, most commonly hockey, baseball, tennis, basketball and vigoro.

Few women in this period restricted themselves to only one sport, most playing several in both summer and winter. Likewise few administrators were prominent in only one area, their skills often being used to promote a host of sports. In New South Wales Olive Peatfield was vice-president of three sports organisations: the New South Wales Women's Amateur Sports Council, the Women's Cricket Association and the Parks and Playgrounds Movement; president of two: the Baseball and Basketball Associations; as well as being the sports secretary of the Young Women's Christian Association. In Victoria Miss L. C. Mills assisted with the inauguration of many sports associations and was president of basketball, baseball, cricket, night basketball, amateur athletics; vice-president of rowing; and life member of hockey, cricket and basketball associations.

Readers of mass circulation newspapers and magazines were kept up to date with the exploits of team players as well as individuals. At the other end of the scale, magazines aimed at middle and upper class women portrayed a different range of sports. The magazine *The Home* cost two shillings and sixpence per month (the *Australian Women's Weekly* cost twopence a week in 1933). Despite its name, from 1920 *The Home* regularly featured outdoor activities for women including golf, tennis, swimming, ice skating, horse riding, cycling, bridge parties, surfing, holidays, fishing, and skiing. Team games received no mention despite the numbers of society women who were players, administrators or patrons. Very little attention was given to the women's part in the Empire or Olympic Games or to competitive swimming and athletics in general. The magazine accepted advertisements from the Bjelke-Petersen Physical Culture School, and from most of the independent girls schools where physical activity as an integral part of studying and school life was emphasised. Advertisements also featured fashions applicable to the above sports and the new 'sportswear' for women.

The extent to which middle and upper class women played sport can also be gleaned from the pages of the 1940 London publication *Principal Women of the Empire: Australia and New Zealand*. They listed 314 women of note, most of whom were from the middle classes, had attended the independent private girls school in Australia and New Zealand and were aged at least forty. Most were politically conservative and from a Protestant religion. Of the 314 women, 183 list some sort of physical activity among their recreations, about six women in ten. These 183 women played 332 sports between them, about two each. As reflected in the pages of *The Home* the most popular sports are tennis and golf, but what the sample illustrates is the diversity of sports played by middle class women, and its importance in the lives of older women. As could be reasonably expected of women in this age group, team games were not a feature, although quite a few alluded to playing them when younger. Here is a breakdown of the sports listed by 183 women:

PRINCIPAL WOMEN OF THE EMPIRE: AUSTRALIA AND NEW ZEALAND 1940

TENNIS	86	SQUASH	3
GOLF	83	TABLE TENNIS/PING PONG	3
RIDING	38	TARGET SHOOTING/SHOOTING	3
SWIMMING	25	CRICKET	2
WALKING/BUSH WALKING/HIKING	20	MOUNTAINEERING/	
		HILL CLIMBING	2
YACHTING/BOATING	11	PHYSICAL CULTURE	2
CROQUET	9	ROWING	2
ICE SKATING/SKATING	6	SURFING	2
SKIING/SNOW SPORTS	6	BASEBALL	1
BADMINTON	3	BOWLS	1
BILLIARDS	3	DECK GAMES	1
CHESS	3	HUNTING	1
FISHING	3	ICE HOCKEY	1
HOCKEY	3	MOST GAMES	1
OUTDOOR SPORTS	3	OUTDOOR ACTIVITIES	1
RACING	3	'TRUE SPORT'	1
		TOTAL	332

Holidays increasingly included physical activity as an integral component. Deck quoits on board the S.S. *Jervis Bay* off the NSW coast, 1937.
STATE LIBRARY OF NEW SOUTH WALES

The ski fields enticed both the experienced and novice sportswoman. Mt Buffalo, Vic, 1918.
MUSEUM OF VICTORIA

Magazines like *The Home*, aimed at middle and upper class readers, often depicted women enjoying the twin pleasures of golf and tennis. Cover illustration by Bertha Sloane, 1 March 1922.

MITCHELL LIBRARY, STATE LIBRARY OF NEW SOUTH WALES

In addition to the one million women who were involved in organised sport, many more included some form of physical exercise in their lives. Hiking clubs were very popular in the 1930s and activities ranged from treks around the capital cities to events organised by Mountain Trail clubs and Bush Tracks clubs. The City Sports Girls regularly went on weekend 'mystery hikes', the first of which in August 1933 took thousands of young women down the south coast to Wollongong, New South Wales.

The Government Railways directed most of their advertising in this period to people taking weekend train and walking treks. In fact more women were beginning to include physical activity as an integral part of holidaying. In summer this meant swimming and beach games. In winter it meant snow sports or mountain treks. Summer holiday resorts began to advertise the range of outdoor diversions available to women. Women at Palm Beach in Sydney could swim, surf board ride and play golf on the local links. On the Great Barrier Reef women could 'turtle ride' as well as swim and fish. The new health and spa resorts advertised 'opportunities for varied sporting recreations' along with their medicinal mineral salts. In winter women could enjoy tobogganing, skiing and skating at places like Mt Buffalo in Victoria, while the wealthier were lured to the 'outdoor playground' of the United States.

For women unable to afford a resort or overseas holiday the outdoors still beckoned. The Easter vacation was a popular time for organised or informal camping expeditions. Places at the annual YWCA camps were in demand among women:

> One of the most popular features of a camping holiday is its lack of heavy expense and the absence of worry over the adequacy of one's wardrobe, ever present when a holiday to some popular resort or to cities is planned.

Sports associations like hockey and cricket eagerly adopted the camp system, employing recognised coaches and holding Easter camps where specific skill training was concentrated on. Regular Easter tennis tournaments were held in many country centres across Australia and usually included a fair share of city players.

The artist Margaret Preston, in her series of wood cuts to celebrate Victoria's centenary sports programme for women, tried to encapsulate as wide a range as possible of women's sports. She depicted a cricketer, a hiker and a woman playing with a yo yo, so symbolising a team sport, a physical recreation or leisure activity for women of all ages and a new fad diversion that young women were drawn to. The first yo yo craze had swept across Australia in 1932.

By the Second World War the 'sportswomen' of Australia had emerged as a recognisable social group. In a 1927 editorial the *Sydney Morning Herald* claimed 'Today it is the girl who does not take part in games of athletic skill who is abnormal: the cult of sport is universal'. The *Everlady's Journal* received many entries to their 1929 competition 'Are women good sports?' The writers emphasised and eulogised women's sporting instincts linking them with Australia's pioneering spirit and the success of the nation as a whole. When another golden era of women's sport blossomed in Australia in the 1950s it came as a surprise and mystery to many commentators — but only to those who had ignored the foundations laid in the 1930s. A whole infrastructure was in place that propelled the daughters of the 1950s and beyond into the world arena. By the 1990s there were few sports in which Australian women had not yet become world champions.

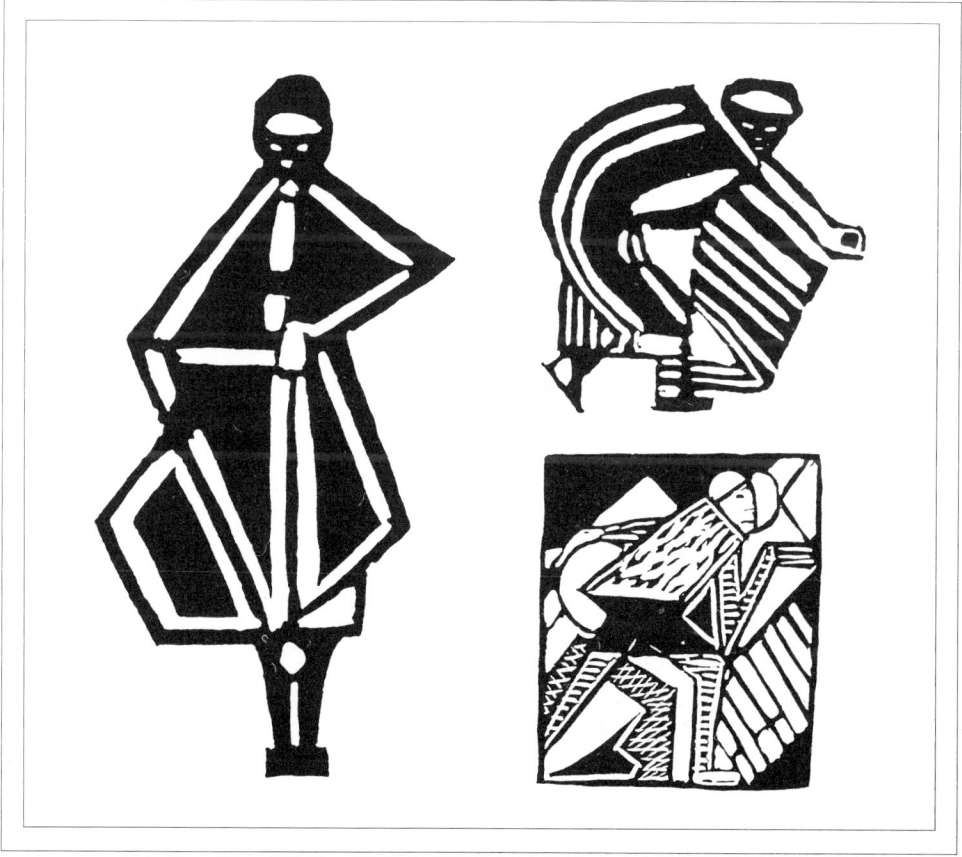

The artist Margaret Preston commemorated Victoria's 1934 centenary womens sports carnival by depicting a wide spectrum of sporting endeavours — the yo-yoer, the hiker and the cricketer. Woodblock prints, 1934.
ART GALLERY OF NEW SOUTH WALES

THE CULT OF
THE PHYSICAL

ALONGSIDE THE GROWTH AND
CONTROL OF ORGANISED COMPETITIVE SPORT FOR WOMEN WAS
ANOTHER FORM OF EXERCISE — PHYSICAL CULTURE. It too was largely run
and controlled by women for women. Already introduced in the schools, it
acquired large numbers of devotees throughout the first half of the twentieth
century. To the one million women who participated in organised sport on
the outbreak of the Second World War must be added a substantial number
who took regular exercise in the form of physical culture.

On the one hand physical culture can be regarded as a restrictive form of
exercise. It relied on traditional, old fashioned values — it was ladylike,
feminine and aesthetic. Its emphasis on grace, deportment, posture and
beauty reinforced rather than threatened women's role in society. In the
nineteenth century women swinging clubs and performing exercises in
'rational' costumes was liberating and daring. Once more strenuous games
and sports were organised by women, physical culture can be seen as
limiting to women's sporting potential. But on another level it cannot be
dismissed so readily. The history of women's sport is dotted with constant
battles for acceptance and recognition. Throughout all these challenges, large
groups of women participated in a form of exercise that built team-work,
discipline and strength and heightened their self-esteem. It provided a basic

The increasing employment of women outside the home led to the belief that their fitness could be in jeopardy.
Railway Institute Gymnasium, 1906.
ANU ARCHIVES OF BUSINESS AND LABOUR

training in flexibility, agility and exercise and proved a strong foundation for sportswomen of the future. Only when it was recommended to the *exclusion* of organised sports was it limiting to women.

As industrialisation increased in Australia the principles of physical culture found their way from the classroom into the broader community as an appropriate arena for urban women. The robust country woman had no need for supplementary vigorous exercise, but it was generally accepted that her sedentary and physically inferior city-bound sister should have instruction in physical culture. The increasing employment of women in the major cities outside the home led to the concern that their fitness and suitability to be healthy vehicles for procreation of the race could be in jeopardy.

The scientifically based Swedish physical culture emphasised the therapeutic and curative principles of exercise as opposed to the more militaristic drill and mechanical movements of the German system. Its exponents had studied anatomy and physiology in London and applied these principles to every movement of the body ensuring the correct development of chest, spine and limbs. Commercial schools were established in the major cities and advertised directly to women. By the end of the First World War physical culturists could be fully trained in Australia. In 1919 Ada Bosworth established a college to train teachers in Melbourne. Miss E.M. Webb and Miss C.M. Lorimer were the principals in 1920 of the 'Open-Air Roof Medical Gymnasium and Physical Culture School' in Collins Street, Melbourne. Calling themselves the 'Premier Training School of the Southern Hemisphere' they advertised widely in women's magazines. By 1921 they were styled the 'Australian Physical Training College for those desirous of becoming teachers'.

The 'Bjelke-Petersen Bros Sydney and Melbourne Schools of Physical Culture, Fencing, Boxing and Jiu Jitsu' also appealed to women through journals and magazines offering 'a large staff of lady instructors and masseuses always in attendance' to treat 'constipation, loss of energy, sleeplessness, nervousness, indigestion, obesity, excessive thinness' and promising 'beauty of form, grace of movement, robust health and vitality'. The ideal woman was not yet the svelte ideal of the late 1920s. The Bjelke-Petersen Bros assured clients 'Our methods for Ladies produce rounded and graceful lines in the Figure'. Nor was physical culture the preserve of the young single woman. Older readers were advised 'No married woman need lose her figure if proper measures are taken to keep the muscles firm'.

Eileen Edwards, the Tasmanian author of *Modern Physical Culture for Women and Girls*, defined physical culture in 1916 as 'the production of a state of health and physical fitness of the body, as well as of the mind, thus producing graceful as well as healthy women'. Australia, Edwards said, was a world leader in physical culture,

this training has been chiefly in the hands of women, and women too, who have gone into the work whole-heartedly and voluntarily. There has not been any need for girls to have compulsory training, and it stands to the credit of thousands of Australian girls that they have voluntarily and with pleasure paid to be trained physically.

The purpose of physical culture she said was not 'to enable a girl to perform some difficult exercises for display purposes' but to promote the 'harmonious development of the whole body'. It was for all classes of women 'maidens, matrons, and even grandmothers'. In a special chapter 'The rejuvenation of society women', Edwards advised non-working women to set aside a month per year of recuperating time. The working woman on the other hand, *has to try to bear the strain of continuous struggle against an overtaxed system. But she has some redress. Her skin is seldom powdered, thus the pores are not clogged. She does not keep such late hours, her habits are of necessity more regular, her living more simple. She has an aim in life, and more often than not she belongs to some recreative club, where she has an outlet for superfluous energy in a good and rational style, to say nothing of Saturday-afternoon tennis or surf bathing.*

But the cautions were ever-present. A chapter on 'Acrobatic Eccentricities' admonished 'you will seldom, if ever, find an acrobatic woman over the age of twenty-five who is not an absolute wreck.'

Despite Edward's assertion that physical culture was not purely for exhibition, perform they did. Her 'troupe' travelled more than 600 kilometres a week through country Victoria giving displays and taking classes. During a visit to Tasmania in 1912 they performed at the Launceston Exhibition,

we had five thousand as an audience on our first evening, and were asked by special request of the Director of Education for Tasmania to give a second demonstration, after which we were asked to give a third evening.

Her popularity was such that by 1916 Amalgamated Moving Pictures had commercially released two films of her work.

Massed physical culture demonstrations and competitions continued throughout the ensuing decades — massed because of the hundreds of young women taking part in any one event, and massed because of the thousands of spectators present. During a demonstration in 1927 the doors of the Sydney Conservatorium had to be shut 'excluding fully as many people as had gathered inside'. In October 1935 the *Sydney Morning Herald* reported, 'Nearly 3500 pupils, mainly girls, took part in the competitions and demonstrations of the Bjelke-Petersen School of Physical Culture at the Sydney Town Hall. Seventy-two clubs were represented, and for the massed drill event 1500 girls exercised with perfect precision.' Interstate competitions attracted many participants and girls competed annually for points in such categories as free arm, marching, rods, clubs and spectacular. Physical culture girls appeared before visiting royalty and swung clubs soaked in flammable liquid and ignited to welcome the American fleet during the Second World War.

Physical culture became more than just a set of exercises for the body and mind. It was increasingly promoted as part of a movement that emphasised the importance of exercises to aid not only women's health but their beauty. In 1913

Demonstration performance at a commercial gymnasium.
NATIONAL LIBRARY OF AUSTRALIA

the *Everylady's Journal* Shilling Library published the third in their series for women entitled *Good Looks and Long Life. A Guide to Beauty and Health in Australasia.* (Others in the series covered cooking, housekeeping and babycare.) In it Jacqueline Gore extolled the benefits of the Swedish system of physical culture in work and play. Women could improve their carriage, walk gracefully, add chest measurement, lengthen their waist and exercise themselves to sleep. Particular wrist exercises were prescribed for women who were violinists, pianists, telegraph operators and typists. Violent exercise in any form was counselled against and emphasis was placed on maintaining the 'delightful roundness and charm' of the feminine form.

Professional swimmer Annette Kellermann championed the cause in 1918 with the publication of her book *Physical Beauty How to Keep It.* In the United States, Harvard University's head of the Physical Education Department had judged Sydney-born Kellermann the 'Perfect Woman', the 'ideal ratio of femininity' after tests had been conducted on the heart, lungs, teeth and eyes of 10 000 American women. Kellermann's book contained advice that promoted exercise, especially swimming, as an integral part of women's beauty and health. Beauty was no longer 'skin deep'. In 1927 Dr Josif Ginsburg, author of the American book *The Hygiene of Youth and Beauty,* told his Australian readers 'we are not very far from the time when the athletic type of woman will be considered the most beautiful.'

In 1935 the London-based movement, the Women's League of Health and Beauty, was established in Australia by Thea Stanley Hughes. Hughes had studied under the league's founder Mrs Bagot-Stack in England where the league claimed over 100 000 adherents. The league recommended physical fitness for all women, regardless of whether they were sportswomen. One hundred Australian members assembled on Manly Beach in December 1935 to give a demonstration of the benefits of physical culture to women of all ages. Hughes told the assemblage,

The league is establishing centres all over the world, and so physical culture is becoming an international sport with everyone on the same side, that of health and fitness. There is as much satisfaction in mastering an exercise as there is in playing a shot correctly in any game.

The League was based in Sydney, and branches were established in Melbourne, Adelaide, Perth and Brisbane. Women were graded into classes comprising three levels, with private lessons, pregnancy classes and classes for the sick also available. Each paid an annual subscription of ten shillings plus one shilling per class. For an additional one shilling and sixpence they received an issue of the magazine *Movement,* written and edited twice yearly by Hughes. The entrepreneurial Hughes also published two books expounding her philosophy. Many women incorporated the programme into their training for sport and special exercises were claimed by Hughes to greatly benefit their performance in individual sports — foot and toe exercises for take-off in cricket, hockey and tennis, plus exercises to steady the nerves of the cricketer, increase the lung capacity of the swimmer and relax the athlete.

The 1930s, however, also saw the rise of national and international fitness movements which were to threaten the established links between physical culture and organised sport for women. Physical training was placed on a more medical and scientific basis with increased emphasis on diet as well as exercise. There occurred a world-wide shift from the Swedish to the German methods of physical culture. In response to what was thought to be an increasing physical and mental degeneration of its people, Germany under the Nazi regime had instituted nationwide programmes of physical fitness. Similar fears were raised in Australia during the Depression. George Dupain, founder of the Dupain Institute of Physical Education and Medical Gymnastics, Sydney, stated in 1933, 'The racial physique as a whole is not improving — it is degenerating. The Great War showed this; hospital records and insurance statistics corroborate it; and the results of modern city life prove it.' Regimes throughout Europe now directed their attention towards the physical fitness of young women — but it was no longer fitness for fitness sake. The future mothers of the race were duty bound to be healthy. More than ever before strenuous competitive sport among women was incompatible with their roles as mothers and nurturers.

Convinced of the Australian population's own degeneration, the federal government established the National Fitness Council in November 1938 and allocated £100 000 over five years. One politician, speaking at Bendigo in 1937, claimed that 75 per cent of all girls employed in factories needed 'physical direction and treatment' and 'urged parents to hesitate before sending their daughters out into the business world unless they were physically capable of standing the strain.' After the outbreak of the Second World War, government financial contributions to national fitness were substantially increased. Combined with these official moves was a new non-official national fitness campaign. The press began to encourage women to 'keep fit at home'. One expert devised 350 separate bar movements so women could attain perfect physical fitness in the home 'with the aid of an ordinary broomstick'. Fencing was promoted as an answer to the problem of keeping women fit. Its rigid rules of practice taught co-ordination of mind and muscle. As a sport it promoted 'brain over brawn' and women could therefore achieve the same high standards as male fencers. Women's

The national fitness movement was promoted by a government concerned with the degeneration of the population.
Brisbane class, 1941.
JOHN OXLEY LIBRARY, BRISBANE

sporting pursuits now needed a purpose. No longer was it merely enough to enjoy the game for the game's sake.

To cater for the new interest in national physical fitness formal qualifications were introduced for teachers. When champion Sydney hurdler Clarice Kennedy wanted to be trained as a specialist physical education teacher in 1929 no course was open to her through the government school system. Kennedy would have to become a general teacher and take one lesson a week of physical education. Kennedy relinquished her teachers' college scholarship and embarked upon a sportsmistress training course offered by a private school. The National Fitness Council promoted new full time courses. The Swords Club of Sydney, re-named the Australian College of Physical Education, was among those who pioneered physical education as a profession for women. The college conducted a two-year training course for women to qualify as a 'Physical Culture Instructress and Sports Mistress'. In 1937 physical education was brought under university auspices when Dr F. Duras was appointed lecturer in physical education at the University of Melbourne. But it proved a double-edged sword. To an audience of women who played competitive tennis, hockey, cricket, baseball and basketball, Dr Duras recommended a choice of fluent and rhythmic exercises as most suitable for

Physical education as a profession. Advertisement from
The Home, 2 January 1940.
NATIONAL LIBRARY OF AUSTRALIA

women, 'dancing, rhythmic gymnastics, javelin throwing, high and long jumping — if not done to excess — archery, skiing, skating, fencing, riding, and above all else, swimming'. Physical education was introduced at the University of Sydney in 1941 with the appointment of Harold Le Maistre as lecturer. The three-year certificate course was held at the Sydney Teachers College, which possessed a fully equipped gymnasium.

For women the activities of the National Fitness Council and the opening of new careers in physical education, while broadening the base of fitness, signalled a push away from competitive sport. In 1940 the Victorian physical culturist George Beattie warned against the adoption of unsuitable exercises and sports for women. He recommended four sporting activities as safe — hiking, archery, horse riding and tennis, the latter only when it was non-competitive! His daughter Joan Beattie, also a physical culturist, had never engaged in competitive sports as she would 'sacrifice feminine charm and run risk of overstrain'. From late 1939 the head of physical education in New South Wales state schools directed that young women were to be taught folk dancing rather than basketball as part of their physical education. The stage was set whereby women of the post-war generation would need to re-establish their right to choose the form of exercises or sports they individually preferred.

After the war most competitive sport in government schools was phased out for girls across Australia and in its place new forms of physical culture and eurhythmic dance were instituted. Classes in eurhythmics (a combination of the Greek words for music and movement) had first been given at Government House, Perth, by graduates of the London School of Dalcroze Eurhythmics. It was taught in some schools from the 1920s. Grecian clad nymphs were to be seen gambolling about the school grounds in imitation of Isadora Duncan. The baby boomer generation began to exercise to music broadcast in special programmes to their schools nationwide. But this new form of exercise was punctuated by military commands either from their teachers or from the airwaves.

Gambolling in school grounds. Eurhythmics class, Maryborough Girls Grammar School, Qld, 1922.
STATE LIBRARY OF NEW SOUTH WALES

Heather Gell was Australia's leading teacher of movement through music. After graduating from the London School of Dalcroze Eurhythmics in 1951 she set up her own Australian school to train teachers in the mid-1950s. Barbara Worledge, a physical education teacher from Sydney, represented Australia at the 1953 Women's Congress of Physical Education and Sport, which was held in Paris. Here she learnt that,

Routine muscle building exercises were out for girls; most countries now looked at physical training for girls through the eyes of the scientist and artist . . . modern dance was the most important factor in developing grace and strength in a young girl.

Worledge thought the American sport of synchronised swimming — a combination of swimming and dancing — had infinite possiblities for Australia. At the 1962 Conference on Physical Education sponsored by the commonwealth government and held in Perth, speakers recommended the extension of non-competitive sports for girls within the school system.

The establishment of movement and physical culture based exercises for schoolgirls had one serious effect. Rather than create generations of fit young women as intended, it produced generations disinterested in physical activity. The elements of fun were taken out of sport and in its place tedious, regimented exercises were substituted. The addition of music made them no more palatable. Exercise for women had come full circle. Many young women escaped from the realm of physical culture as soon as possible.

The cult of the physical still dominates some areas of women's sport. There is a direct connection between eurhythmics and the graceful sports recently introduced for women at an Olympic level — especially synchronised swimming and modern rhythmic gymnastics both introduced in 1984. Even the modern aerobic dance, practised more for weight control, owes its origins to physical culture. Women need to have equal access to a far greater range of physical activity than that represented by aesthetic exercises emphasising grace, beauty and femininity.

KHAKI SPORTSWOMEN

1939–1945

BY THE SECOND WORLD WAR THE 1930S GENERATION OF SPORTSWOMEN WERE WELL AND TRULY ENTRENCHED IN ORGANISED SPORT. Although all international sports tours and most national sporting championships ceased during the war years, women's participation in sport continued to thrive. Women who had previously belonged to factory or social sporting teams hastily joined service teams during the war. As more and more women were moved into industry, recreational activities were organised. The war promoted team sports but it also did much to encourage a higher level of physical fitness among women.

When war was declared in September 1939 the sportswomen of Australia were as genuinely keen to play their part as any. Under the newspaper headline 'Our Sportswomen are Ready. Training and Discipline at the Service of Australia', the various women's sports associations declared,

Sportswomen throughout Australia are ready to give their service in this time of national emergency. They are among the most highly organised groups in the community. They are young and energetic. Moreover, the discipline of field, and course, and river in their sporting spheres has taught them to be ready for emergencies.

Having faced decades of resistance to their efforts, the women's sports associations now recognised that their very existence could be threatened in time of war. They were anxious to help and anxious to ensure that erosion of their hard won sporting independence did not occur. They hastily justified the need to keep women fit and to maintain high citizen morale through games,

The majority of the thousands of sportswomen within the metropolitan area are business girls. Many of them work in factories, and with the extra pressure of work in all industry anticipated within the next few months, some leisure recreation will be the more necessary. Moreover, if the girls are kept fit by their games, they are better prepared to give more service in the community. . . The sporting organisations feel that they are in touch with every group, and thus can more easily provide war work for them.

Their fears were certainly well founded. Male-controlled sports organisations had used the international situation as early as 1934 to ban women from the nation's rifle ranges.

The offers were not hollow rhetoric. Raising money was something sportswomen did regularly and did well. Throughout Australia they banded together during the war to raise money for the patriotic funds and to co-ordinate war work. By 1943 the Women's Golf Union recorded that it had raised more than £20 000 and donated 86 000 articles to the Australian Comforts Fund (ACF). Members also packed annual Christmas hampers for the troops. Women bowlers made or supplied 33 500 articles to the ACF and the Red Cross Society. Special competitions were arranged to raise money and a tournament held in 1944 raised more than £100 for the Prisoners of War Appeal. Women cricketers, including many state players, travelled to soldiers camps throughout Victoria to play fund-raising matches against men. Over three years members of the New South Wales Women's Amateur Sports Council raised £1500 for the war effort.

Thousands of women enlisted in Australia's services and were required to have the same general level of physical fitness as male personnel. The military of course had a penchant for drill, marching and physical education of all kinds. Drill sergeants were appointed and usually drawn from service women with experience in physical training, whether through sporting associations or through organisations like the Girl Guide movement. The author of *Australian Women at War* Patsy Adam-Smith reported,

Contrary to expectations, it was found that the WAAAF [Women's Auxiliary Australian Air Force] learned to drill more quickly than their male counterparts, they swiftly assimilated the air force atmosphere and were 'rapidly transformed from a motley collection of young women from different backgrounds (be it country or town) into an efficient, disciplined body, able to carry out orders without confusion.'

Doris Carter, a former Olympic hurdler, was in charge of training courses for the Women's Auxiliary Australian Air Force. Recruits were taken on camps or bivouacs to assess their potential. The hurdler Clarice Kennedy lectured in physical education and led exercises with the Army Education Service at Victoria Barracks. Servicewomen were encouraged in sporting recreations such as table tennis and ice skating. Tennis and squash courts as well as swimming facilities were also available depending on their station. Sporting teams were organised and entered in the local competitions under their service names and occasionally inter-service competitions were staged. Former Australian cricketer Nance Clements organised a WAAAF cricket and softball team. On the second anniversary of the formation of the WAAAF in 1943 a sports carnival was held with units competing for pennants and a cup. Dressed in khaki shorts and blouses, WAAAFs also gave public demonstrations of physical culture to boost war loan tallies.

In 1943 Kathleen Gordon, the Commonwealth National Fitness Officer in charge of Women's Physical Education, was appointed to assist in instructing Australian Women's Army Service (AWAS) personnel in physical training. At the Physical Training School in Melbourne she evolved a standardised form of training to be used for women. Supervisors and instructors underwent a six week practical course at the school and were then able to train other instructors in their units. Gordon devised an instruction manual, mostly based on the British standard of physical training, which was printed by the department of health in conjunction with the defence department. Entitled *Physical & Recreational Training for Australian Womens Services*, it was published in 1944 and included sections on set exercises, organised games and relaxation. The level of intensity of each exercise varied with provisions made for new recruits and for those who lived in barracks or where no ground work was possible.

As in peacetime, women factory and munition workers were provided with sporting amenities to attract them to the job and help keep absenteeism down. Workers at a Melbourne textile factory played deck tennis and ten pin bowls on their factory roof. A multitude of sports teams were formed and inter-factory competitions held. Special war time exercises were devised for women working

full time in a factory or office and still providing domestic duties at home. These
'rationalised' exercises were designed to give a woman 'just the amount of activity
or relaxation she needs, to the muscles that need it, in the time she can afford —
and no more than her weary body needs to restore it.'

Motor cycle messengers of the National Emergency Services. These women supplied their own uniforms and motor
cycles. Sydney, c. 1942.
AUSTRALIAN WAR MEMORIAL

On the home front sportswomen formed themselves into organisations to advance the war effort. In 1940, 300 expert horsewomen formed a cavalry corps in Melbourne. They were an auxiliary of the Australian Women's Legion and were trained to replace men during a national emergency in such tasks as carrying despatches over rough country. The corps consisted of volunteers and their membership included 'shop assistants, typistes, mannequins and society girls'. Women cyclists, under the direction of Australian cycling champion and world record holder Valda Unthank, formed themselves into a Women's Cyclists Messenger Service and trained out of the Air Raid Precautions (ARP) Centre at Coburg, Victoria. Among other things, the women practised cycling in gas masks and aimed to provide communication between vital points of ARP areas in the event of air raids. In accordance with strict rationing of petrol many women used bicycles during the war, especially nurses and women from the Land Army who travelled from their hostels to local farms each day.

After learning of the exploits of an Englishwoman who captured a German pilot, the Victorian Women's Clay Target Shooting Club formed themselves in 1941 into a unit to train for defence against attack by parachute troops. Many women were already expert in handling guns and their membership was said to consist of 'musicians, manicurists, nurses, salesgirls, typistes and plain wives'. The enemy stood no chance if they had parachuted onto the roof of the Water Board building in Pitt Street, Sydney, where 150 women of the Small Arms Club trained each lunchtime. A fully-equipped miniature range was constructed for their practice complete with reduced sized targets, matting and wooden shooting mounds.

American Army nurses stationed in Australia were offered the facilities of women's tennis and golf clubs during their off duty hours. Many also became keen horsewomen, 'probably spurred on by those of their number who have cantered round the wide open spaces of Arizona'. Fencing was a common pastime, especially after the arrival in Australia of Second Lieutenant Muriel Guggolz who had represented the United States in fencing at the Olympic Games in Los Angeles in 1932. The major sporting influence of American nurses, however, was their introduction into Victoria of the game softball in 1942. A cross between rounders and baseball, softball had caught on to such an extent that within two years the Victorian Women's Softball Association was formed. It had a total membership of 250 players with 20 teams in regular competition. By 1944 softball was made a compulsory part of the University of Melbourne's physical culture course and was adopted across the state in various schools and colleges. The National Fitness Council promoted interest in the game Australia-wide. The popularity of the sport was explained in 1944 by the first president of the association Irene Burrows. Softball, she said,

All service personnel were required to have a high standard of physical fitness. The women's services employed former Olympic athletes, including Doris Carter, to run their fitness programmes.
NATIONAL LIBRARY OF AUSTRALIA

is speedy and has the same teamwork, science and sportsmanship [of baseball] but has the advantage of requiring less elaborate equipment, less playing space and is suitable for all ages and both sexes. It is inexpensive to play and provides good exercise for the amateur athlete.

Softball soon displaced other women's games and cricket in particular lost many members to the sport after the war. Another sport to start during the war was polocrosse. In 1940 women from the Ingleburn (NSW) Horse and Pony Club ploughed and hand planted a field for their use.

Vigoro game, Brisbane 1940.
JOHN OXLEY LIBRARY, BRISBANE

With the fittest men absent from the beaches, Australia's women played a vital role in surf lifesaving during the war. Conveniently forgetting the ban they had placed on women receiving the bronze medallion, Surf Lifesaving Officials appealed to women to fill the depleted ranks. Victorian honorary secretary, Mr E. Pleydell, told the *Argus* in summer 1940:

The girls are fully prepared for their responsibilities and are most enthusiastic. They have always played an important part in the life-saving movement, and their training, identical with that undergone by the men, is sufficient to enable them to take their place in patrols.

Women lifesavers took over duties across Australia and by 1944 were keeping the reels turning in Western Australia. Their actions were universally praised:

for clubs to remain active and maintain a standard of efficiency, the women members have been called upon to carry on and do 'the heavier types' of life-saving work that was previously undertaken by the men. They now patrol the beaches, carry out rescues, render any necessary first aid, and, in addition, take their share in instruction of new and younger members.

No wonder women were surprised when the Surf Lifesaving Association of Australia refused to grant them official recognition in the calmer waters of 1946.

The war of course interrupted the careers and training of many sportswomen. Athletes such as Western Australian Shirley Strickland and tennis players like Nell Hopman, chose to place their careers on hold as they participated in essential war work. Wilma Fowler, a promising Victorian golfer and tennis player, joined the Women's Land Army in 1943. The Victorian superintendent of the land army was Kitty McEwen, one of Victoria's top golfers. Fowler always travelled to her country placements with two or three golf clubs and a bag of balls for practice to 'keep the swing going and so forth'. After the war she returned to her golf but took up nursing when she discovered that it was not possible for her to become a professional golf teacher.

Despite the fact that national and international competition was cancelled for the duration of the war, many sportswomen kept training with the same dedication they had exhibited before the war. For some it was business as usual. Queensland athlete Joyce Brewer even interrupted her Sydney honeymoon to compete in the 1941 New South Wales 880 yards championship. Local athletic and swimming clubs for women were kept alive and the competition they provided must have gone a long way towards producing the crop of Australian women post-war champions. 'Graduates' from the 1938 Empire Games were encouraged to remain in active competition. Young women like swimmer Marjorie McQuade were noticed in 1944 as potential stars of the future. McQuade was unbeaten in her age group and won the Victorian 55 yards freestyle under-14 years race while still ten years old. Empire Games runner Irene Talbot and hurdler Thelma Peake remained

Petrol rationing introduced many more to bicycle clubs. Women's cycle racing continued throughout the Second World War. Empire Amateur Wheelers, Brisbane 1939.
JOHN OXLEY LIBRARY, BRISBANE

star athletes throughout the war with Talbot a former member of the Shell Women's Amateur Athletic Club joining the recently formed Melbourne Women's Amateur Athletic Club in 1941. In 1942, 21-year-old Charlotte McGibbon broke the

Australian javelin throw record of 118 feet with a massive throw of just over 131 feet. Although McGibbon left competitive athletics after the war to become a trainer herself, she still insisted on mowing the lawn 'to exercise her arms'.

Twenty-year-old Rhoda Cavill gave up competitive swimming during the war when her father Dick Cavill died. She took over the management of his pool and turned professional to teach swimming. Champion pre-war swimmers Judy Joy Davies and Evelyn De Lacy continued competitive swimming during the war, with De Lacy taking a few months off for the birth of her child. Nineteen-year-old Elsie Williams continued her assault on Australian cycling records and clinched the 32 kilometres record in 1941 on her special custom built bicycle. Sport was not only the preserve of young women. Forty-eight-year-old runner Kathleen Harney made a comeback to competitive club running in 1941, (but not before taking the medical examination her husband insisted upon) and 45-year-old rower Nellie Walsh stroked the Victorian women's four in 1940.

One woman oblivious to part of the war was cyclist Pat Hawkins of Perth. From February 1941 to February 1942 Hawkins made an attempt on the year's cycling world record of 29 603 miles held by Mrs Billie Dovey of England. Hawkins was only off the road for seven weeks of the twelve month period and claimed a distance of 45 402 miles. But one week later supervising officials found what they called 'certain irregularities in Miss Hawkins's log sheets' and refused to recognise the record. One wonders if she ever rode a bicycle again.

The war ultimately did not have the same effect on Australian women that it did on women athletes overseas. They finished the war with their sporting organisations still in place and thriving, and were individually physically unaffected by food rationing. They suffered little deprivation or dislocation as was the case for European women.

The real test and challenge for Australian sportswomen was not the war itself, but the post-war orchestrated push to return them to the domestic hearth. Their fit young bodies were now required as breeding machines for the future baby boomers, not as competitive athletes.

GOLDEN WOMEN

AT THE OLYMPIC, EMPIRE AND COMMONWEALTH GAMES,

1912–1990

IF YOU WERE FORCED TO ISOLATE THE ONE SPORTS ARENA IN WHICH AUSTRALIAN WOMEN HAVE HAD THE MOST SPECTACULAR SUCCESS, IT WOULD HAVE TO BE THE GAMES. Four hundred and eighteen women have represented Australia at the Olympics, winning 26 gold, 20 silver and 21 bronze medals. Five hundred and twenty-two women have competed at the Empire Games, later renamed the Commonwealth Games. Together they have won 137 gold, 119 silver and 102 bronze. Many more have been denied the chance to compete. The history of the Games has been in reality the history of swimmers and athletes. But even within these sports, events have been restricted. Although the number of events for women has crept up from year to year, large gaps still exist. Women are yet to enjoy a full Olympics or Commonwealth Games. The history of the Games has also been the history of young women competitors. For a plethora of reasons women have retired early from competition.

Many theories have been proffered to explain the extraordinary success of Australian women at the Games. In national terms, women's medal tallies have almost been an embarrassment considering the encouragement and resources directed elsewhere. But put in a historical perspective, women's success at the Games is perhaps no more outstanding than their success in every other sporting arena. When it comes down to international competition it is the individual who stands alone on the starting blocks. Fortunately for Australia, individual women know how to win. Fortunately, they also know how to fundraise.

The following is a brief survey of the history of women's sport at the Games from 1912 to 1990 — the even years of international competition.

1912 Olympic Games: Stockholm, Sweden

According to a contemporary newspaper account,

The ladies got off to an excellent start and Miss Durack at once went to the front. . . Miss Durack unfortunately ran into the side of the bath, but kept on swimming without losing any appreciable time.

Fanny Durack (left) and Mina Wylie (right), Australia's first women Olympians. Durack won the gold medal and Wylie the silver medal in the 100 metres freestyle at the 1912 Olympic Games. If two other swimmers had been sent, rather than two chaperons, Australia could well have won another gold medal in the 4 x 100 metres relay.

Fanny Durack's slight detour in the final of the 100 metres freestyle was the first, but by no means the last, time that Australian women would come up against seemingly impervious and immovable man-made objects in their quest for Olympic glory.

Sarah 'Fanny' Durack was born in Sydney in 1889, her parents were both publicans. After a mishap in the surf on a holiday in Newcastle, New South Wales, at the age of nine, she obstinately taught herself to swim at Sydney's Coogee Baths during 'ladies hour'. She had mixed success as a schoolgirl swimmer but after regular competition won the New South Wales 100 yards title in 1906. She dominated Australian swimming until the 1910-1911 season when 12-year-old Mina Wylie trounced her in the 100 and 220 yards freestyle and the 100 yards breaststroke. Mina (Wilhelmina) Wylie's father ran Wylie's Baths at Coogee and was the Australian underwater distance champion. As a child, Mina was part of her family's aquatic act and could swim with her hands and feet tied. Durack turned the tables on her younger rival the following season. In the process she captured three world record times. By 1912 both young women were deserving of Olympic Games selection.

For the first time in history two women's swimming events, the 100 metres and 4 x 100 metres relay, were scheduled for the Olympic Games in Stockholm, Sweden. Despite this, the all-male Amateur Swimming Association Olympic Committee selected seven men but no women to represent Australia. Immediately under challenge from women's organisations, they justified their omission of Durack and Wylie by arguing that it was too costly to send women to Stockholm for one race. Not only did the gentlemen try to prevent the women competing, they withheld any financial assistance. Individual women as well as women's organisations rallied behind the champions, opening a subscription which paid all of Durack's and part of Wylie's fare. The money allowed Durack to sail for Stockholm several days after the official team with Wylie following three weeks later. Both were accompanied by chaperons, a 'necessary' restriction on 1912 sportswomen. Two more swimmers and Australia could have won the relay.

In Stockholm 27 women contested the 100 metres freestyle event. Wylie was drawn in the third heat. She won her heat and created history as the first Australian woman to compete at an Olympic Games. Durack won the fourth heat in a new world record. Exactly 1 minute 22.2 seconds after the start of the final on Friday 12 July, Fanny Durack possessed the first gold medal in women's swimming; 3.3 seconds later Mina Wylie secured the first silver medal and Australian women had a perfect record.

The First World War caused the cancellation of the 1916 Olympics scheduled for Berlin, so Durack and Wylie continued their rivalry in Australian pools with

Durack breaking a further eight world records. Both toured the United States in preparation for the 1920 Antwerp Games. Mina Wylie never again reached Olympic selection standard despite a remarkable domination of Australian swimming championships for 20 years. On three occasions she won every women's event at the national championships (100, 220, 440 and 880 yards freestyle, 100 yards breaststroke and 50 yards backstroke) in 1911, 1922 and 1924. Wylie spent her life teaching and died in 1984 at the age of ninety-three.

1920 OLYMPIC GAMES: ANTWERP, BELGIUM

Lily Beaurepaire, the only Australian woman to compete at the 1920 Olympic Games.
LA TROBE COLLECTION, STATE LIBRARY OF VICTORIA

Two women, Fanny Durack and Lily Beaurepaire, were originally selected in the Australian team for the Antwerp Olympics. Durack had come back from defeat in American competition and was determined to gain revenge and defend her Olympic title. A week before she was due to depart, a burst appendix, complicated by typhoid fever and pneumonia, robbed her of the opportunity. She retired at the age of 29, but continued swimming for pleasure until her death in 1956. She received little attention in her home country until 1990 when a public subscription was raised to place a commemorative plaque on her untended grave at Waverley Cemetery in Sydney.

1924 OLYMPIC GAMES: PARIS, FRANCE

The male-controlled Amateur Swimming Association resisted the claims of women swimmers.

1928 OLYMPIC GAMES: AMSTERDAM, THE NETHERLANDS

The formation of the Federation Sportive Feminine Internationale in 1921, and their successful staging of international women's athletic games, forced the reluctant Olympic Committee to include women's athletic events at the 1928 Olympics. Australian women had not participated in these international meetings. The 1928 Olympics included the 100 and 800 metres, 4 x 100 metres relay, high jump, and discus. Four Australian women were selected for the Games; three swimmers and one athlete. The first women's athletic representative, Sydney sprinter Edie Robinson, was placed third in the semi-final of the 100 metres and fifth in her heat of the 800 metres. Robinson began her athletic career at the age of 17 while an apprentice in Hordern's Clothing Factory. She was spotted at the firm's annual sports day picnic and three weeks later won the 75 and 100 yards New South Wales state championships. No controlling women's amateur athletic association existed in Australia until 1932. Furthermore, Australian women were disadvantaged internationally as they did not compete locally on the harder cinder tracks used at the Olympic Games. A fifth Australian woman Thora Dennis (older sister of future 1932 gold medallist Clare Dennis) was also selected as a freestyle swimmer, but was deemed too young at 14 years of age to travel overseas.

These Olympics were dogged by controversy both in Amsterdam and Australia. Officials removed the 800 metres race for women athletes from future Olympic competition, claiming it had caused 'distress' to the participants, despite medical evidence and eye-witness accounts to the contrary. Canadian delegates led by an Australian-born manager also tried to eliminate women's track and field events completely. The manager of the Australian team Les Duff seemed to agree with this view. He quarrelled repeatedly with chaperon Mabel Springfield and submitted on his return a report critical of the diet of female competitors. He was clearly uncomfortable around women, requesting that in future 'women athletes should travel on a separate boat, and be housed in a different establishment'.

1930 EMPIRE GAMES: HAMILTON, CANADA

It was unfortunate, given this country's open hostility to women's athletics, that Canada was chosen to host the first Empire Games. No athletic events were scheduled for women. Instead a separate Canadian women's championship was held 'in conjunction' with the Games which Australian women were unable to attend. No Australian women were selected for the Empire Games swimming events.

1932 OLYMPIC GAMES: LOS ANGELES, USA

Two months before the March 1932 Olympic Games Australian swimmer Clare Dennis cemented her selection by breaking the world 200 metres breaststroke record at the Sydney Domain baths. Although only 15 years of age, such an achievement made her impossible to overlook. Controversy followed her to Los Angeles. In 1930 the Randwick-based swimmer had been disqualified in the New South Wales freestyle championship for not swimming in her lane and also disqualified in the breaststroke race for touching with one hand instead of two. By 1932 Dennis was New South Wales and Australian breaststroke champion, but nearly didn't make it past her Olympic heat after controversy erupted over the design of her official Australian swimsuit. Dennis won the heat and the protest, and went on to touch first (with both hands) in the Olympic final thus securing Australia another swimming gold. Her teammate Bonnie (Philomena) Mealing won a silver medal in the 100 metres backstroke.

The Australian team of four women also included swimmer Frances Bult, the first Olympic representative from Victoria. A schoolgirl from Merton Hall, Bult had set a 100 yards Australian freestyle record which stood until 1949. Sprinter Edie Robinson had been overlooked in selection in favour of Eileen Wearne who had run a 'plucky race' but was eliminated in her heat.

The unrivalled star of the Games was undoubtedly Texan Babe Didrikson who won both the 80 metres hurdles and the javelin. Unashamedly strong, Didrikson challenged world assumptions regarding the supposed femininity of women athletes, an issue which has continued to plague women's competitive sport. Back at home, Australian women competitors were praised for their 'feminine' appearance, the report from officials explaining Wearne's defeat stated that she, 'was not quite class enough in her event. The masculine type of girl has an advantage over the feminine type — the class that Miss Wearne represents. A perfect little lady and a credit to the team.' Better to be a perfect lady than a medallist! Everything that women's sports administrators had lobbied for was under challenge as women's success began to threaten male views on what was a 'normal' woman. Italian women athletes had already been barred from competing at the 1932 Olympic Games by a decision of a group of doctors who claimed that 'athletics, particularly running, are unsuitable for Italian women'. Long time misogynist and Olympic President Count de Baillet-Latour continued his opposition to the inclusion of women at the Olympics during a visit to Australia in October 1932. He too argued that athletics was detrimental to women's health, nonsensically adding 'If women want sport, I think they should have their own Olympic games'.

1934 EMPIRE GAMES: LONDON, ENGLAND

As women gradually began to establish official control over women's sport in general, they were in a far better position to lobby for the inclusion of women at the Empire Games. At the invitation and expense of the New South Wales

Women's Amateur Swimming Association, British swimming champion Joyce Cooper had toured and competed in Australia in 1933. The efforts of women officials had resulted in the Australian British Empire Games Association agreeing to send 12 competitors to London 'irrespective of sport or sex'. The way seemed clear for women's equal participation, or was it? The years 1933–1934 had been among the most successful for Australian sportswomen. In swimming, the Olympic medallists Clare Dennis and Bonnie Mealing had retained their winning form, the latter defeating Joyce Cooper and lowering her own Australian backstroke record. Lesley Thompson had captured the Australian diving title and Edna Davey excelled at all long distance swimming events. On the track and field Edie Robinson and Eileen Wearne filled one and two in both the 100 and 220 yards Australian championships in record time. Cora Hannan shattered the Australian shot-put and discus records and Clarice Kennedy established her dominance in the hurdles and quarter-mile events. All times compared favourably with world standards and women were confidently predicting that a minimum of four of the 12 places available would be for women.

When the selections were announced, the all-male committee chose only Clare Dennis and Lesley Thompson. Although not one athlete had been selected the major surprise came with the exclusion of Olympic backstroke medallist Bonnie Mealing, who was a certainty to capture Empire gold. Dennis spoke out against the decision, telling the press 'she has just as many claims as I have'. She was backed by women's swimming officials who lamented 'it is difficult to know what the selectors expect from candidates for selection when Bonnie has done everything required of her'. It was a decision made even more unpalatable by the failure of some of the male members of the squad.

In London on the 6th August 1934, 17-year-old Clare Dennis became the first Australian woman to compete at an Empire Games and, like her friend and mentor Fanny Durack, she settled for no less than gold by easily winning the 200 yards breaststroke. Twenty-year-old Victorian schoolteacher Lesley Thompson won silver medals in both the springboard and highboard diving events. Clare Dennis continued her domination of Australian breaststroke swimming in 1935 and 1936.

1936 OLYMPIC GAMES: BERLIN, GERMANY

Small-mindedness once again dogged the selection of Australian sportswomen for the 1936 Olympics in Berlin. Initially only one woman, backstroke champion Pat Norton, was selected. Several weeks later high jumper Doris Carter was added to the list and finally Clare Dennis, freestyle swimmer Kitty Mackay, and the first Western Australian, long distance swimmer Evelyn De Lacy, recieved the official nod. Dennis later withdrew because of a foot injury. Disappointed at not being able to defend her Olympic title, she turned professional, taught swimming and took up the sport of shooting. With Clare Dennis's withdrawal, four women made the journey. Schoolteacher Doris Carter had nearly missed the Victorian championships when she was refused leave by the Victorian education department. Forced to drive her Baby Austin through the night to the championships she remarkably retained all her titles for high jump, sprints, hurdles and discus. None of the four women had experienced overseas competition before and none won medals at the Games. In fact Australia's whole contingent of 33 only managed a solitary bronze medal. Such a poor showing was attributed to the fact that overseas competitors had adopted more scientific training methods.

The 1936 Games proved to be the last Olympics before the outbreak of the Second World War. In the pre-war Olympics, 15 women had been selected to represent Australia, winning four medals. These 15 seemed destined to be the last as pressure once again surfaced to ban women from competing at the proposed 1940 Tokyo Games. Even before the Games, Hitler had attempted to prohibit German women competing in athletic events. After the 1936 Games the International Olympic Games Committee met to digest the red herrings of women's sport — was it medically safe, was it ladylike, did it make the Olympics too unwieldy. Such attitudes were fuelled by some ignorant comments made throughout the world, like those of Russian marathon runner Paavo Nurmi whose remarks were reported widely in Australia,

I simply cannot bear to watch a female contorting her body in a javelin contest, convulsing her features, and gritting her teeth in a race, and attempting to clear a high jump with sprawling limbs. Such events should be forbidden. . . I am not opposed to all of the women's Olympic events. I admired the wonderful performances of the Dutch swimmers. Such contests do not prevent women from remaining ladies.

Despite the realistic fears among women sporting officials in Australia that the controversy 'would destroy all ambition in the younger athletes and swimmers', and after decades of negative attitudes and unfair selection procedures, young Australian sportswomen still continued to train and strive for the Olympics.

1938 EMPIRE GAMES: SYDNEY, AUSTRALIA

Doubt was cast as early as 1935 on the participation of women at the 1938 Empire Games. Traditionally the host country was entrusted with the responsibility of determining the final programme but the secretary of the British Empire Games Federation announced in 1935,

The general impression in London is that women's events may not figure prominently in Sydney. This is due partly to the difficulty of fully representative women obtaining long leave, and also to the relatively small proportion of women athletes in Australia.

Fortunately neither observation was correct. By far the most significant event in women's sport before the Second World War was the decision to hold the 1938 Empire Games in Sydney. Not only did such a move circumvent (most) selection problems, it provided incentive for thousands of sportswomen and for the first time allowed Australia to enter competitors in relay events on the track and in the water. Because the Games were held in February (the height of the Australian competitive season), Australian women, especially schoolgirl juniors and teachers, had the opportunity to reach peak fitness over the Christmas break.

Women were still restricted to two groups of events — athletics and swimming — but in them the Australians produced what was described as a grand triumph. Australia emerged the premier women's nation. The *Sydney Morning Herald* described it as 'a marvellous performance, overseas managers might well ask why they had not heard more of the Australian women athletes.' No one shone brighter among the 'galaxy of talent and record breaking achievements' than Western Australian athlete Decima Norman. Described as running 'like a bullet from a gun', Norman shot to international fame at the Sydney Games. She entered five events and won an unprecedented five gold medals — 100 and 220 yards, long jump, 440 yards relay and 660 yards relay. Although producing her outstanding times as early as 1935, Norman had been overlooked for 1936 Olympic Games selection as Western Australian athletes were not eligible for nomination.

Decima Norman was born in Tammin a wheat belt town in Western Australia on the 9 September 1909. A superstitious athlete, she selected her lucky number nine as her Empire Games number. Fortunately no one questioned the exact origins of her superstition too closely as Norman gave her official age as twenty-one, when in fact she was twenty-eight. Anticipating discrimination, she had no trouble convincing anyone of her youthful prowess as she swept all before her. After the Games she remained in Sydney to continue preparations for the 1940 Olympics where experts believed she would win a minimum of three gold medals. The war, however, forced her to forgo her Olympic dreams and she returned to Western Australia where she became a businesswoman and did much to promote women's athletics in that state.

Apart from Decima Norman, Australia boasted an array of medallists and

West Australian athlete Decima Norman won five gold medals, including one for the long jump, at the 1938 Empire Games in Sydney. Her achievement was not equalled until swimmer Hayley Lewis performed at the 1990 Commonwealth Games. Norman was also a state hockey player, surf lifesaver and tennis player. Photograph by Max Dupain, *The Home*, March 1938

champions. Thirty women competed, 14 of them receiving medals. In athletics Joyce Walker (NSW) ran second to Norman in the 100 yards and Australia won the 220 yards trifecta with Jean Coleman (NSW) second and Eileen Wearne (NSW) third. Queensland athlete Thelma Peake, the only married woman representing Australia, won gold for her part in the 660 yards relay and bronze for the long jump. Isobel Grant (Vic) won silver in the 80 metres hurdles and Joan Woodland (WA) won gold in the 660 yards relay.

In the pool Evelyn De Lacy (WA) won the 110 yards freestyle with Western Australian teammate Dorothy Green second. De Lacy, Green, Margaret Rawson (NSW) and Pat Norton (NSW) won silver in the 4 x 110 yards freestyle relay and the team of De Lacy, Norton and Valerie George (Vic) won bronze in the 330 yards medley relay. Norton, a 1936 Olympian, took her annual holidays to coincide with the Games and was rewarded by also winning the 110 yards backstroke final. Irene Donnett (Vic) won gold in the springboard diving and bronze in the highboard, with Lurline Hook (NSW) taking gold in the highboard diving.

Many junior women performed creditably including several breaststrokers coached by Clare Dennis. All the former Olympic representatives showed the value of their experience. Like Dennis, Evelyn De Lacy turned to coaching, an occupation she still enjoyed in 1990 at Sydney's Bronte Baths. One competitor achieved note of a different kind in later life. Promising New South Wales schoolgirl breaststroker Margaret Dovey 'who has many interests other than swimming', and could only train in her summer vacation, came a creditable sixth in the 220 yards breaststroke final, an event she later recalled (as Margaret Whitlam) with pride.

The war eventually ended the international careers of the women competitors, but a strong sporting foundation and a belief in widespread rather than individual achievement had been created. Once given their chance Australian women rose to the occasion and the world was to see the Australian flag raised in victory ceremonies in many future Games.

1948 OLYMPIC GAMES: LONDON, ENGLAND

It was to be a further ten years before international competition for Australian women was restored. When it did resume, it was without pre-war champion Decima Norman, but her running spikes were to be amply filled by another woman from the West. The gap of 12 years between Olympic Games had also seen a number of selection procedures changed that would benefit the representative claims of women. Each association affiliated with the Olympic body now nominated their own representatives. Their nominations would be accepted if they had reached Olympic qualifying standard, and it would then be the association's responsibility to raise the necessary funds to send their competitors. Nine women proved their claims for the 1948 Olympics in London; five athletes and four swimmers. For the first time the standard of women sprinters was high enough to send a relay team and two New South Wales runners, June Maston and Betty McKinnon, were selected specifically as competitors in the 4 x 100 metres relay. Running with Shirley Strickland and Joyce King, they returned with a silver medal.

The 1948 Olympics witnessed the first international appearance of 23-year-old nuclear physicist Shirley Strickland. Perth-based Strickland had risen to prominence in the 1947 West Australian and 1948 Australian athletic championships as a sprinter and hurdler. After only one season of competition her performances automatically selected her as Australia's number one ranked athlete for the Games. Strickland's illustrious nine year career at the top of world athletics was never free from some form of public criticism. On her arrival in London

Shirley Strickland winning the 80 metres hurdles at the 1956 Melbourne Olympic Games. She became the first Australian athlete to win gold at successive Olympics and the first woman to win the same track event at successive Olympics. After the Games her Olympic medal tally, from a career that began in 1948, stood at seven.
NATIONAL LIBRARY OF AUSTRALIA

former Olympian-turned-sportswriter Harold Abrahams claimed she was not of Olympic standard. How wrong could one man be. Strickland returned home with three medals — silver for the 4 x 100 metres relay, and two bronze medals for the 100 metres sprint and 80 metres hurdles. She came fourth in the final of the 200 metres. Abrahams ate his words, 'She is one of the finest athletes in the world' he said. Strickland also had the distinction of being the first Australian woman to win a medal in athletics at an Olympic Games. She was to win a total of seven medals in Olympic competition. Human error robbed her of an eighth — in 1975 a chance re-examination of the photofinish of her 1948 Olympic 200 metres final revealed that she had in fact come third rather than fourth.

Other Australian women staying at Army Hut Thirteen of war-torn London's Olympic 'village' had cause for celebration. Seventeen-year-old swimmer Nancy Lyons, originally named as a reserve, won the silver medal for the 200 metres breaststroke. All-rounder Judy Joy Davies broke the world 100 metres backstroke record in her heat but had to be content with a bronze medal in the final. The 1948 Games also witnessed the first appearance of 13-year-old swimming sensation Marjorie McQuade. Students at Fort Street Girls High Sydney had much to cheer about — co-pupil Judy Canty was Australia's representative in the long jump and both Maston and McKinnon were Fort Street Old Girls.

1950 EMPIRE GAMES: AUCKLAND, NEW ZEALAND

In 1949 the New South Wales Women's Amateur Athletic Association invited Dutch champion Fanny Blankers-Koen to compete in Australia. Blankers-Koen had won four gold medals at the 1948 Olympics for the 100 and 200 metres, 80 metres hurdles and 4 x 100 metres relay. Her success in the local Australian competition was regarded as a mere formality by many. In her first 100 metres race she came up against a 17-year-old 'typist' from Lithgow, New South Wales, who thrashed the Olympic champion by a metre. To prove it was no fluke she repeated the dose one week later over the 100 yards distance. Disappointed at not gaining selection in the 1948 Olympic team, the young Marjorie Jackson made the most of the visit and established herself as Australia's premier sprinter.

When the team was announced for the 1950 Empire Games, Marjorie Jackson was among the 23 women selected. Although a smaller women's contingent than that at the 1938 Games in Sydney, the women amassed 20 medals between them, half of them gold. Jackson scooped the track. She won every race she entered: the 100 yards, 220 yards, 440 yards relay and 660 yards relay. Her success forced Shirley Strickland to be content with silver medals in the sprint distances and to concentrate on the 80 metres hurdles, which she won. For the very first time Australian women won all four relays, two on the track and two in the pool, proving their depth of talent. Olympians Marjorie McQuade and Judy Joy Davies, the 110 yards freestyle and backstroke champions respectively, each won three gold medals. Three Australian women also entered the first fencing competition at an Empire Games with Catherine Pym securing the individual foil bronze medal.

1952 OLYMPIC GAMES: HELSINKI, FINLAND

In anticipation of their local heroine's appearance at the 1952 Olympic Games, the people of Lithgow built a cinders track for Marjorie Jackson to train on. On it she wore her hand-made kangaroo leather running spikes, each pair costing her a month's wages. As the Helsinki Games were held in the northern summer Jackson was forced to do the bulk of her training through the Lithgow winter — typified by fog, rain and sleet. Interspersed with training was the constant need to raise funds for her trip abroad.

Ten women made the journey to Finland, but none had more success than the dedicated Jackson. Already holding the world record time for the 100 metres sprint, Jackson led all the way to win Australia's first athletic gold since 1896 and the first ever by an Australian woman. The cheer in the grandstand that Jackson heard was nothing like the noise that erupted in Lithgow as the townspeople sat by their radios. The locals reportedly used more electricity on that night than any other night in the town's history.

Behind Jackson the indefatiguable Shirley Strickland captured bronze with Winsome Cripps of Australia fourth. Cripps is perhaps unfortunately remembered more for her part in the 4 x 100 metres relay in which the last baton change robbed Australia of a certain gold medal. Jackson also blitzed the field to win the 200 metres sprint. Shirley Strickland was not to be denied Olympic glory. She won the 80 metres hurdles in world record time. Confusion reigned as Strickland stood on the Olympic victory dais to receive her medal. The Finns, uncertain of Strickland's continued use of her maiden name, included every name she ever had on the scoreboard, thus 'Strickland de la Hunty Shirley Barbara' flashed before her.

Back in Australia both women were accorded heroines welcomes. When Marjorie Jackson arrived in Sydney, people lined the road between the airport and her hometown Lithgow, 150 kilometres away, to cheer her.

1954 EMPIRE AND COMMONWEALTH GAMES: VANCOUVER, CANADA

By choice, the 1954 Games were Marjorie Jackson's last international competition. Shirley Strickland's athletic career almost came to an unplanned end. Strickland had given birth to her first child in 1953, but by 1954 was back at peak condition and keen to defend her Empire and Olympic hurdles titles. During the Australian qualifying trials for the hurdles, Strickland thought she heard a false start signalled and remained on the blocks only to discover the double sound had been an echo. Disappointed, Strickland attempted to enlist support for her inclusion in the Games team and offered to pay her own way. Public opinion turned against her and at 29 she was accused of denying younger competitors a chance, and of neglecting the needs of her child. Fortunately for Australia, Strickland withstood the pressure to retire permanently knowing she had not yet reached her peak.

Marjorie Jackson topped off her athletics career in Vancouver with a perfect record — gold in the 100 yards, gold in the 220 yards and gold in the 4 x 100 yards relay. Thus she was never beaten at an individual event in international competition, scoring a perfect six out of six. At 22 years of age she announced her retirement.

Only 13 women were sent to Vancouver, the smallest contingent since 1932. The *Australian Women's Weekly* launched a special fund to raise money to help send the women. The efforts of readers of the women's magazine were not in vain for the Games heralded the arrival of a new swimming star, 15-year-old Lorraine Crapp. Still a schoolgirl at MLC Burwood, Crapp, a sprint as well as middle distance swimmer, had swept the board in the 1954 Australian championships beating both Marjorie McQuade and Judy Joy Davies. A product of the new year-round fitness training principles, Crapp won the 110 yards freestyle and the 440 yards freestyle and captured a bronze in the 330 yards medley relay.

The Australian women secured ten medals at the Games, a tally dominated by golds courtesy of Jackson, Crapp and diver Barbara MacAulay. Brilliant Sydney sprinter Marlene Mathews, who 'ran like a greyhound' but was destined to have a career punctuated by injury, also made her first appearance in Vancouver. But it was to be a brief debut. She had only completed 50 yards of her 100 yards heat when a hamstring injury caused her to withdraw.

1956 OLYMPIC GAMES: MELBOURNE, AUSTRALIA

Just as the 1938 Empire Games in Sydney had done so much to promote women's sport in Australia before the war, the 1956 Olympic Games held in Melbourne rocketed Australian sportswomen to national prominence and acclaim. The term 'golden girls' was over-used but aptly described the success of the Australian women who continued to outshine and outperform their male team mates. Forty-four women represented their country and they easily dominated the competition both on the track and in the pool and gave Australia its best result, third overall.

The year 1956 was indeed a memorable one for many Australian sportswomen. Swimmer Lorraine Crapp had broken 17 world records even before the start of the Olympic Games! Going into the Games she held the records for 100 metres, 200 metres, 220 yards, 400 metres, 440 yards, 800 metres and 880 yards. This made her the favourite for the only two women's individual events — the 100 metres and 400 metres. She won gold in the 400 metres, and silver in the 100 metres. The honours in the sprint distance went to a woman who was to become the greatest Olympian of all time, Dawn Fraser. From the moment she won her first gold medal, she

Toast of Australia – "The Girls"

The Australian swimming trifecta for the 100 metres freestyle at the 1956 Olympics. (L-R) Faith Leech (bronze), Dawn Fraser (gold) and Lorraine Crapp (silver). They also combined with Sandra Morgan to win the 4 x 100 metres freestyle relay in world record time. *Australian Women's Weekly*, 19 December 1956.

NATIONAL LIBRARY OF AUSTRALIA

captivated public attention but was destined to be the centre of controversy. Headstrong and opinionated, Fraser clashed repeatedly throughout her career with swimming officials in whose attitude she detected a fair amount of class prejudice towards her 'rather scrimpy education in a very unfashionable suburb'. Bitterly, the Balmain star later wrote:

Australian officials don't like swimmers to question their decisions or their attitudes. Ideally, they'd like to use athletic puppets — but they're willing to settle for young schoolchildren who are happy to let the grown-ups do all the thinking . . . Enough remarks have been made at times about my 'background' to indicate that officials think I ought to feel very grateful that they even let me into swimming.

The youngest of eight children, Dawn Fraser grew up believing, like so many other successful sportswomen, that she could tackle anything physical. She began serious swimming training and in 1951, at the age of 14, defeated Lorraine Crapp before being banned for 18 months for allegedly breaking her amateur status. Back on track, she received the benefits of the revolutionary swimming training based on rigorous conditioning that was being developed in Australia. Forced to watch Crapp (who was a year younger than Fraser) and the other swimmers leave for the 1954 Empire Games in Vancouver without her, she began defeating Crapp again by 1955. The 100 metres Olympic final between the two was very close. At the turn Crapp was ahead and according to Fraser 'we were stroke for stroke over the last few yards, and it seemed to me that we hit together. Neither of us knew who was the winner'. But it was Dawn Fraser who was number one in the world. The swimmers had pushed each other so hard that both were under world record time. Crapp turned to Fraser, grinned and said, 'It makes our relay team look pretty good'. Although the women's 4 x 100 metres freestyle relay had been on the Olympic programme since 1912, 1956 was the first year an Australian team had been entered. Fraser and Crapp teamed with 100 metres bronze medallist Faith Leech and Sandra Morgan to win the gold medal in world record time.

Out at the Melbourne Cricket Ground (MCG) world records also toppled. Betty Cuthbert, born the same year Decima Norman won five gold medals at the Sydney Empire Games, virtually took over the mantle of women's athletics where Marjorie Jackson left off. Coached by 1948 Olympic silver medallist June Maston (now June Ferguson), 18-year-old Betty Cuthbert began a series of victories that were to earn her the tag 'Golden Girl' and prove her to be Australia's greatest athlete. In the final of the 100 metres sprint Cuthbert said she:

Betty Cuthbert, Australia's greatest athlete. *Argus*, December 1956.

never relaxed for a fraction of a second and kept driving as hard as I could till I felt the little white tape break in two. Towards the end my mouth was open so wide it began hurting but I thought 'You can't stop to shut it now'. So it stayed open till I thought my jaws were going to split. I'd done it. I'd won.

Before Cuthbert's second gold medal in the 200 metres final, a Melbourne newspaper predicted victory. She recalled:

I picked up the paper on the morning of the final and there, covering the whole front page of The Argus, *was a glorious action photograph of myself in colour with the words 'Betty Cuthbert — Golden Girl' superimposed down the side of it.*

She struck a third gold medal and another world record with Norma Croker, Fleur Mellor and Shirley Strickland in the 4 x 100 metres relay, a combination that inexplicably omitted 100 metres bronze medallist Marlene Mathews.

Fortunately for both Betty Cuthbert and Dawn Fraser, the champion Australian sprint hurdler Shirley Strickland made a comeback at the Melbourne Olympics. Both young women have acknowledged the help and advice imparted to them by the seasoned and experienced Strickland. Described as a housewife (nobody asked her about her thesis on cosmic particle detection) Strickland, now 31 years old and the mother of one child, won the 80 metres hurdles championships to become the first woman in history to successfully defend an Olympic title. Strickland's path had not been an easy one. She continued to be taunted with claims that she was too old and even received crank letters before the Games. By the end of the Games her personal Olympic tally stood at seven medals.

At the conclusion of the Olympics, Australia's 20 women athletes had won four gold and three bronze medals and the public could not help but notice that the men's team, although 55 in number, had only secured two silver and two bronze. Suddenly the press was hunting down the reasons for women's ascendancy. Where had they come from? Weren't sportsmen our great national heroes? Wasn't sport dangerous and unfeminine for women? To those who had kept themselves ignorant regarding the rising generations of women champions such questions were puzzling. Sportswomen knew the answer. Every woman swimmer since Fanny Durack and every sprinter since Decima Norman knew what was possible. One lone male hinted at the answer. Writing to the *Sydney Morning Herald* in December 1956 he said:

In 1956 the media ran out of superlatives to describe the performances of Australian women at the Games. Marlene Mathews (left) won bronze medals in the 100 and 200 metre sprints and Betty Cuthbert (right) won gold medals in the same events. *Australian Women's Weekly*, 12 December 1956.

NATIONAL LIBRARY OF AUSTRALIA.

Many are guessing as to why our girls showed so splendidly in the Games. . . I would guess that the outstanding strength of our sportswomen has lain in their morale. Anyone who knows the self-reliant energy and unselfishness of some of their organisations raising funds for their grounds and equipment, and even for overseas tours, by vigorous voluntary effort, must be impressed by their enterprise and good citizenship. I recall the day, some years back, when a very dangerous surf swept out the greatest number of bathers ever recorded, and the lifesavers were reported next day as saying that the behaviour of the women in this peril was markedly better, on the whole, than that of the men. I should be surprised if this outstanding spirit is not reflected in their athletic performances.

The writer was C.E.W. Bean who had been the war correspondent and historian of the Anzacs at Gallipoli. It was he who had done most to create the Anzac legend. Perhaps if fate had dealt him a journalistic assignment in 1956 rather than 1915, the Australian legend of heroism might have been based around a completely different tradition!

1958 EMPIRE AND COMMONWEALTH GAMES: CARDIFF, WALES

Much was expected of the Australian women at the 1958 Games. Twenty-one made the journey to Cardiff, and they returned with 20 medals. Dawn Fraser set a new world record in the final of the 110 yards freestyle and the team of Fraser, Lorraine Crapp, Alva Colquhuon and Sandra Morgan won the 4 x 110 freestyle relay. Fourteen-year-old Ilsa Konrads defeated Fraser in the 440 yards, the only other individual freestyle event available for women. Konrads had come to Australia as an emigrant from Latvia at the age of five. Another newcomer and medal winner was Polish javelin thrower Anna Wojtaszek-Pazera who had stayed in Australia after the 1956 Olympics. Her relocation had caused no apparent difficulties in her training, she won in Cardiff with a new world record. Beverley Bainbridge became Australia's first gold medallist in the 110 yards butterfly.

Athletics honours at the 1958 Games belonged at last to the persistent Marlene Mathews, who, according to the *Australian Women's Weekly*, had just celebrated her first wedding anniversary with a Chicken Maryland dinner and a night at the pictures. Injury ridden for most of her athletic career, the Burwood-born athlete who had attended Sydney Girls High School, peaked in 1958 to win double gold in the 100 yards and 220 yards. Betty Cuthbert, herself struggling with injury, finished in fourth place in the 100 yards and second in the 220 yards. With the retirement of Shirley Strickland, South Australian Norma Thrower emerged as the 80 metres hurdles champion and Michele Mason won the women's high jump.

Australia had its best result in the fencing with the women's national fencing champion 19-year-old Barbara McCreath winning silver in the individual foil. Despite a surplus of £1000 in the Empire Games Fund officials had inexplicably not selected McCreath. She travelled to Cardiff on money raised in door-to-door collections and purchased her own official track suit and uniform. After the Games she had to work as a typist to earn money for her passage home.

1960 OLYMPIC GAMES: ROME, ITALY

Injury robbed both Betty Cuthbert and Marlene Mathews of any chance of success at the 1960 Olympic Games. Brenda Jones won Australia's only track and field medal capturing silver in the reinstated 800 metres race. Although the number of events for women had increased, international pressure was still being applied to expand the range to what the Soviets claimed would be a 'full Olympics' for women.

Twenty-two-year-old Dawn Fraser and 21-year-old Lorraine Crapp, now called the 'old ladies' of swimming, were members of the 27 strong team. Fraser produced the only gold medal performance, successfully defending her 100 metres freestyle crown, and won silver in the 4 x 100 metres freestyle and medley relays. Crapp, who had officially retired after Cardiff, made a comeback but her controversial omission from the 100 metres freestyle, and the discovery of her 'secret' marriage, made for an unhappy Games. Fraser, ever ready to challenge injustice, also managed to antagonise swimming officials and was punished by being omitted from forthcoming overseas experience building tours.

1962 EMPIRE AND COMMONWEALTH GAMES: PERTH, AUSTRALIA

International competition returned once more to home soil in 1962 resulting in the selection of a record 46 women competitors. Australian women won 33 medals, including eleven gold, watched by special home-town guests Decima Norman and Shirley Strickland. Although Dawn Fraser dominated the swimming winning four gold medals, a number of other stars emerged in the pool and on the track. Victorian Pam Kilborn won gold in the 80 metres hurdles and long jump and Sue Knight won both the highboard and springboard diving. Medley, sprint and long distance swimmer Linda McGill began her Games career by winning gold in the medley relay, silver in the 440 yards individual medley and bronze in the 110 yards butterfly.

Golden Dawn — and golden sunset. At the 1964 Tokyo Olympics Dawn Fraser won her third consecutive gold medal in the 100 metres freestyle — a feat never equalled by any competitor in any Olympic Games. She also received a controversial 10 year suspension from Australian swimming officials, which prevented her from contesting the 1968 final. *Australian Women's Weekly*, 28 October 1964.

NATIONAL LIBRARY OF AUSTRALIA

1964 OLYMPIC GAMES: TOKYO, JAPAN

On the 27 October 1962 Dawn Fraser created world headlines by being the first woman to break the minute for the 100 metres freestyle. The Tokyo Olympics were to make her an 'immortal' and also see her banned from competition swimming for ten years. At 27 she was nicknamed 'granny' by her teammates. For the third Olympics in succession Fraser qualified for the final of the 100 metres freestyle. Suffering from a recent asthma attack Fraser used an open turn instead of the faster tumble turn, and battled all the way to win her third consecutive gold medal — a feat never equalled by any competitor in any Olympic event. In the celebrations that followed, Fraser, accused of stealing a Japanese flag from the Palace, earned a controversial ten-year suspension from swimming officials. It was rescinded four years later, but not in time to allow her to compete at the 1968 Olympics where many believed she could have continued her gold medal spree. Fraser won the 1964 final in 59.5 seconds. Four years later, in her absence, Jan Henne of the United States won the 1968 final in 60 seconds.

The addition of the 400 metres event to the women's athletic programme for the first time in 1964, enabled Betty Cuthbert to prove herself once again the golden girl. Her recurring foot injury had at last been diagnosed accurately as a dislocation, and once corrected she concentrated on the new distance. Running the last 100 metres of the 400 metres race as if she were in a sprint, Cuthbert drew ahead and won her fourth Olympic gold medal, a fitting finale to her athletic career. Of the 42 women present in Tokyo high jumper Michelle Brown won silver, 80 metres hurdler Pam Kilborn won bronze, and athletes Judy Amoore and Marilyn Black won bronze in the 400 and 200 metres respectively.

1966 EMPIRE AND COMMONWEALTH GAMES: KINGSTON, JAMAICA

Twenty-eight women made the trip to the Caribbean and they won 24 medals. Without Dawn Fraser, Kathy Wainwright was the only swimmer to win a gold medal, setting a world record in her heat of the 440 yards freestyle and bettering it in the final. Diane Bowering-Burge from South Australia took on the athletics mantle, winning the 100 yards, 220 yards and anchoring the victorious 4 x 100 yards relay team. Pam Kilborn was also a member of the relay team as well as winning the 80 metres hurdles. Judy Amoore-Pollock won gold in the 440 yards and silver in the 880 yards, Michele Mason won the high jump and Margaret Parker won the javelin. For the first time a women's badminton team was included and Australian fencers won a silver medal in the team foil.

Raelene Boyle congratulates the Canadian team on their relay victory at the 1982 Commonwealth Games in Brisbane.
Boyle retired after the Games with a total of seven Commonwealth gold medals to her credit.
OVERSEAS INFORMATION BRANCH

1968 OLYMPIC GAMES: MEXICO CITY, MEXICO

Australian women continued their good showing in the sprint hurdles at the 1968 Olympics under the guidance of new assistant manager Shirley Strickland. Strickland was among 41 officials sent with the team — compared with only 24 women competitors! Pam Kilborn was the favourite for the 80 metres hurdles, but had to be content with a silver medal after the event was won by the youngest ever Olympic track and field gold medallist, Maureen Caird. Seventeen-year-old Caird trained under Betty Cuthbert's coach June Ferguson. From a working class Sydney family, Caird did it the tough way. Throughout her career she was plagued with stomach pains and nose bleeds and acquired a reputation as being something of a hypochondriac. After retirement her stomach pains were diagnosed as cancer. Caird won the hurdles in an Olympic record time, never to be bettered as the hurdles distance was extended to 100 metres in the 1972 Olympics.

Many competitors struggled in the rarefied Mexico City atmosphere, but not so asthma sufferer Lynn McClements. Considered an outsider for the 100 metres butterfly, McClements improved greatly in the weeks leading up to the Games and drew inspiration from training swims and time spent with Dawn Fraser. She became the first Australian to win gold in the butterfly event and she also won a silver medal in the 4 x 100 metres medley relay. After a meteoric rise the West Australian retired in 1970 after a swimming official disqualified her for having an alleged technical fault in her kick. Another swimmer to gain individual distinction was Karen Moras who won a bronze medal in the 400 metres freestyle event.

The 1968 Games saw the first appearance of the 17-year-old schoolgirl athlete Raelene Boyle who started her 'rickety roller coaster ride that would roar on relentlessly and sometimes erratically for 14 years'. The Victorian sprinter was catapulted into world athletics limelight by equalling the world records in her 100 metres and 200 metres heats but she had to be content with a silver medal in the final of the 200 metres.

1970 COMMONWEALTH GAMES: EDINBURGH, SCOTLAND

Although Australian women had carried the day in many Commonwealth contests, 1970 was the first time a woman was accorded the national honour of carrying the Australian flag at the head of the team. It was Pam Kilborn who held the flag aloft as the team entered the Meadowbank stadium for the start of the Games. Australian women, wearing their official gold dresses in the bleak Edinburgh weather of the opening ceremony, had their best games ever. The 32 women left the Edinburgh Games with an astonishing 38 medals, 17 of them

Sue Howland won the gold medal in the javelin at the 1982 Commonwealth Games.
NATIONAL SPORT INFORMATION CENTRE

Australian hockey forward Julei Pereira in action, 1990.
NATIONAL SPORT INFORMATION CENTRE

Swimmers Tracey Wickham (left) and Lisa Forrest (right) each won two individual gold medals at the
1982 Commonwealth Games, Brisbane.
OVERSEAS INFORMATION BRANCH

matching the colour of their official dresses.

Pam Kilborn successfully defended her sprint hurdles title, winning the event, now over the extended distance of 100 metres, for the third time in succession. By forcing Maureen Caird into second place she reversed the placings of the 1968 Olympics. The young Petra Rivers surprised many by winning the javelin throw. But it was Raelene Boyle who took the track honours. The confident sprinter won triple gold in the 100 metres, 200 metres and anchor leg of the 4 x 100 metres relay.

The majority of the medals, however, were won in the pool. Australia possessed an extraordinary depth of swimming talent winning the 4 x 100 metres freestyle and medley relays. Karen Moras was the star of

In 1974, 12-year-old Michelle Ford swam the fastest time in the world for her age group over 100 yards freestyle. Six years later she won an Olympic gold medal in Moscow for the 800 metres freestyle.
NATIONAL LIBRARY OF AUSTRALIA

the Games winning three individual freestyle gold medals, 200 metres, 400 metres and 800 metres, as well as breaking her own world record in the longer distance. The sensational Moras finished almost a lap ahead of her nearest rival and carved nearly seven seconds off the world record. New South Wales swimmer Beverley Whitfield also won three gold medals, including the 100 metres and 200 metres breaststroke.

1972 OLYMPIC GAMES: MUNICH, GERMANY

These Games belonged to Shane Gould. Swimming with an unusual arm-action and an old fashioned two-stroke kick reminiscent of Fanny Durack, the 15-year-old started the Games with every freestyle world record to her credit, the 100, 200, 400, 800 and 1500 metres. Gould was born in Brisbane the day after the opening ceremony of the 1956 Melbourne Olympics. Assisted by a resting heartbeat of only 40 beats per minute, she had trained religiously since the age of nine, covering enough kilometres per day to make Fanny Durack look like a land-lover in comparison. Shane Gould was under pressure to perform. In an attempt to out-psych the 15-year-old, American competitors wore T-shirts saying 'All that glitters

Still with braces on her teeth, teenager Shane Gould won
five medals, including three
gold medals, at the 1972 Olympics.
NATIONAL LIBRARY OF AUSTRALIA

is not gould'. But glitter she did, winning three gold medals — for the 200 metres, 400 metres, and 200 metres individual medley, all in world record time — one silver medal for the 800 metres freestyle and bronze for the 100 metres. One year later she quit competitive swimming. In her wake she left Karen Moras. Relegated to number two behind Gould, (and complaining that their coach used her as a workhorse for her younger rival) Moras also announced her retirement.

Medley swimmer Gail Neall was another young woman to reach her peak at the Munich Games. A schoolfriend of Shane Gould, she won a silver medal in the 400 metres individual medley at the Edinburgh Games. That medal gave her the incentive to continue and she was rewarded with a gold medal in Munich in the 400 metres individual medley. Inspired by the performances of Dawn Fraser, Wollongong swimmer Beverley Whitfield repeated Clare Dennis's 1932 victory by winning the gold medal in the 200 metres breaststroke, to which she added a bronze medal for the 100 metres breaststroke.

The most successful athlete was Raelene Boyle who won two silver medals for the 100 metres and 200 metres sprints. Boyle, defeated by East German Renate Stecher on both occasions, lamented 'I'm sick of looking at her back'. In all, 27 women went to Munich, including sisters Karen and Narelle Moras.

1974 COMMONWEALTH GAMES: CHRISTCHURCH, NEW ZEALAND

A record 51 women made the journey across the Tasman. Athlete Raelene Boyle and swimmer Sonya Gray won the prestigious individual double gold; Boyle for the 100 and 200 metres sprints and Gray for the 100 and 200 metres freestyle. Australia won silver medals in three of the four relay events for women, winning the 4 x 100 on the track by courtesy of Boyle, Denise Robertson, Jenny Lamy and Robyn Boak. Middle distance runner Charlene Rendina emerged as the 800 metres champion and Petra Rivers successfully defended her javelin title.

Champion Debbie Flintoff-King continued the tradition of outstanding Australian athletes.
NATIONAL SPORT INFORMATION CENTRE

Walker Kerry Saxby holds the most number of world records by any athlete in Australia's history. She won gold at the 1990 Commonwealth Games in the inaugural 10 kilometres walk.

NATIONAL SPORT INFORMATION CENTRE

Another young woman, a product of what was being called by now the Australian water-baby production line, was 13-year-old Jenny Turrall. Kept almost peter-pan-like by her coach, the 42.5 kilogram Turrall won the 400 metres freestyle and came second in the 200 and 800 metres. Olympian Gail Neall was third in the 200 metres butterfly and Beverley Whitfield gained a silver medal in the 200 metres breaststroke. Sandra Yost won the 200 metres butterfly. In all, Australian women won 29 medals, ten of those gold. Australia's first woman shooter, Yvonne Gowland, won a gold medal in the mixed small bore rifle event.

1976 OLYMPIC GAMES: MONTREAL, CANADA

Hit by retirements and disqualification the 35 Australian women in Montreal returned with no medals to their credit. Raelene Boyle had moved to Western Australia to be coached by Shirley Strickland. Tipped for gold, Boyle got off to a slow start in the 100 metres and was unable to recover. Determined to improve her start in the 200 metres semi-final, she broke twice and was automatically disqualified. At 13 Tracey Wickham, holder of the Australian 400 metres title, was one of the youngest swimmers to represent Australia. Although eliminated in the heats, Wickham gained valuable experience as did her team mate Michelle Ford. Shock waves spread through Australia after the team's disappointing performance. Unfortunately official moves to bolster Australia's across-the-board sporting failure were discriminatory and did little to concentrate on the historical source of medal victory — the women. No women athletes were nominated by the athletic union for Olympic track and field scholarships in 1977. Women had to wait until the Australian Institute of Sport opened in 1981 before receiving encouragement.

1978 COMMONWEALTH GAMES: EDMONTON, CANADA

Canada was not the kindest place for Australia's women athletes. Raelene Boyle won a silver medal in the 100 metres and was forced to withdraw through injury from the 200 metres. Illness cost champion long jumper Lyn Jacenko a place in her event, but some track and field pride was regained through the performances of Boyle's longtime rival Denise Robertson who won the 200 metres, Judy Canty who won the 800 metres, Katrina Gibbs who won the high jump and Gael Mulhall who defeated Romanian-turned-Canadian Carmen Ionescu in the shot put. Mulhall also won a silver medal in the discus.

Tracy Wickham was easily the most impressive swimmer. A veteran at 15, Wickham won the 400 metres and 800 metres freestyle from her regular Australian rival Michelle Ford, as well as winning silver in the shorter 200 metres distance.

But Wickham didn't just win her longer events. With electrifying swims the Queenslander set new world records in both the 400 metres and 800 metres. She improved upon these times later in 1978 and her records stood for an incredible nine years. Ford was compensated by winning a gold medal in the 200 metres butterfly. Debra Forster won the 100 metres backstroke. Gymnastics was included for the first time and four Australian women led by Broken Hill gymnast Marina Sulicich performed creditably for a fourth in the teams event. In all, 42 women attended the Games and won 28 medals, eight of those gold.

1980 OLYMPIC GAMES: MOSCOW, RUSSIA

Bowing to political pressure, 17-year-old Tracy Wickham was one of the selected Australian competitors who did not go to the Moscow Games; Raelene Boyle was another. In doing so Wickham forfeited what appeared on paper a certain gold medal in the 800 metres freestyle. This medal, however, was brought back to Australia by Michelle Ford. Ford was the most successful of the 27 Australian women who eventually made the journey to Moscow. Ford had herself broken the 800 metres world record early in 1978, but had been eclipsed at the Edmonton Games by in-form Tracy Wickham in what were described as the most sensational swims of the Games. In Moscow, Ford won the 800 metres in a new Olympic record time as well as winning the bronze in the 200 metres butterfly.

1982 COMMONWEALTH GAMES: BRISBANE, AUSTRALIA

By the time of the Brisbane Games, sprinter Raelene Boyle had extended her preparation to contest the 400 metres event. At 31 years of age Boyle was chosen as the runner to deliver the traditional Queen's message. Entering the QEII stadium Boyle received the applause of the 60 000 strong crowd. Four days later the tumultuous noise of the crowd brought her home in the 400 metres final in what she described as the 'biggest thrill of my life'. That day she retired with seven Commonwealth gold medals to her credit. Australia's other gold medal winners of the Games were 400 metres hurdler Debbie Flintoff, heptathlete Glynis Nunn and javelin thrower Sue Howland. Petra Rivers, making a comeback to the javelin, won the silver medal and Gael Mulhall won silver medals in both the discus and shot put.

Resilient Tracy Wickham reasserted her dominance in distance swimming by winning both the 400 metres and 800 metres freestyle. Wickham retired from competition with a total of four gold and two silver Commonwealth Games medals. Michelle Ford won the 200 metres butterfly. Lisa Forrest won gold medals in both the 100 metres and 200 metres backstroke and Lisa Curry won gold medals for the 100 metres butterfly, 200 metres individual medley and 400 metres individual medley. Jenny Donnet won the springboard diving, an event her mother Barbara MacAulay had won at the 1954 Vancouver Games. For the first time archery and lawn bowls were included for women, but the former at the expense of gymnastics. In addition Wendy Ey was appointed manager of the athletics team, the first woman to hold the head position. In all, the Australian women won 35 medals, 15 of those gold.

1984 Olympic Games: Los Angeles, USA

Controversy once again surrounded the selection of some competitors and Michelle Ford, although swimming into form, was prevented by the Australian Swimming Union from defending her Olympic title, despite intervention by the federal minister of sport on her behalf. Glynis Nunn intensified her training in the seven-event heptathlon after her win in the Commonwealth Games. The event had previously contained only five components but had been extended in 1981. Her personal dedication paid off and she was rewarded with the Olympic gold medal at Los Angeles. After the Games she announced her retirement from the heptathalon. The track and field team was managed for the first time by a woman, Wendy Ey. Gael Mulhall (now Martin) won a bronze medal in the shot put event.

Australia's success in the pool came from Suzanne Landells in the 400 metres medley and Karen Phillips in the 200 metres butterfly who both won silver medals, with a bronze medal to Michelle Pearson in the 200 metres medley. Women's rowing had been included in the Olympic programme for the first time in 1976, but amid controversy, no Australian women's crews had been recommended until 1980. The coxed four returned with a bronze medal. A record 71 women went to the Los Angeles Games.

1986 Commonwealth Games: Edinburgh, Scotland

These Commonwealth Games saw the inclusion of two new sports for women — rowing and synchronised swimming. The rowers had outstanding success. The women's eight won gold, the coxed four and lightweight four both won silver, the coxless pair won bronze and lightweight sculler Adair Ferguson won gold.

On the track Debbie Flintoff won double gold in the 400 metres and 400 metres hurdles, Lisa Martin won the marathon and Gael Martin won the shot put and discus. In the pool Suzie Baumer won the 200 metres freestyle and Suzanne Landells won double gold in the 200 metres individual medley and 400 metres individual medley. The women's 4 x 200 metres freestyle relay also won a gold medal. Georgina Parkes won gold in the 200 metres backstroke. The women's fours won a silver medal in lawn bowls.

1988 OLYMPIC GAMES: SEOUL, KOREA

These were the first Olympic Games in ten years unaffected by major political boycotts. Eighty-seven women went to Seoul to contest 72 women's events and 14 mixed events. Australia's women rowers were not so fortunate. Earlier in the year the Australian Rowing Council's selection committee had refused to name any women in the train-on squad for the Games, claiming that none met the selection criteria, a reasonable observation until it was discovered that selection trials for women had been conducted with faulty timing equipment and that the Council had already decided the year before not to allocate a coach for women's crews at the Games.

Given the opportunity, many women at Seoul delivered memorable performances. The most outstanding was the finish by 400 metres hurdler Debbie Flintoff-King who visibly mustered every ounce of energy to lunge and pass the leader on the line to win the gold medal. Media photos of the dedicated Flintoff-King training on her Victorian farm with a deadweight car tyre attached to her waist by a harness as she ran through the paddocks helped explain her inner reserves. Lisa Martin won Australia's first medal in the gruelling marathon event by finishing second. Martin had openly (and justifiably) criticised officials for allocating first and business class air seats to themselves and relegating athletes to economy class on the flight to Seoul. The women's hockey team emerged as the surprise of the Games by winning the final against South Korea. Hockey had been introduced for women in 1980. Wendy Turnbull and Liz Smylie won bronze medals in the tennis doubles, an event restored to the Games after its exclusion in 1924. Another new event for women was cycling in which Julie Speight represented Australia. Julie McDonald was the most successful swimmer winning a bronze medal in the 800 metres freestyle.

1990 COMMONWEALTH GAMES: AUCKLAND, NEW ZEALAND

The Auckland Games witnessed the re-emergence of one of Australia's swimming champions and the creation of another. Lisa Curry, a veteran in the pool at 27 and the mother of one child, had returned to vigorous training. She had retired after the 1984 Olympic Games but came back with a vengeance winning a further four Commonwealth gold medals — in the 50 metres freestyle, 100 metres butterfly, 4 x 100 metres freestyle relay and 4 x 100 metres medley relay — as well as a silver medal in the 100 metres freestyle. But it was 15-year-old swimmer Hayley Lewis who stole the show, winning the most number of medals by a woman in Commonwealth Games history. Her five gold medals were won in the 200 metres freestyle, 400 metres freestyle, 200 metres butterfly, 400 metres individual medley and the 4 x 200 metres freestyle relay with a bronze in the 200 metres individual medley. Other gold medallists were Nicole Livingstone in the 100 metres backstroke, Julie McDonald in the 800 metres freestyle and Karen Van Wirdum in the 100 metres freestyle.

Other outstanding gold medallists were Jane Flemming in the long jump and heptathlon (despite originally gaining selection in only the long jump), Kerry Saxby in the inaugural 10 kilometres road walk, Lisa Marie Vizaniari who won the discus and Lisa Martin who won her second consecutive Commonwealth gold in the marathon ahead of co-Australian Tani Ruckle. The women's fours bowling team of Daphne Shaw, Marion Stevens, Dorothy Roche and Audrey Rutherford won the gold medal, Kathryn Watt won the 72 kilometres cycling road race, Jenny Donnet won the three metres springboard diving and Monique Allen won the uneven bars gymnastics. Controversy over team numbers nearly denied the women's 4 x 100 metres athletic relay team of Monique Dunstan, Kathy Sambell, Catherine Freeman and Kerry Johnson the chance of winning their gold medal.

* * *

Such a survey, by necessity, has omitted the thousands of successful performances Australian women have achieved over the years in international competition other than the Olympics and Commonwealth Games. Nor can it possibly survey the number of women who were Australian champions. Many champions and potential champions faced years of economic hardship and sacrifice to attend the ever increasing number of international competitions. Many more of them had success in the odd as well as the even years.

As the number of events for women gradually increased in both the Commonwealth and Olympic Games Australian women made the most of their opportunities. At every international competition since 1896 (the first modern Olympics) fewer women than men were selected to represent their country and in some instances more officials than women competitors were sent with the Australian teams. Invariably women returned with more medals than the men. In fact Australia's consistent prominence in the sporting world has relied on its women competitors. Since 1912, when Australian women first competed at the Olympics, women have comprised about 18 per cent of competitors but won over 40 per cent of gold medals. But such comparisons are fruitless. Except in a few cases women do not compete against men, they compete against each other and their medal tallies are significant irrespective of the greater number of men competing or the men's lower medal count. Where women do compete with men is in the areas of encouragement, employer support, scholarships and financial backing. In these areas women have consistently lost out to men.

The women who make it to an Olympic or Commonwealth Games are the tip of the sporting iceberg. The real tragedy is with the women who did not receive enough encouragement and support to continue with their training. Some swimmers slip through the net of prejudice and some sprinters hurdle the barriers and outrun the discrimination, but many more women achieve a level of success and retire, often well below their peak. The pressures on Shirley Strickland to retire were enormous. Others like Betty Cuthbert and Raelene Boyle came back as 400 metres specialists to continue their athletic careers. Officials in the Australian swimming and athletic unions have preferred to deal with younger women. Mature women athletes who have their own opinions and who celebrate their victories are far more threatening to the officials than younger competitors. As a result women are not encouraged to stay in their sports, many shine brightly then disappear. Sports like athletics and swimming are acceptable for women, but only while young, as golden girls not golden women.

AUSTRALIAN WOMEN AT THE OLYMPIC GAMES

YEAR	LOCATION	COMPETITORS	GOLD	SILVER	BRONZE
1896	ATHENS	0	N/A	N/A	N/A
1900	PARIS	0	N/A	N/A	N/A
1904	ST LOUIS	0	N/A	N/A	N/A
1908	LONDON	0	N/A	N/A	N/A
1912	STOCKHOLM	2	1	1	-
1920	ANTWERP	1	-	-	-
1924	PARIS	0	N/A	N/A	N/A
1928	AMSTERDAM	4	-	-	-
1932	LOS ANGELES	4	1	1	-
1936	BERLIN	4	-	-	-
1948	LONDON	9	-	2	3
1952	HELSINKI	10	3	-	1
1956	MELBOURNE	44	7	2	3
1960	ROME	27	1	3	1
1964	TOKYO	42	2	2	3
1968	MEXICO CITY	24	2	3	2
1972	MUNICH	27	5	3	2
1976	MONTREAL	35	-	-	-
1980	MOSCOW	27	1	-	1
1984	LOS ANGELES	71	1	2	3
1988	SEOUL	87	2	1	2
	TOTAL	418	26	20	21

AUSTRALIAN WOMEN AT THE EMPIRE AND COMMONWEALTH GAMES

YEAR	LOCATION	COMPETITORS	GOLD	SILVER	BRONZE
1930	HAMILTON	0	N/A	N/A	N/A
1934	LONDON	2	1	2	
1938	SYDNEY	30	10	5	4
1950	AUCKLAND	3	10	6	4
1954	VANCOUVER	13	6	3	1
1958	CARDIFF	21	9	6	5
1962	PERTH	46	11	10	12
1966	KINGSTON	28	8	10	6
1970	EDINBURGH	32	17	10	11
1974	CHRISTCHURCH	51	10	10	9
1978	EDMONTON	42	8	11	9
1982	BRISBANE	65	15	13	7
1986	EDINBURGH	75	12	11	16
1990	AUCKLAND	94	20	22	18
	TOTAL	502	137	119	102

OUTDOORS IN THE OUTBACK

BY THE TIME WE TROTTED INTO THE PADDOCK THAT HAD BECOME A SPORTS GROUND FOR THE DAY, THE MARRIED LADIES' RACE WAS BEING ANNOUNCED. 'Hold the reins', Mum told Mick, and she sprang to the ground. In a few minutes she was racing down the unmarked track, her shoes in one hand, the other holding her hat on her head. Sixteen women were in the race. The men came over from the wood-chopping arena to watch. We could hear Dad shouting, 'Come on, Birdie! You little beauty!' And Mum had won. Then she came back to the jinker, took up the reins and drove over to the post-and-rail enclosure where harness horses could be rested. 'Put your hat straight', she reprimanded me. 'Wherever will people think we've come from!'

Women growing up in rural Australia had a different experience of physical activity. As children they would often walk or ride long distances to school, swim in the local dam or creek and go fishing or yabbying. At small one-teacher schools they would play a wide range of sports to make up the team numbers. As young women they would participate in the local picnic sports days and country fairs and, depending on their circumstances, possess their own horse. They would visit neighbours who had constructed a homestead tennis court for social matches. They would travel to agricultural shows in the country and in the cities. If they attended boarding school they might also

The women's cotton winding race at the McCulloch Park picnic, Broken Hill, NSW, c. 1910.
BROKEN HILL CITY COUNCIL

be sent for dressage lessons. If country educated they might dream of being buckjumpers or rodeo riders. They would form teams to play against other districts or against visitors. As adults they would attend the country race meetings and own and train race horses themselves. At the fair they would enter the 'married women's races' and a few novelty races like the egg and spoon and cotton winding races. They might join the activities of the local golf club. They would dress appropriately and practically for life on the land. In short, women in the bush had no need for the physical culture movements of the cities. They obtained their outdoor exercise every day of their lives in their work and were also likely to pursue some sort of physical activity for their leisure and recreation. Medical men were far less likely to try and explain to a country woman that physical exertion of any kind was dangerous for her child bearing!

Growing up in the 1920s, in an area just north of Shepparton in Victoria, Patsy Adam-Smith remembered 'there was never a time in our lives when we couldn't ride'. Children who did not own horses would ride those of their friends during the week at school. At home on the weekend they would ride the harness horses. Judith Wallace, raised in the New England district of New South Wales, recalled the gift of two ponies to her and her sister by an aunt:

she had transformed our lives. From then on we practically lived on horseback. . . for their chief value was not as pets, but as a means of transport, of getting about the ten thousand acres and being able to participate in the life of the station.

141

Young country women were born in the saddle; Maude Colless at the Walgett show, NSW, c. 1910. More than fifty
years later she leapt onto a horse and galloped off — leaving two city-born
granddaughters wide-eyed and lost for words.
STELL COLLECTION

Side-saddle riding was unthought of, especially as a child's saddle was
considered an unnecessary expense. Many girls simply hitched up their dresses
and threw a bag or a folded rug on the back of the horse. For young women it was
a carefree time. 'As we entered our teens we became as rough as the young horses
we rode', Wallace explained,

> *We never wore shoes except when we were riding, and not always then, and, although
> our parents insisted that we change into dresses for dinner, during the day we wore
> checked shirts and ragged overalls, or threadbare jodhpurs. All of our games were
> tomboy games.*

Breaking-in or helping to break-in horses was common among women in the
bush, as were other challenges. At the Adelong (near Tumut, New South Wales)
Church of England sports day in 1931, two local girls, Dorothy and Meg Campbell,
won the bullock-riding competition. The local newspaper reported they 'rode
their bullocks to a standstill'. Rough riding was a sport with American rather than
British origins. Agricultural shows often featured women trick riders, such as the
'daring, fascinating, dashing rodeo cowgirls' from America who toured the

Margaret Doyle of Boggabilla at the Murrurundi Open Draft rodeo, NSW, 1938. Photograph by J.A. Smith.
STATE LIBRARY OF NEW SOUTH WALES

country in 1939. Twenty-two-year-old Violet Skuthorpe, whose father had pioneered buckjumping in Australia, was rough riding champion in 1942. In New England Judith Wallace remembered:

Gill and I wanted to be good roughriders, a sport that was very popular in the district . . . we encouraged the newly-broken horses we were riding to buck by jumping straight onto them and digging our spurs in while their backs were still cold . . . At the local rodeos they had calf riding for boys and we were determined to be the first girls to try it out. We practised by rounding up some yearlings . . . neither of us lasted longer than three bucks, but that was a reasonable effort for calf-riding, which was never a very successful sport as it is nearly impossible to get a good grip with the knees on a calf's back. The next time there was a rodeo on we thought we would try our luck. However, when we went up to the chutes and asked to be included, the men looked at us in disbelief and embarrassment and we never did get a turn. Mother was rather disappointed.

Women throughout Australia persevered, formed themselves into organised associations and competed at rodeos in events ranging from steering to Rodeo Queen, the latter requiring a well groomed horse and an expensive western outfit. Kitty Gill of Tamworth, a 'slim attractive mother of two children', won the Australian women's buckjumping championship held at the Warwick Rodeo in Brisbane in 1951. The following year she travelled to New York to compete in the Madison Square Rodeo. Cowgirl associations flourished among young women from horse-owning families. A group of 40 women from the then semi-rural Bossley Park formed a Cowgirls Association to teach each other the skills of rodeo riding. During the week they were to be found 'in schools, offices, shops, working as sales reps'. Their ages ranged from 15 to 50 and they practised and competed regularly. According to Patsy Adam-Smith, among the real horsewomen of the Australian bush 'hunting pink, riding breeches and black velvet caps were unknown'.

Wealthier country women maintained their links with the more formal side of horse riding, even after they had moved to the city. Country and semi-country girls boarding schools established riding as a school sport. Many women owned and operated riding school businesses. Around Sydney, for example, riding schools were established in the 1920s and 1930s by women on the North Shore, at Centennial Park, Kensington, Canterbury and Cronulla and in 'semi-country towns' like Medlow Bath in the Blue Mountains, Bowral and Camden. With the increasing popularity of the motor car and other recreations, riding in the cities went out of fashion for a time but was revived to the delight of the *Sydney Morning Herald* which welcomed the sight once again of the 'fair riders' who,

make pleasing pictures of the young Australian womanhood which evidently finds the saddle more thrilling than others find golf or tennis. Indications are that cross-country horse and rider are definitely coming back into their own as features of typical Australian life, and the advance of the sport will be welcomed with open arms by a community which is essentially British in its tastes.

As well as belonging to hunt clubs, women competed in equestrian events at agricultural shows. The Royal Agricultural Society's show held in Sydney at Easter attracted a number of competent country and 'semi-country' horsewomen. The majority of women in Australia by the 1930s rode astride, but occasionally, because of the difficulty and additional skill required, a side-saddle event was retained as one of the women's events. In 1914 at the Sydney show Mrs Stace of Forbes, New South Wales, won an event with a jump believed to be a world record

Despite the misleading gender-specific title, many women regularly competed at bushmen's carnivals. Mrs J.P. Brunner of Singleton clearing the sticks at the Scone Bushmen's Carnival and Show, Scone, NSW, c. 1934.
STATE LIBRARY OF NEW SOUTH WALES

for side-saddle jumping, clearing a 6 foot 7 inch (2 metre) hurdle. From the 1950s women were accorded the status of judges at equestrian events and in 1956 the first woman, Gwen Stead, was chosen as groom-in-charge of the Olympic horses. In 1964 a woman was selected for the first time as a competitor at an Olympic equestrian event. She was Bridget Macintyre of Muswellbrook, New South Wales. Macintyre had grown up, and still lived, on her family's cattle station. She had established herself as a champion in the mixed show-jumping event. Another Olympic and Commonwealth Games sport with strong links to the country was shooting. Many women representatives were drawn from country areas, including the world champion Judy Trim from Narrandera, New South Wales. A gun was a constant companion for women in the bush.

Notwithstanding the inaccurate gender-specific title of a 1986 publication on horse racing, *Gentlemen of the Australian Turf*, women played a significant part in the horse racing industry in Australia. Despite their equestrian skills, women were barred from holding a jockey's permit in Australia until 1979. But that did not mean there were no women jockeys. Violet Murrell won the blue ribbon for best

More convenient than shopping at the nearest butcher.
Vida Tubb, Quaker's Hill, NSW, 1920.
STATE LIBRARY OF NEW SOUTH WALES

woman rider over hurdles at the 1928 Sydney show having 'ridden everything since I was five'. Finding the situation in Australia unfair as 'girls are really doing the worst of the work. They break in the green horses as a hunter for men to compete with later as racers', she travelled to England to compete as a jockey at amateur race meetings. She raced in the Newmarket Town Plate, an annual race for women jockeys in England. When the *Everylady's Journal* asked her in 1929 if riding interfered with her domestic life, 'she shook her head with a sunny smile and replied: "I help my husband with the horses and he gives me a hand with the house. It's turn and turn about."'Bill Smith, a Queensland jockey who owned his own racehorses, won a series of races including the St Leger Quest in 1902, the Jockey Club Derby in 1903 and the Victorian Oaks in 1909–1910. Described as roughly spoken and given to constant swearing, he was regarded as an eccentric as he refused to change with the other jockeys. After his death near Cairns in 1975, it was revealed that Bill Smith was a woman and she was buried as Wilhelmina Smith.

Many wealthy women owned racehorses, the most prominent and successful in the 1930s was Lorna Utz whose horse *Sylvandale* brought home her colours in enough races to place her at the top of the woman-owner stakes. Mrs R.L. Buxton in Victoria owned the 1929 winner of the Caulfield Cup and Mrs E.E. Jolly of Adelaide owned the winner of the Port Adelaide Guineas. Mrs D.L. Clayton 'although a business executive in the city finds time to visit her stables at Mascot each day'. In summing up their performances in 1935 the *Sydney Morning Herald* commented, 'women owners, women breeders, women racing enthusiasts, for so short a history, have been remarkably successful'. For August–September 1953, 70 individual women were owners of horses who were winners or placegetters at the Sydney racemeetings alone. In 1950 a record five women entered horses in

Australia's most prestigious race, the Melbourne Cup. Three women had already owned winners of the Cup: Mrs E. Widdis with *Patrobus* in 1915, Mrs A. Jamieson with *Catalogue* in 1938 and Mrs J.J. Kitson with *Skipton* in 1941.

Women were breaking into other areas of horse racing, usually an easier task in country rather than urban centres. In South Australia a woman was appointed the first racing club steward in the early 1930s. She was followed by Kathleen O'Mara who became secretary of the Grafton Race Club, New South Wales, in 1933. O'Mara claimed in 1961 that she found nothing unusual in a woman doing that job, 'Nor, these days, do Grafton racegoers, owners, trainers and jockeys raise an eyebrow when they discover a woman taking nominations and organising the hundred and one details connected with a race meeting.' In Queensland Frances Leichney was appointed the secretary of the Downs Racing Club at Toowoomba in 1935.

The long tradition of women as expert horsewomen in Australia was re-endorsed in 1986 when 17-year-old outback Queensland schoolgirl Fiona Forster won the gruelling Winton to Longreach horse ride. She was the fourth woman in the ride's six-year history to win the 200 kilometres race. She beat a field of 65 riders. Women's part in the heritage of outback Australia has been overlooked, even in the modern era. In 1990 a fund was established to redress the imbalance at the Stockman's Hall of Fame museum in Longreach, Queensland, which had been opened in 1988. The most common cause of complaint by visitors to the museum was the lack of attention paid to the deeds of women.

Women grew up in the country able to play a wide range of team games. It was common for families to lay their own homestead tennis courts or at least know a neighbour who had. Patsy Adam-Smith's father, 'put down a court on the sun-baked red ground and painted lines on it with whitewash and encircled it with wire netting, which also served for the net. Neighbours came from far and near to play'. Too hot to play in the heat of the day, tennis parties were often more about socialising than sport, although women had a chance to test their skills against city players in the annual country week tournaments. These tournaments were first arranged by women's sports administrators in the late 1920s and early 1930s to give country players better access to competition in all sports. Budding tennis players in country centres had to rely on the benevolence of tennis court owners or an understanding of their needs by the local council. Champion tennis player Margaret Court who grew up in Albury, New South Wales, ironically attributed her superb volleying skills to her inability to find a court to play on legally. She and three friends would sneak onto an Albury court, only one-third of which was visible from the clubhouse. The other three would play at the obscured end, while Court had to stand at the net and prevent balls passing her.

Country tennis club, Curlewis, NSW, 1907.
STATE LIBRARY OF NEW SOUTH WALES

Evonne Goolagong received her start in tennis with the visit of a one-week country tennis school to rural New South Wales. This, she later commented,

gives kids from the bush an opportunity for first-rate instruction, a chance to learn a game that is a social focal point, for country families drive miles to play at courts in the small towns. Almost every town has a court or two.

She felt the ties to her country town Barellan strongly,

I think the feeling of not letting down the home-folk is strongest in those who come from the country towns. Everybody in our home-town knows us, and frequently, as in my case, the townspeople have contributed financially to make coaching and travel possible.

Gambling on more than fashion. Advertisement from *The Home*, June 1920.

Goolagong never lost the perspective of her country origins. When she first played at Wimbledon she described it as 'twenty-eight times the population of Barellan. You could fit the inhabitants of my town into a corner of the standing room sector, and they wouldn't be noticed.' International circuit player Jan Lehane from Grenfell, New South Wales, was another tennis player to be spotted at a country coaching week.

Cricket for women in Australia had originally started in the country centres and spread to the city. Young women at small schools often grew up proficient in the finer points of a variety of games. If country towns possessed one thing other than a pub, it was plenty of open space. Patsy Adam-Smith recalled her schooldays,

The school was next to the Waaia recreation ground, a great paddock containing a fine football field, cricket oval, two tennis courts, a basketball court and a rounders field. . . We could use all these playing fields, indeed a wooden stile was built over the s c h o o l fence to make access easier. As well, our own school ground was a quarter of a mile long and had basketball and tennis courts. Though I was useless at all sports this extravagant abundance didn't upset me. After all, one has to be bad not to gain a place in a team where there are only nineteen children in the school. Using every girl we had we still must impress boys to get a basketball team and opposition. And in turn, the boys pressganged us girls in eight-a-side football and cricket. My sister Mickie was one of the best footballers in the school.

Women cricketers at Hall, near Canberra, in 1908 played against their only available opposition — males. To compensate for the handicap of women's cumbersome dresses, men played with pick handles instead of regular cricket bats. When the women's cricket association was formed, city players made an effort to get to the more remote areas to play against women. Margaret Peden the captain of Kuring-gai and New South Wales (and later Australia) took her club team on an annual tour to Goulburn, Collector, Queanbeyan, Moss Vale, Berry, Wollongong, Junee and Temora. The women pitched tents, cooked their own meals and played matches in all the towns they visited. When the English women's cricket and hockey teams visited Australia they visited many country areas, drawing large crowds and often having local public holidays declared in their honour. In the 1930s only one Australian woman representative cricketer was a country player — opening batter Ruby Monaghan of Wollongong, New South Wales. But the tradition continued. In 1986 Lyn Larsen from Lismore, New South Wales, was appointed captain of the Australian women's cricket team. Don Bradman, himself a country boy, lost his wicket in 1931 to Eileen Thornton of Newcastle, New South

Wales, during a charity match. The 20-year-old Thornton bowled Bradman 'a well-pitched ball with plenty of nip from the pitch', to become what the *Newcastle Herald* claimed was 'the only girl in the world to secure Bradman's wicket'.

Other country sportswomen were given the chance to prove their skills in regular country week competitions in hockey, basketball, baseball and croquet. Umpiring courses and umpiring examinations for hockey were also held in conjunction with the hockey week programmes. Such endeavours often involved large numbers of country women. In 1934 over 400 country players from rural Victoria made the journey to Melbourne to compete in a croquet contest.

From the beginning of the women's golf associations in each state, annual trophies were awarded for the country champion, a prestigious title. Country women often did not have access to the level of tuition available in the cities. The 1933 country champion of New South Wales, Vedas Ebert from Griffith, did not have the advantage of a golf professional at her home club from whom she could take lessons. Undaunted, she purchased a book on golf, pored over its contents and carried out the instructions to the most minute detail. She practised every

Women were always full-time lifesavers and swimming instructors to their children. Armidale, NSW, 1929.
STATE LIBRARY OF NEW SOUTH WALES

stroke before her wardrobe mirror, and became the most outstanding player at her local Griffith club. Her dedication was even more praiseworthy considering she was a lefthander and all the instructions were therefore back-to-front.

Young country women taught themselves to swim in the local dams, bores and creeks, braving both leeches and prying male eyes. Mothers often acted as lifesavers at the local swimming hole. Before swimming pools were constructed, towns would conduct their swimming competitions at the local river. In Bassendean, Western Australia, women were excluded from the annual swimming races. They responded by forming their own club and conducting their own swimming programme in the river. Every country girl knew the skills of yabbying in the local creeks and many women were enthusiastic anglers. Women in Yass, New South Wales, in 1933 celebrated a record trout catch made by Miss Stuart in the Goodradigbee River, close to Burrenjuck Dam. Aboriginal women living in rural Australia already possessed the skills of swimming and intimate knowledge of the rivers and creeks. Jessie Street who grew up on a station on the upper Clarence River in northern New South Wales recalled,

Summertime fishing and boating on the Paroo River, Qld, 1908. Every young country woman learned the skills of fishing and yabbying in the local creeks, rivers and dams.
STATE LIBRARY OF NEW SOUTH WALES

I used to swim in the river with some of the aboriginal women whom I admired immensely as they could swim underwater for quite a distance and come up in unexpected places. They would find baby platypuses in their nests and bring them out for me to see.

Free spirits in stockinged feet. Country folk often rallied behind their champion women athletes. Broken Hill, c. 1910.
BROKEN HILL CITY COUNCIL

Picnic races and church fairs were a common occurrence in the country. Before the formation of the athletic associations, country championships would often be billed as state championships. Thus in 1911 at the old showground in Goulburn, New South Wales, Miss A. Moore won the '100 yards championship of NSW from Mrs F. Drennan in 13 $^3/_5$ seconds'. Many Australian athletic champions originated from country areas where the local population was often called on to help fundraise and finance expensive interstate competitions and overseas trips. In honour of their origins, Olympic gold medallist Marjorie Jackson was dubbed the 'Lithgow Flash', and Australian sprint champion Debbie Wells was called the 'Emmaville Express'. Those who were not destined to be international champions were just as content to run at the local sports.

Over the years the traditions of women's sport in the country have come under threat as new areas of leisure and recreation have opened up. Young women continue to roam the countryside swimming and riding horses, but twentieth century diversions have also intruded into their lifestyles. Although still able to play competitive sport and represent their area, state or country, women in rural

Australia have not been able to keep up their interest in sport on a social level. A survey of rural women in 1989 revealed that,

women with families regretted they did not have more time for outdoor sports, especially team activities, but the demands of children and husbands got in the way of practice times. A number of women who liked individual outdoor sports never indulged in them.

To counter this trend the federal government produced *The Rural Woman's Guide to Fitness and Well-being* in 1990. Women who in the past could ask their families to 'hold the reins' while they competed in the Married Ladies Race were no longer winners. In the harsh economic reality of the country, the rural lifestyle has changed and women and their sporting pursuits have been the losers.

SPORTSWEAR

THE STORY OF THE CLOTHES WOMEN WEAR TO PLAY SPORT IS REMINISCENT OF THE OLD QUIP ABOUT THE ABILITIES OF THE DANCERS GINGER ROGERS AND FRED ASTAIRE: THAT GINGER COULD DO EVERYTHING FRED DID, BUT BACKWARDS AND IN HIGH HEELS! One of the crucial issues in women's ability to play sport has been the design and nature of their clothing. Controversy has raged over the appropriateness of their dress. Clothing performed both a restrictive and a liberating role in women's sport and the adoption of more rational dress correlates closely with the establishment of more vigorous sports. Fashion reflects women's role in society. It is both an outward reminder of their limitations and an inward reminder of society's restrictions.

It is surprising that women and men could move at all, let alone play sport, in some of the fashions of the nineteenth century. As could be expected, the style of dress of colonial women closely followed that current in Britain at the time, with occasional concessions being made to the climate in the form of lighter weight material. In the 1840s women of all classes were laced, petticoated and bonneted in every shade of grey imaginable in a style of dress that emphasised the 'droop' or bustle. These dresses proved almost impossible to walk in. By the middle of the century the crinoline, a cage of wire hoops, had been adopted and gave more freedom to the legs. But the crinoline could employ over 14 metres of material in a single dress and was cumbersome and impractical. Some women rode to country balls with their crinolines tied in a figure eight. From the 1850s riding habits were available in the colonies. Because women rode side-saddle, riding habits consisted of trousers worn under a skirt topped with a separate jacket. By the 1870s women's conventional dress was no more practical. It incorporated tied back skirts and a bustle. The overall circumference was smaller, but a sweeping train and leg-of-mutton sleeves had been added which severely restricted movement. A laced bodice, now heavily boned and with brass hook-and-eye to allow even tighter lacing, meant that the clothing restricted breathing. The seemingly 'delicate' nature of women in this period can be attributed to the tightness of their corsets.

Dress constraints could determine the winner of a sprint race. Bonegilla, Vic.
STATE LIBRARY OF NEW SOUTH WALES

When the new sport of tennis was introduced in the late 1870s, no concessions were made to women players who remained corseted, bustled, hatted and sometimes even gloved. At first very little rapid movement was allowed without tripping, but skirts were gradually raised which permitted some chasing and vigorous stroke play. Women's clothing became less hampering and restrictive with the influence of the English Aesthetic and Rational Dress Movements. But the standard order of the day was still voluminous skirts and wide brimmed cabbage tree hats.

The real breakthrough, however, came with the introduction of the gym tunic in Australia. This form of rational dress had been adopted in the physical education academies of England and was brought to the colonies by their disciples. Once established in the independent girls schools (at first within the private confines of the gymnasium), gym tunics eventually came to be considered appropriate dress for physical activity of all kinds. The dress standards of young women could also be freer than that of older women.

Towards the end of the nineteenth century numerous social changes occurred that were to have a significant bearing on women's dress. A sewing machine for the home was available and women could make their own clothes from paper patterns sold through such firms as Madame Weigel's. Clothes made from paper patterns were, by necessity, simpler than those ordered from a manufacturer. With the growth of large retail emporiums, women could purchase a wider range of clothes suitable for a variety of occasions.

Side-saddle bicycle riding was possible — provided you never had to pedal uphill!
Annie Dawson Wallace, Sydney, 1899.
STATE LIBRARY OF NEW SOUTH WALES

The invention of the safety bicycle, which was popular among women, also caused a loosening of strict dress rules, if not stays themselves. Most women who had previously ridden their horses side-saddle found it totally impractical to continue doing so on the new 'metal horse' (although side-saddle bicycle riding was not completely unknown). Geography dictated that a rider had to pedal at some stage of the journey. Special bicycling clothes, usually incorporating bloomers, were advertised for women. Tights were commonly worn under the bloomers. As skirts in general began to rise to permit more movement, the ankle and leg remained thickly covered in non-transparent stockings.

To indulge in the pastime of sea bathing women donned special costumes. These consisted of drawers and a separate jacket belted at the waist. Connie Miller who

'The suit's natty white-tape trimming did nothing to counteract the monstrous effect cotton stockinette can achieve, when wet, on the human shape'. *Melbourne Punch*, 23 January 1919.
NATIONAL LIBRARY OF AUSTRALIA

grew up in Perth during the early part of the twentieth century described her costume:

> *My first suit was a navy cotton stockinette two-piecer. Its shapeless pants finished two inches above my knees and its sacklike, short-sleeved top ended about ten inches below my hips. The suit's natty white-tape trimming did nothing to counteract the monstrous effect cotton stockinette can achieve, when wet, on the human shape. And the mob cap of yellow oiled silk into which I pushed my long thick hair looked like an over-ripe pumpkin.*

The swimming champion Annette Kellermann had set Australian and world record times in her long distance swims. She completed several gruelling long swims in Europe and while touring America in 1907 was arrested by Boston police for wearing a one-piece skirtless bathing suit. She argued that the bathing suits of the day were as dangerous as having lead weights tied to you while swimming. When Fanny Durack and Mina Wylie competed at the 1912 Olympics in Stockholm they wore green caps and green cloaks which they shed to reveal one-piece neck-to-knee costumes.

After the First World War women's sport underwent an accelerated growth which was accompanied by an equally rapid change in sporting attire. Standards improved markedly across all sports and by 1935 the *Sydney Morning Herald* acknowledged 'it is an outstanding fact, coincident with the greater freedom of the modern sporting attire, that a greater degree of skill and accomplishment has been shown.'

Young women who first began playing hockey in Australia wore their ordinary clothes — long skirts, high collars, and large hats fastened precariously on to the head with long and deadly hat-pins. Coloured silk sashes were worn to distinguish the teams. A generation later hockey players roared with laughter when treated to an 'old-timers' match replicating the fashions of the early 1900s in which each player,

favoured a voluminous ankle-length black skirt, high-necked white blouse, white cotton stockings, a straw boater gaily decorated with a tangerine band, a sash of the same hue . . . and a magnificient pair of high-buttoned black boots.

The spectators were again convulsed with laughter at the appearance of the umpires 'in trailing white frocks, lace collars of great size, black hats with immense feather boas, all complete with furs'. By 1909 the women's hockey association decreed that players would wear sports tunics for their games, similar to those worn by schoolgirls. Before the start of each hockey match in the 1930s a ritual measuring of the tunics took place which, according to the rules, 'must be not less than one inch, or more than four inches, from the ground when kneeling'. The only other sportswomen to adopt the tunic were basketballers. With it they wore a white blouse (the sleeves of which they were permitted to roll up) with a tie and black stockings.

Other sports faced more difficulty in determining their uniforms and it was not until the arrival in Australia of overseas players with alternative fashions, or the return home of touring sportswomen with new ideas, that uniforms in all sports were codified.

The development of the basketball uniform had a long way to go. Kaniva, Vic, c. 1935.
MUSEUM OF VICTORIA

Pioneer cricketers were hampered in their movements by their voluminous skirts. Such was the nature of their clothing that it is not known for sure whether early cricketers wore pads to bat in. Nurses playing during the First World War somehow wore batting pads outside their ground length nursing uniforms. Gradually the skirt was shortened to just below the knee, a length that still proved incommodious in pads. Trousers or bib and brace overalls were adopted by some cricket teams as a solution. It was not until 1934, and the visit of the English women cricketers, that the uniform was finally agreed upon. The English wore the divided skirt which, while looking like a neat pleated skirt, afforded greater movement to the player. To this they added a short sleeved open neck shirt. The Australians embraced the new style enthusiastically and by the time of the 1937 tour to England the Australian captain Margaret Peden had drafted and sent the uniform pattern to each Australian player. Not so enthusiastic were the women's thoughts on the white lisle stockings to be worn under the divided skirts. One player from the 1930s kept numerous pairs and used them, in accordance with the accepted custom of the day, to dress the bodies of relatives who died — a use she considered far more appropriate! Women were not permitted to wear cricket caps and instead wore white wide-brimmed hats. (Many years later an astute male cricketer successfully marketed these same hats.)

Australian tennis fashions were also determined by outside influences. The first challenges to convention were made by Americans. In 1905 May Sutton daringly rolled up her long sleeves at Wimbledon and in 1909 Hazel Hotchkiss at the US championships wore a short sleeved dress made especially for tennis by her mother. The exposure of women's elbows met with considerable disapproval, but this reaction was nothing compared with what awaited South African Billie Tapscott who appeared on court in 1929 without stockings. American player Helen Jacobs was the first to wear tennis shorts and heartily recommended them as 'she felt a distinct improvement in her game and a far easier swing and action in all strokes'. Although shorts were never permitted at Wimbledon, Jacobs sparked a controversy which had the top Australian players evenly divided regarding the wearing of shorts or skirts. Joan Hartigan and Nell Hopman wore shorts as soon as the Victorian Lawn Tennis Association lifted their ban in 1933. Both had toured overseas and brought back to Australia 'attractive pleated linen shorts'. But in the long run, tennis shorts never enjoyed the popularity among women in Australia that they did in America.

The shorts adopted by tennis players were regarded as less 'severe' than those worn by women athletes and rowers. In 1935 the Baptist Minister of Granville in Sydney objected to women athletes running in shorts at the first annual field day conducted by the New South Wales Christian Endeavour Union at Parramatta. While he argued that only 'the severest prude would be idiotic to cavil' at shorts being worn in the privacy of a gymnasium he thought it 'an admirable opportunity for our Christian maids to set a more exalted standard . . . Hence my request to our girls to be arrayed as feminine athletes have done until the last decade.' Officials considered his request unreasonable, 'shorts give competitors greater freedom of movement, particularly in running, and offer less wind resistance than the divided skirts'.

Clarice Kennedy started her hurdling career in the late 1920s in pleated bloomers that blew out like balloons when she ran. While at Fort Street Girls High School, she obtained special permission from the headmistress to discard her stockings when she made an official attempt to break the Australian sprint hurdles record. Kennedy first wore shorts in 1930, one year after leaving school, and remembered writing to various police stations asking permission to be seen in shorts at venues under their jurisdiction.

Australia's first woman Olympic athlete, Edith Robinson, was issued in 1928 with an official uniform consisting of a white half-sleeve jumper with green and gold bands around the neck, sleeves and hem, and a pair of knee length black bloomers. Aware of the styles worn by other women competitors, Robinson knew that the cumbersome uniform would put her at a disadvantage. On the boat voyage to the Games in Amsterdam she borrowed a portable hand-operated sewing machine from a passenger and, with another team member turning the handle, she converted the issued garments into a short sleeve blouse and shorts.

It was years until a track suit was issued to all Australian competitors or before one could even be purchased in Australia. Most athletes shivered in thin competition uniforms, donned home-made track suits or threw a coat over their shoulders. Such arrangements were not conducive to good performances and many injuries probably resulted from such practices. In 1936 women athletes wore the new 'sweat suits' for the first time at an Olympic Games. The *Argus* newspaper described them as 'long slacks and pullovers which they don over their shorts and shirts when not competing'.

Track suits were not always strictly for warmth. In 1933 the acting secretary of the Brisbane YWCA had approved shorts for athletics provided a wrap was 'donned on the field preparatory to leaving the ground'. Mavys Opperman, 'wife of the famous Australian cyclist', writing for the newspaper *Sportswoman* in 1936 recommended shorts for bicycling, provided women carried 'a special button-up skirt, which can be slipped on quickly when the rider has dismounted'.

A similar double standard operated regarding women's bathing costumes. In a 1933 front page story headlined 'Oh Mr Alderman What Can We Wear?', the *Australian Women's Weekly* questioned the need for the shire councils to 'take notice of the area of material per person used in the latest bathing costumes'. The Cronulla Council in Sydney had charged three women with unseemly conduct after they left the beach in their backless costumes. The council had stipulated that a wrap be worn by women on their way to and from the beach. Sandringham Council in Melbourne went a step further and banned backless costumes on the beach itself. At the 1936 Olympic Games Australian women swimmers wore black bathing suits which had 'skirts reaching to a regulation length down the thigh, and are not backless'.

Tasmanian badminton players who visited Adelaide for a tournament in 1934 were so impressed by the versatility of the shorts worn by the other players that they 'revelled in the freedom' and refused to return to wearing skirts. In 1935 the International Fencing Federation banned skirts being worn by women and stipulated black 'knee-breeches reaching to and buttoned below the knee'. Baseballers chose plus fours (also called apple catchers and knickerbockers) for their sport because 'they give the complete freedom of action necessitated by so strenuous a game, yet they could scarcely be regarded as lacking in modesty by the most scrupulous observer of the conventions'.

The removal of the constrictive suspender belt left a lasting impression on Jean Ryder and Brenda Scott at Belmont, NSW, 1928.
STATE LIBRARY OF NEW SOUTH WALES

The practical aspects of sporting attire did not always win through. On the golf course women resisted attempts to introduce plus fours. They continued to wear long pleated skirts, despite the visit in 1935 of an English women's golf team who declared:

We wear the usual conventional golfing kit, but it is quite acceptable that slacks, long rainproof trousers are permissible for wet-weather play. This is much more practical than windswept or wet clinging skirts.

Similarly conservative, the women's bowling association ruled that 'All players in association matches must wear white or cream dresses with long sleeves, white shoes and white stockings.' Not even coloured underclothing could be worn while playing. One bowler who daringly donned a low-back frock incurred the displeasure of her association and had to be lent a coat to complete her match. Short sleeves were banned because it was thought they would not suit elderly players, and as a club official explained, 'If we do not allow short sleeves, even to the elbow, it is not likely that we would allow a low-backed dress'.

Perhaps of even greater importance than what sportswomen wore on the outside, were the restrictions placed on them by their underclothing. Many suffered in the name of convention. Elizabeth Ryan, Wimbledon doubles champion between 1914 and 1934, recalled the clothes rack in the women's changing room, 'Alongside the dresses it was not unusual to see whalebone corsets, stained with blood in places'. It was not always the white lisle stockings that women cricketers objected to so much as the constrictive suspender belt needed to keep them up in pre-pantyhose days.

After the First World War a further radical change came over women's clothing with the development of sportswear fashions. These bore no direct relation to the type of clothes appropriate for women to wear on the sportsfield. It was a range designed for everyday wear that used as its theme freedom of movement. During the war women had been disinclined to spend more than was necessary on clothes. Once the war was over women became pawns in the high fashion stakes of manufacturers and the bait was freedom. Fashion photography began to feature women in the latest 'creations' holding a tennis racquet or set of golf clubs. Women were photographed at the beach in a wide range of swimming fashions. *The Home* told its readers in 1921, 'When much of one's time is spent in sea water the least one can do is to dress for it'. Beginning in the 1920s stores like David Jones promoted a range of women's clothes for swimming, walking, playing croquet, tennis and golf, fishing, motoring and riding as well as something called a 'river frock', all of which were totally impractical for the purposes specified. A 1923 article in a women's magazine, illustrated by a sportswoman, stated, 'Surely one can play a better game in garb designed for perfect freedom of movement and designed deliberately also to look well!' The new clothes, while promising liberation, caught women up in a fashion spiral that was never to release them. It had been discovered that sporting imagery could be used to sell clothes to women.

Once created, the new marketing strategy was exploited with gusto. Companies like Dunlop shoes produced a whole range of footwear for the active woman. Described as 'fashionable sport shoes' they featured crepe soles and wedge heels and were available for 'sport, leisure or beach'. Parker Shoes designed a new 'out-of-door' range for 'golf and country' wear. Prestige offered special 'outdoor hosiery' for 'we active women'. Kestos Brassiere Co produced a bra 'for all sports wear'. To the fastidious woman it gave 'comfort and allows her complete freedom of movement. . . knowing that only when feeling and looking her best is she able to play her best'. To match her new sports clothes the fashion conscious woman also had a whole range of accessories featuring sporting motifs, including scarves, brooches, buttons and clasps. Gone were the cameos of the former generation and in their place 'designs indicative of women's new interest in sport'. Gift ideas for women now included new ranges of sporting equipment whose,

general appearance has improved tremendously. They are now not merely a part of the game, but attractive-looking as well. Golf balls are put up in smart, colourful boxes. Tennis racquet covers are brightly striped or patterned.

The sale of such gifts was not reserved for the professional:

it is not necessary for people to be very proficient at sport before they can appreciate as presents those goods which belong to it. Often the least proficient players are the most enthusiastic, and whether one plays well or not, one needs equipment.

The Second World War brought women an even greater level of economic independence — and advertisers were ready for them. More insidiously, the incorporation of sport into the everyday lives of Australian women caused a not-so-subtle shift in the way sportswomen were treated in the media. Women's sport in the 1930s had been taken seriously by a new generation of women journalists, but once it was seen as a marketable commodity it was doomed to trivialisation. The reporting of women's sport shifted to a concentration on clothes, accessories and colours, rather than performance, competition and ability. Sport for women was acceptable as long as they looked nice while participating — a difficult prospect for either sex while grimacing, straining and sweating. The change in emphasis was no accident. The mass circulation *Australian Women's Weekly* had ceased reporting women's sport as sport in 1937. Its place in the magazine had been taken over by mass commercialism and a new interest in consuming. Any references to sport were now laced with special attention to the clothes or appearance of the sportswomen. During the war the women's supplement to the *Sydney Morning Herald*, which featured a regular article on sport, ceased publication. After the war its place was taken by the new *Sunday Herald* in which women's sport was relegated to the 'Women's Section' while male sport was reported in the 'Sports Section'. Suddenly what sportswomen looked like, what they wore and what they did in their private lives became more important than what they achieved. The trend was copied in all major newspapers and women's magazines across Australia. The fashionably dressed, slim and attractive woman became the sporting woman's supposed role model.

The new fashions of the 1940s were briefer than ever. Jantzen swimming costumes launched their 'Be attractive while you're active' campaign with suits made of rayon, with a built-in cross over bra and a 'deep V back for ample sun exposure'. Before the war separate bras had been worn under some knitted woollen suits. A new panty-girdle called 'Sports Tights' was designed by La Mode Corsetry 'ideal for the miss of today an active hard-hitting tennis ace' or a golfer 'with a full free swing'. It featured detachable suspenders designed for sportwomen who needn't wear stockings. In 1947 the women's cricket association ruled that players should wear white socks rather than white stockings. While such rule changes appeared like a move towards greater freedom, it was an illusion if sportswomen were told by advertisers to still wear the corset without the stockings! Doris Magee, author of the 'Women In Sport' column of the *Sunday Herald* pushed the new line. In a 1953 article titled 'More glamour in clothes' she informed her readers:

> *Sportswomen are turning their attention more and more to the introduction of glamour into sportswear and uniforms. The drab schoolgirl uniforms for active competitions are now a thing of the past. Women tennis players made headlines at Wimbledon with their sports attire, and the world's leading dress designers are now giving tennis togs their serious attention. The Australian sporting public demanded 'more glamour for our Olympic girls' . . . Now women athletes are turning their attention to brightening up their officials.*

But not all sportswomen were so impressed with the practical aspects of the new 'glamour'. Champion tennis player Margaret Court refused to wear clothes designed by Teddy Tinling, one of the world's leading tennis dress designers:

I think they are inclined to be impractical. . . I wore his frocks during the 1961 and 1962 tours, but I found that I was not comfortable in them. One day on Wimbledon's centre court the shoulder strap of the frilly creation I was wearing persisted in slipping off . . . Not long after this match had finished I confronted Teddy and asked him to make me something simple and practical. 'I feel like a pretty little doll on the court in these clothes. They are uncomfortable,' I told him. . . I now wear skirts and shirts by Fred Perry. My sentiments on tennis dressing are shared by many of the other players on the circuit, including the two American girls Billie-Jean Moffitt and Karen Susman, who agree that trying to be a centre-court fashion plate and play championship tennis at the same time is too difficult.

After winning the first of her 16 consecutive British women's squash championships, Heather Blundell (later McKay) also criticised high fashion for sportswomen, 'I think some of those dresses must be a bit uncomfortable,' she said, 'for squash, anyway. I always wear shorts and a loose top. Then I don't have any distractions while I'm playing.' Australia's women bowlers also stood their ground amid much derision and mocking. In 1953 V. Froud, in a letter to the editor of the *Sydney Morning Herald*, defended her sport against the encroachment of fashion, 'We go onto the green to enjoy friendship and play the game, not to worry about looking glamorous.'

Women continued to be bombarded with new products, new fabrics that would not shrink or fade, new ranges of styled-for-action shoes and new underclothing that they could go bowling, skiing and even surfing in. Australian women were the first to wear coloured uniforms at the Olympic Games when they departed from the traditional white in 1952 and wore what was described as 'sunshine yellow'. Critics attacked the women's uniforms of nearly every team to leave the shores. In 1974 the Commonwealth Games uniform for women was described as 'totally sexless'. Linda McGill thought the jacket 'ready made for a ladies' bowling team' and a fashion editor thought 'the girls will look more like a middle-aged croquet team than the cream of Australian sportswomen'. The *Australian* newspaper warned 'The girls better win some medals over there, because they won't be winning any hearts in that uniform'.

The fashion debate continued with few sane voices to insist upon women's right to simply play sport in clothes that were practical and functional. The clear distinctions between fashion and sport were blurred for women in Australia. Sponsors insisted that sportswomen should look glamorous in order to attract the corporate dollar. Individual women were easier targets to market than team players, about whom the word uniform denotes how they look as well as what

Bowlers vehemently resisted change to their uniform — 'we go onto the green to enjoy friendship and play the game, not to worry about looking glamorous' — but gradually pants have become more acceptable among their ranks. Canberra, 1987.
OVERSEAS INFORMATION BRANCH

they wear. Changes inspired by the media and the sponsors were made in the non-uniform sports — golfers' skirts became shorter, track and field costumes tighter and 'feminised' with sequins, and swim suits were cut higher and higher in the leg. New sports such as aerobics, triathlons and beach volleyball come already marketed with a fashion component, the latter called volleywear. The balance between practical sports clothing and glamour has been lost or confused, and in the process attention has been removed from the achievements of the few sportswomen who actually receive media coverage. Long skirts and tight whalebone corsets may have hampered the sporting aspirations of earlier generations but in their wake other fashion constraints, perhaps more insidious, restrict the modern sportswoman.

The improvement in comfort of women's outer sports garments meant nothing if manufacturers encouraged them to wear a pantie-girdle underneath. Advertisement from the *Australian Women's Weekly*, 18 December 1948.

Equally Suitable

for all Sports Wear

The fastidious woman relies upon the subtle touch of the Kestos Brassiere to accentuate and safeguard her natural beauty. Kestos gives comfort and allows her complete freedom of movement. Wisely she wears a Kestos Brassiere, knowing that only when feeling and looking her best is she able to play her best.

Kestos Elastic Straps
may be obtained separately
at 6d. per pair

KESTOS
BRASSIERES

Trade Enquiries to
Kestos Brassiere Co., 3-11 Howard St.,

As sport became incorporated into the lives of Australian women manufacturers and advertisers were ready for them. Advertisement from *The Home*, July 1934.

MEDICAL AND SOCIAL HURDLES

I<small>N WOMEN'S SPORTING LIVES</small>
<small>THERE ARE PLACED A NUMBER OF HURDLES</small>. To cross these hurdles requires a great deal more dedication and commitment than it takes to run on the straight and narrow path reserved for sportsmen. These hurdles are marked medical intervention, menstruation, marriage, sexuality, pregnancy, motherhood, age, appearance and body image.

MEDICAL HURDLES

When women were first admitted to universities in the 1870s some medical men attested that women should not study during menstruation as it would drain their vitality. Mental strain, the men argued, would affect the reproductive functions of women. With such ignorance being propagated in relation to mental exercise, it was almost inevitable that men would get an attack of the vapours at the notion of physical exercise for women. But their opposition proved more than just bloodymindedness. It effectively restricted women's participation in sport.

Much of the debate was conducted elsewhere, but Australian women were keenly aware of the pseudo-medical controversy regarding women's sport.

Pressure from women's sporting organisations forced the introduction of women's athletic events for the first time at the 1928 Olympics. The 100 metres and 800 metres were included on the programme. But after the 800 metres had been run, officials considered that women had shown too much 'distress' and amid controversy removed it from the Olympics. The removal of the longer race (until 1960) effectively robbed women of a career in athletic running, as sprinters often move to a longer distance and so keep form for years.

Earlier in 1928 the French Ministry of Public Instruction had decreed that all French sportswomen entering a public competition or championship must have a medical certificate and sports licence testifying to their fitness. The *London Morning Post* reported:

The French girl has of recent years flung herself into sport with such whole-hearted abandon that critics had begun to fear that the general health of the country's womanhood would suffer as a consequence.

Association football (soccer) and cross-country running were said to be the two most popular sports with women. The department proposed to 'regulate this enthusiasm' and introduced a compulsory medical test, 'of a searching character, in which the state of the candidate's heart, lungs, and other respiratory organs, as well as age, weight, height, and more obvious details have to be given'.

Across Europe in the 1930s the rising fascist dictatorships decreed that sport was dangerous for women. Hitler imposed a ban on strenuous sport for women and Mussolini, with the backing of the Vatican, prohibited running and football. 'Fascist girls must be prepared to discharge missions of wives and mothers, and learn how to rule the household. They may take such exercise as improves their figures, but no more', the new regulations stated. In 1934 the British-based Women's Amateur Athletic Association responded by organising their own inquiry into the effects of strenuous sport on women athletes. The results refuted the objections made to women participating in endurance events. The association arranged their own international long distance races for women, keen to prove 'girls are not made of cotton wool, and have stamina and perfect health'.

It was clearly in the interests of fascist dictators, attempting to keep women biologically oppressed, to ignore such findings. But the fascists were not alone. Respected medical authorities in England also refused to accept that women should engage in energetic sports. As would be the case for future generations of male doctors and scientists involved in this issue, their presumptions were not based on scientific evidence, but on the simple belief that if sport was straining for men it would be even more so for women. A rather emotional reaction for men trained in science! Dr Adolphe Abrahams, the honorary medical officer to the British Olympic Games team, typified this reaction. When he addressed the British Association for Physical Training in London in 1935 he outlined the nerve-strain on the male athlete and continued,

> *I would expect it to be much worse in the case of a girl or young woman. One visualises a higher type of nervous system, much less likely to stand up against the same strain. For that reason I have never hesitated to inveigh against Olympic games for women, and I am strongly against highly competitive lawn tennis. Of course, I may be wrong. A lady doctor I know tells me that I am. She holds that women are more flexible and adaptable than men. That is the point at which we differ. I may be old-fashioned, but I must say that when I visualise collapse and exhaustion in a male — an unpleasant enough spectacle in some circumstances — I cannot bring myself to believe it cannot be worse in the case of a woman.*

There was plenty of negative visualising back home in Australia. A motion at the 1929 annual meeting of the Country Women's Association proposed that the association should obtain a 'scientific medical investigation' to ascertain whether strenuous sport had an injurious effect on the health of growing girls. Dr Margaret Anderson returned from the Women's International Medical Congress at Stockholm in 1935 with a warning against women doing weightlifting and wrestling (how many of them were doing so, to warrant such an announcement in Australia?). While Anderson approved of competitive athletics in general she did not believe that 'the adolescent girl should go in for too much competitive sport or athletics while she is studying for important examinations, though normal exercises and games are essential'. Direct from Sweden, she recommended physical culture, bicycling and riding, though never side-saddle which is 'apt to make one hip higher than the other'. In short, all exercise was beneficial provided women were medically examined first.

So from the middle of the 1930s most women participating in competitive sport in Australia were theoretically to be medically examined. In Victoria, the Victorian Women's Amateur Athletic Association ruled that each member had to be examined every two years, and new members within one month of joining a club. They also reserved the right to submit any woman to an examination at any time. All rowing clubs insisted that women be medically examined as well as being able to swim. Before leaving for England, the 1937 Australian women's cricket team were subjected to two medical examinations, the cost of which had to be borne by the players themselves.

Although the rulings were made by associations sincerely concerned that no woman should do herself harm, how many women would have wanted to submit themselves to such an examination regularly? If male athletes were not examined and women were, it automatically placed some doubt on women's athletic ability where no doubt should have existed. A glance at the statistics for men being rejected by the military in Australia during the Second World War reveal that approximately 20 per cent of the potential recruits were rejected on medical grounds. Were 20 per cent of women who wanted to participate in physical activity prevented by their doctors? How many women who nowadays play sport would have been restricted by either the criteria of the examination (based on male doctors' visualisations) or the personal attitude of the (male) doctor. Special examinations were never organised or carried out under the jurisdiction of the sporting groups concerned — the parameters of tests were left to the discretion of women's own general practitioners.

How sincerely women's organisations took the need for medical examinations is difficult to judge. Organisations that were fighting for grounds, funding, recognition, media coverage and Empire and Olympic representation were unlikely to bow to disputable medical pressure. Perhaps medical intervention was a price they were prepared to pay to permit women to play sport. If so, they must have felt genuinely threatened by hostile male attitudes to sportswomen in the community. Certainly statements by Dr Anderson that weightlifting and wrestling should be prohibited, in reality give women carte blanche to indulge in as much physical activity as they desired. And in 1938 the same Victorian athletic association that required two-yearly examinations restored the broad jump (long jump) to their athletic programme on 'medical advice that no harm will come to a normal healthy girl from broad jumping'. *The Australian Women's Weekly* assured its readers in 1936 that women did not suffer from 'athletes heart', an over-exertion condition that plagued sportsmen. Once strict control was seen to be in place, women could indulge in a greater range of sports than previously allowed.

In fact many Australian women had taken up sport because they were in some way physically incapacitated. Born in 1887, champion swimmer Annette Kellermann was never a strong child. She was diagnosed as having rickets, but her condition was more likely to have been polio. As a result she wore leg braces from an early age. Her mother took her for swimming lessons that proved so beneficial she discarded the leg irons by the age of fifteen. Her water cure induced a love of swimming which she continued as a professional career. Olympic champion Dawn Fraser realised at the age of ten that swimming eased her asthma. The breathing discipline developed in the water helped her deal with her attacks and she would visit the baths as often as possible. Olympic gold medal butterfly swimmer Lynn McClements had overcome infantile asthma and was one of the few athletes at the 1968 Mexico Games unaffected by the rarefied air in Mexico City. Olympic swimmer Frances Bult, a physiotherapist, used water therapy to cure patients during the infantile paralysis epidemic. Joan Hammond, a champion golfer as well as an opera singer, injured her left arm as a child and took up golf to strengthen it. Kay Cottee, the first woman to sail around the world solo and non-stop, did so with a congenital heart murmer, a small hole in the heart and pulmonary stenosis. Other women prominently supported the medical benefits of sport for women. Addressing women at the Farmer & Co. retail business girls' luncheon, the champion 1938 Empire Games athlete Decima Norman was asked the question: Are athletics good or bad for women? She replied,

From my own experience, I can say that they are definitely beneficial. During the seven years in which I have been playing hockey and training for athletics, I have had no illnesses except a few minor colds, and I have never felt better in my life. Also, from my experience as a business girl in a large firm in Perth, I have noticed that

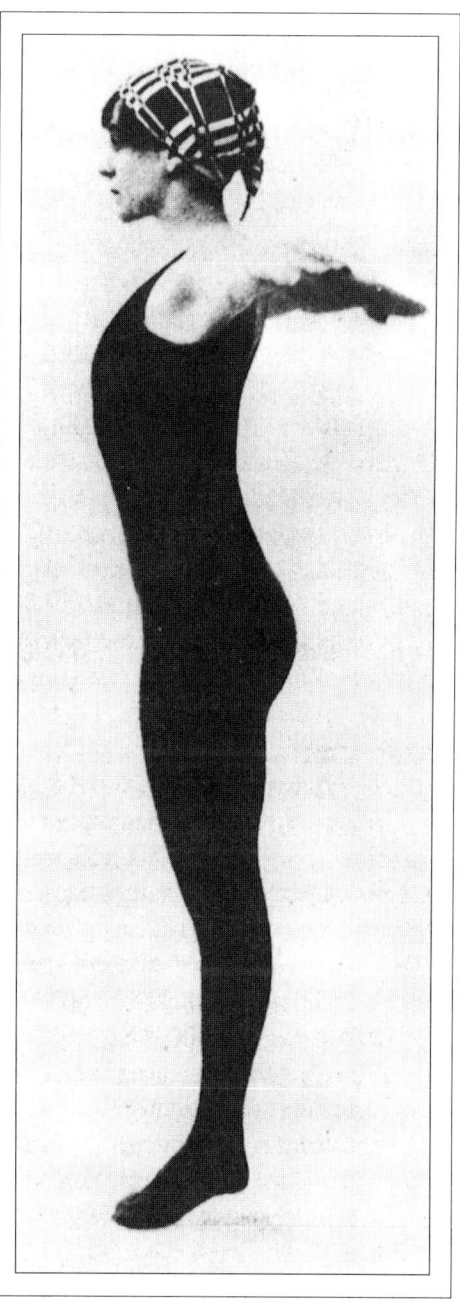

Rather than allowing a medical condition to keep her out of sport, Annette Kellermann was among the women who took up sport in order to improve their health.

those girls who play some form of sport are the ones who are brightest at the end of a long day, and who are the most alert and quick-thinking generally in their daily work.

During the Second World War women proved once and for all that they were capable of taking on so-called men's jobs, and it was no coincidence that after the war medical testing to screen out women athletes ended. But men's visualisation of what they thought was women's physical inferiority never really ceased. Women were welcomed into the surf lifesaving movement during the war and successfully carried out line and reel rescues. When the men returned from the war it was a different story. In 1953 the Surf Life Saving Association suddenly felt 'that women are not strong enough physically to carry a heavy belt and line or to swim competitively in surf races'. An attempt was made to exclude women from the sport of parachuting as it was thought few of them could exert the 22 pound pull required to open the parachute. (The award covering women in the Australian Women's Land Army during the war specified the maximum weight they were allowed to carry as 35 pounds, an upper limit that was rarely adhered to.) Even as late as 1988 the lifesaving movement in Queensland banned women from competing in beach flag events (where contestors sprint and dive on the

The attitudes of the medical world have often been employed to prevent women from competing in sports like surf lifesaving. Coffs Harbour, NSW, 1931.
STATE LIBRARY OF NEW SOUTH WALES

sand) on advice from their medical committee who stated 'Females contesting flags risk damage to breast tissue and the development of painful lumps which could be a source of worry'. That boys obviously stood as much chance of being hurt diving in the sand conveniently escaped their notice. In fact, the danger of damage in sport to male genitalia (which Adrianne Blue described succinctly as 'a sitting duck') greatly exceeds the danger to the female body. Women in all sports need less protective gear than males and individual sports such as cricket, boxing, running and cycling could be easily classified (or visualised) as simply too dangerous for males to compete in. The fact that men have rarely been prohibited from competing in sports because of medical danger places in a social perspective attempts to exclude women on medical grounds.

Another medical examination reserved especially for women was the so-called sex test introduced for all women Olympic candidates in 1968. Sprinter Raelene Boyle described her experience at the hands of the medical interventionists when she was tested in 1968 at the University of Melbourne's *veterinary* clinic:

A squadron of doctors prodded, poked, quizzed and studied me for those eight-and-a-half hours. It was an ordeal that I was totally unprepared for . . . I was required to reveal written and oral information about myself that I had not even disclosed to my mother . . . The humiliation was dreadful, and reached a depressing point when the female members of the team were ordered to subject themselves to a sex test to prove their femininity. There were three parts to this trauma. The first involved pricking a finger with a needle to obtain a blood sample. Then followed scraping of the inside of the mouth for a saliva specimen. It was the third step which really stirred up my indignation. Each competitor's pubic region was visually examined by a male doctor to ensure that it was, in fact, a woman's hair formation. It was frightfully disconcerting, at 16, to walk into a room with a much older guy and be told: 'Pull your pants down.'

Medical men have not ceased their interest in women's sporting bodies — they continue to poke, prod, test, measure and evaluate. The performance of the female athlete remains as interesting a topic to them today as it ever was. To challenge women's athletic capability or even to compare it with males serves to reinforce all men's superiority over all women when this is not in fact the case. Some women and men are fit, strong, athletic and healthy and some women and men are unfit, sedentary and unsuited to exercise. Fitness or athletic ability has never been the exclusive preserve of one sex.

SOCIAL HURDLES

Never far from the undercurrent of pseudo-medical debate were a range of social issues for sportswomen in Australia which have also hindered their participation. While sport has generally been tolerated in the lives of Australian women, this acceptance has in fact been restricted to an ideal. The ideal sportswoman is assumed to be young, slim, single, attractive, successful and with no responsibilities, hence the title 'golden girl'. Sport is often seen as a phase that young women go through before they settle down to their more serious roles in life. In open defiance of this are women who continue to play sport once they no longer fit the ideal. To compound this situation the rules of sport are not designed to cater to women of all ages, conditions and shapes, as they are for men. This makes sport seem somehow less appropriate for a number of women. Their bodies challenge predetermined notions of what is acceptable as a sportswoman.

BLOODY GOOD SPORTS

The introduction of the tampon to Australia in the 1950s was probably one of the most significant events in sportswomen's lives. Menstruation had the potential to formally and informally prevent all women exercising to their full ability every day of the month for about 40 years of their lives. Sex education has never been a strong point in Australian society. Myth, uncertainty and error have permeated the knowledge women have of their own bodies. When young women began to join organised sports clubs it was the first time many of them had access to any kind of reliable information regarding menstruation. Similarly in schools it was traditionally the role of the sportsmistress to pass on information regarding personal health. Warnings have always been paramount. In her 1918 book *Physical Beauty How to Keep It*, Annette Kellermann reminded women, 'I do not wish you to get the impression that the strenuous exercises that I have recommended are to be indulged in at the time of your menstrual periods.'

The role of the manager was an essential one when sportswomen first began travelling interstate or overseas to compete. The team manager was most often an older woman who had had experience in dealing with young women in such organisations as the Young Women's Christian Association. During an overseas tour by a women's sporting team before 1939 it was not uncommon for the manager to note the dates of each woman's period and make selections as to who would play in scheduled games accordingly, irrespective of whether individual women felt inconvenienced by menstruation.

Some women's most reliable information about menstruation came from advertisements. In the late 1950s the Tampax and Meds brand tampons came on the market in Australia. Tampax advertisements told women for the first time that they could now, 'Swim any time of the month. Don't let "problem days" hold you back from basking on the beach, from looking and feeling your best in a bathing suit, from *even going in swimming!*' In response, the Meds brand adjusted their advertisements to also include the possiblity of swimming.

Little family-based knowledge regarding menstruation was totally infallible, even as late as the 1950s. Dawn Fraser, born in 1937, related that when she first started bleeding her mother told her she should never wet her hair. Her father contradicted this and told her she should never wet her feet. Confusing advice for a swimmer. The trained medicos were even less reliable. In March 1958 the mass circulation *Australian Women's Weekly* presented a liftout entitled *Handbook to Health*, sponsored by the British Medical Association. It contained the following advice for young women:

The most popular myth about periods is that a girl should not bath or swim during them. There is nothing to stop her. It is perfectly normal and safe in every way to have a shower or a sit-down bath and to swim in the later stages, but if she swims it's good advice not to swim in any enclosed pools or doubtful water, to keep out of heavy surf, and not to dive deeply. The simple reason for this is that surf or pressure in deep water could force bacteria internally and perhaps cause infection. Doubtful water could also be a source of infection.

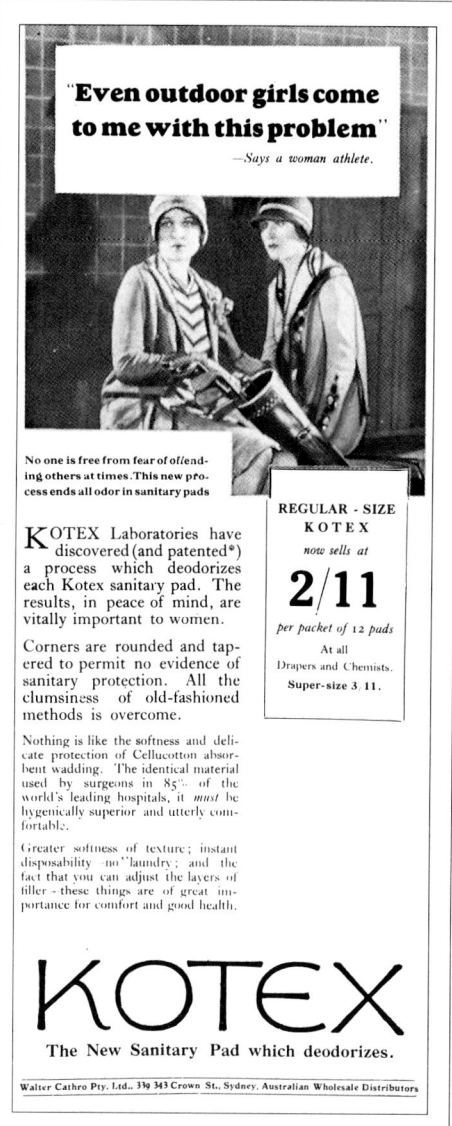

Women have had to endure decades of myth and uncertainty regarding menstruation and sport. Advertisement from *The Home*, December 1929.

With medical advice like that emanating from the BMA who needed myths? In her autobiography published in 1965 Dawn Fraser reassured her female readers, 'it's possible to swim hard at any time. If a girl aims for maybe a year at a certain event, and then finds that it's occurred at what is a difficult time for her, I believe she should still be able to do her best.'

But uncertainty, misunderstanding and embarrassment still revolve around menstruation. Many women perform at their peak even while bleeding and certainly many gold medals have been won by Olympians who are menstruating. But the rules of sport do not cater for the woman competitor — Evonne Goolagong-Cawley commented that a tennis player risks forfeiting a match if she leaves the court suddenly when struck by what she called a 'periodic malady' and must rely on the understanding of the umpire to let her continue playing. Coyness remains in our society regarding menstruation. Individual sportswomen are not used by advertisers to endorse either tampons or pads. Kay Cottee, who sailed solo non stop around the world in 1988 for 189 days and 32 minutes, modestly omitted any reference to tampons or pads in her book's exhaustive 11 page list of everything she packed for her journey.

RETIREMENT RINGS

Only recently has debate begun centring around sport and pregnancy for women. Prior to this it simply wasn't an issue or concern. Social conventions dictated that a woman should resign from competitive sport on marriage, so the question of pregnancy and sport never arose. The decision to retire bore no relation to whether a woman was at her peak, or had yet to reach her full potential. Just as she was expected to resign from her job on marriage (if she was a teacher or in the public service she was sacked) so too did she resign from competitive sport. Those that didn't faced hostile reactions and felt the need to justify their decision.

Marjorie Jackson had proved herself the undisputed fastest woman in the world at the 1952 Olympics. She delayed her retirement after her marriage to enable her to compete at the 1954 Vancouver Empire Games where she won triple gold. Twenty-two-year-old Jackson reiterated her retirement announcement on her arrival home. At the airport her husband was asked 'How is Marjorie with a broom?' To which he replied, 'As a matter of fact, she's a better wife than she is a runner.' In a retrospective on Jackson's life in 1973 the *Australian* headlined their story 'The solid gold suburban mum'. Reassurance that a champion athlete is still a normal woman is a continuing need in our society.

Just as sportswomen in Australia 100 years before had been accorded names like equestrienne and cricketress, women in post-1945 Australia were most often

"Better wife than she is a runner"

Marj. Jackson in gold-medal class as homemaker

By HELEN FRIZELL, staff reporter

Just before Marjorie Jackson, the fastest woman runner in the world, arrived back in Australia from the Empire Games in Vancouver, someone asked her husband, Peter Nelson, "How is Marjorie with a broom?"

Peter replied, without hesitation, though a little shyly: "As a matter of fact, she's a better wife than she is a runner."

AND now Marjorie is to become a full-time wife and no longer a runner.

The finishing line for her career as Australia's foremost athlete was at Kingsford Smith Airport, Sydney — and she crossed it on her return from the Games, to repeat in front of the cheering crowds and whirring newsreel cameras that her days as a runner are over for good.

Instead of training five days a week as a runner, Marjorie will concentrate upon training as a housewife and as a business woman — for she is in partnership with her husband in his newly opened sports shop at Unley, South Australia.

"And this is the last time for us, too," said her father, Mr. W. Jackson, who with his wife and daughters Norma and Beryl waited quietly in the lounge of the air terminal for Marjorie's plane to touch down.

In the years since 1948, when Marjorie flashed to fame as a sprinter and went on to win nine Gold Medals at Helsinki Olympic Games and at the Empire Games, Canada, the Jackson family from Lithgow has become accustomed to the triumphal return of its third daughter.

This time they did not join the crowds on the tarmac, but waited in a room with photographers and pressmen, hearing from outside the cries of "Good on you, Marj!" which heralded her approach and the coming of the rest of the team.

Into the room came Marjorie, wearing a lot of pink orchids from Honolulu round her neck, a soft pull-on white hat, the green Australian blazer, a grey dress, and

leather court shoes which matched her benedictine-tan shoulder-bag.

Hardly had she had time to hug and kiss her family before she was whisked away, to be confronted by microphones and cameras. While she talked, I watched her, gaining

THE HUSBAND, Peter Nelson. At home in Adelaide Peter has been preparing the sports store he and Marjorie have opened.

the impression that most of the photographs I had ever seen of Marjorie Jackson had done her less than justice.

She is tall, with a good figure, and slender nyloned legs which have carried her to victory in sprints all over the world. Her hair, medium brown, curled at the back of

her hat, and as she talked over the microphone she winked happily at her family and friends who stood by.

About her, though, one can sense a feeling of reserve, which seems a characteristic of her family. The reserve goes with a pleasant, natural dignity and lack of emotional fireworks.

Even now, after years of being a world celebrity, Marjorie seemed slightly nervous, betraying this by the movements of her hands, which alternately tugged at the back hem of her blazer or went up to settle the orchid lei in position. As she did this, I saw that she wore coral-pink nail polish, and caught the glint of the gold wedding ring upon her finger.

When the radio interviews were over, I managed to speak for a few moments to 23-year-old Mrs. Peter Nelson—who now firmly signs all autograph books as "Marjorie Nelson" and not as "Marjorie Jackson."

"I'm having a day with my family in Lithgow," she said, "and then I am flying down to Peter in Adelaide. The day I get there he is opening up the shop. We're going to sell sports goods, radios, and electrical supplies. I think that my job will be to keep the books and accounts, so I'm glad that I had accountancy training when I worked in Lithgow."

Peter Nelson, the former Olympic cyclist, whom Marjorie met at the Olympic Games, has also retired from cycling to set up shop.

The Jacksons whisked their daughter from the airport into a waiting car. Before they left, Mrs. Jackson told me that they'd decided to drive straight through to Lithgow—about a four-hour journey over the Blue Mountains—without stopping for meals.

"We'll all have something along the way," she said. "I've filled a couple of vacuum flasks with hot drinks, and we cut a pile of ham sandwiches, so Marj. won't be hungry. And, in case it gets cold, we've brought rugs to put over us.

"Her room at home is just the same as it was before she married. The bed's made up, and she'll have breakfast in bed tomorrow morning. Then, just the day at home, seeing her old friends, and she'll be off to join Peter."

Now all of Marjorie's cups and prize medals have been packed, and will soon follow her to South Australia.

For, from now on, Marjorie Jackson, M.B.E., holder of world sprinting records, is quitting the sporting fields to become Mrs. Peter Nelson, housewife.

Our Irish parades

Our Irish fashion parades, which will be presented in Sydney in association with Mark Foy's, will be launched with a gala opening night at Prince's restaurant on Monday, October 4.

Tickets, at four guineas each, are available at the box office on the main floor of the Piazza building, Mark Foy's store, Liverpool Street.

There will be morning and afternoon parades in the Empress Ballroom at Mark Foy's from Tuesday, October 5, to Friday, October 8, commencing at 11 a.m. and 2.30 p.m.

Special business girls' sessions will be held in the Empress Ballroom at 6.30 p.m. on Friday, October 8, and at 10 a.m. on Saturday, October 9.

Tickets for all these parades are 10/- each and are also obtainable from the box office at Mark Foy's.

THE WIFE, Marjorie Jackson. Wearing the official Australian blazer and uniform for the last time, Australia's star runner arrives at Kingsford Smith Airport, Sydney, on her return from the Empire Games in Vancouver. At the airport Marjorie reiterated her determination to retire into domesticity.

Athletes like Marjorie Jackson had to compete against more than just the other runners in the race. *Australian Women's Weekly*, 25 August 1954.

NATIONAL LIBRARY OF AUSTRALIA

described as housewives. The term 'housewife' in this era was actually interchangeable with 'married'. Feature articles on sportswomen always made reference to their domestic status. (This became easier as women's sport was removed from the sporting pages and placed in the women's section.) When Fanny Blankers-Koen, Dutch champion and holder of four gold medals in athletics from the 1948 Olympics, visited Australia in 1949 she was described by the press as the 'Flying Dutch Housewife'. Michele Mason-Brown winner of a silver medal at the 1964 Olympics was headlined 'Sydney Housewife Second in High Jump at Games' despite the fact that she worked as a clerk as well as training for the Olympics.

Women were asked to emphasise their normality in the eyes of society — even if you didn't fit the ideal, at least if you said you did it was acceptable. Thelma Peake, a champion Queensland athlete before 1939, was asked by a women's magazine 'What comes first — your athletic career or your home?' To which she replied 'My home decidedly. Athletics is only a bad second if it comes to a question of choice between the two.' Clearly her home didn't come first if she was pursuing a career in athletics. She was simply juggling the different aspects to her life.

A generation earlier women were subjected to medical examination to continue competing, now women were subjected to social examination. The Australian public has known the marital status, domestic status, cooking, sewing and cleaning ability, number of children planned of every woman who has competed at the elite level of international sports. These are the details we are told even today. Test yourself: think of five women and five male Australian champions anytime after 1945 and see for which group you know more personal details, and information that is unrelated and irrelevant to their sport. Sportsmen have generally been allowed to keep their private lives to themselves and have that right respected.

Most women succumbed to the retirement rings of marriage, often not realising that there were other choices. Those that didn't were subjected to a public scrutiny, and their personal lives were held under the microscope of public opinion. Many champions and potential champions were lost to Australia as women retired or subsumed their sporting careers to those of their husbands.

REAL WOMEN?

For the woman who didn't marry (and even for some who did) there was always the hurdle of the sexuality issue to contend with. Many sportswomen have borne the brunt of innuendo and most retreat in silence. As sportswomen train harder their bodies openly contradict and challenge society's perceptions of femininity, regardless of their sexuality. Some individuals compensate for this by adopting more obvious and outward signs of traditional femininity like frills, makeup and jewellery.

Society has often breathed a loud sigh of relief upon the marriage of prominent sportswomen. Women who compete in body building and weightlifting have been quickest to promote their marriage plans. Some women have been unfairly taunted all their lives. Dawn Fraser (who refused to retire) remembered,

> *The rumours built up steadily over the next couple of years . . . and they did me irreparable damage. When I was accused of misconduct — unspecified, of course — in Rome, they flared again. And they were renewed when my engagement was broken after eighteen months. They were hurtful rumours, and the terrible thing was that I had no way of fighting against them. How can you combat a whisper? You can't walk around announcing to people, 'Look, I'm not masculine. I've got muscles, sure. But I'm not masculine.'*

Questioning their sexuality is just another way to keep women out of sport.

Although some Australian sportswomen have been accused of taking drugs (and some women have been convicted and banned), the main community opposition to anabolic steroids for women has not been that they help them to cheat, but that women become more masculine in appearance.

TWO VERSUS ONE

The medical debate on whether sport was too strenuous for women was centred around how it would affect women's later reproductive life. After the 1952 Olympics a group of Finnish doctors thoroughly examined their women athletes to determine whether strenuous sport had been harmful. The doctors announced the training and competition had caused no harm. Contrary to their suspicions, they found that the hard training had in fact strengthened the women's abdominal muscles which the doctors thought would contribute to well-being during pregnancy and childbirth. In 1943 the New South Wales Department of Public Health recommended in their booklet *Healthy Motherhood* that,

> *Regular exercise should be practised daily, and, in addition, outdoor exercise taken regularly. Any exercise to which you are accustomed may be continued so long as it continues to be a pleasure and does not leave a feeling of fatigue or tiredness.*

They had prefaced this statement with the following warning in italics, 'N.B. — Housework by itself is not sufficient.' The tone of the exercises emphasised moderation as the keynote.

So exercise was conducive to pregnancy; it could prepare and tone women who were to become mothers. But what about competitive sport during pregnancy?

Both Margaret Court and Evonne Goolagong-Cawley played championship tennis while pregnant. Neither saw any reason to cease until inconvenienced. Goolagong-Cawley remembered, 'Through my first pregnancy I didn't feel pregnant. I was running, playing tennis and swimming a lot — I didn't feel awkward.' The 1936 Olympic swimmer Evelyn De Lacy swam regularly to within a fortnight of her daughter's birth. Modern champions like Lisa Curry also continue training through their pregnancy unwilling to lose hard won fitness. Many overseas women have won sprint races when newly pregnant and completed marathons while six months pregnant. Some women have even experimented with the benefits to be derived from a pregnancy/abortion cycle in the quest for the elusive competitive edge.

Although research confirms that women need not cease exercising during pregnancy, the majority of women still spontaneously decrease their exercise level. *The Sydney Morning Herald* in 1990 featured an article (in their sport pages) in which Lisa Curry's coach stated he believed that Curry had achieved everything she had set out to and should retire. But the article was headlined 'Coach advises pregnant Curry to retire from top grade swimming'. Curry's pregnancy was irrelevant to the story, but the headline linked the two for readers.

Society's message for women to automatically stop exercising while pregnant fell on deaf ears in Newcastle, New South Wales, in 1975. Senone Stephenson won the Newcastle A-grade squash grand final while fully eight months pregnant. Interviewed after the game she said 'I am pretty fit and it seemed natural for me to keep playing'. The match was described as a 'tiring one-hour-10-minute-marathon' for both players. Stephenson came back after being down two sets to win with a scoreline of 7-9, 6-9, 9-3, 9-6, 9-5, but complained lightheartedly that her opponent had over-utilised the drop shot! 'I can get around the court pretty fast', she said, 'but that drop shot really takes it out of me'.

After giving birth, women receive the same negative messages as pregnant women. Evonne Goolagong-Cawley who had a caesarean section recalled,

I wasn't supposed to exercise for six weeks after, but I started running on the beach at about four weeks — very slowly. I felt like an old woman, sort of bent over, but I wanted to sweat again. I couldn't wait to get out and do something. Going that long without exercise was driving me crazy.

MOTHERHOOD IN MOTION

The first to challenge the conventional notion of motherhood and sport was champion sprint hurdler Shirley Strickland. Strickland, who was born in 1925, won three Olympic medals at the 1948 Games, won the 1952 Olympic gold medal for 80 metres hurdles, married in 1953 but did not retire. She kept competing amid taunts to step aside and let 'some one younger have a go'. But worse was to come for public opinion. She temporarily retired to have her first child and then came back to regular competition in 1955. At the 1956 Olympics, at 31 years of age, she successfully defended her 80 metres hurdles title watched by her three-year-old child. Tennis players Margaret Court and Evonne Goolagong-Cawley both won major championships after having children.

They knew what other Australian women were to find out — that not only could women with children still compete at the top level, but that motherhood could actually enhance performance. In short, that motherhood and sport did mix. Since that time, and with the broadening of community attitudes to women, a whole generation of women competitors can pursue a sporting career and have children. Women from a broad range of sports are now not so much making 'comebacks' as continuing their careers. In 1990 former world champion distance Swimmer Tracey Wickham began training for marathon swimming after the birth of her daughter. Lisa Curry won a further four gold and one silver medal at the 1990 Commonwealth Games watched by her daughter. Curry claimed that after childbirth she had been able to push herself through new training thresholds as the pain just did not compare. Curry gave birth to another daughter in late 1990 and resolved to make a further bid for the 1992 Olympics. Marathon champion Lisa Martin gave birth to her daughter in 1990, a mere blink in her

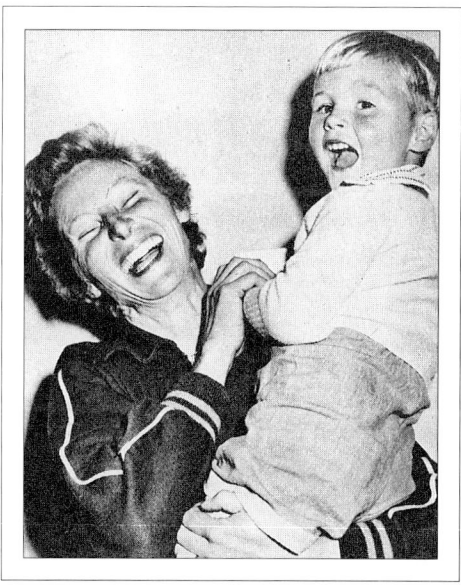

While Shirley Strickland's three-year-old child Pip barracked 'Come on, Mum' from the stands during the 80 metres hurdles final at the 1956 Melbourne Olympics, others in the crowd taunted her to retire and let someone younger have a go. Strickland challenged society's views on women athletes by returning to competition and winning, not only after marriage, but after motherhood, *Australian Women's Weekly*, 12 December 1956.
NATIONAL LIBRARY OF AUSTRALIA

preparation for the 1992 Olympic marathon. Rower Adair Ferguson won the single sculls at the national regatta six months after giving birth and equestrian Vicki

Roycroft was placed fourth in the world one year after the birth of her child. As women's sport grows, and more veteran and senior age competitions are inaugurated, more women can extend their sporting careers. But the trend to continue in sport has not been restricted to top competitors. The example of successful women filters through to encourage all women, no matter what sporting ability, to play on.

The major issue concerning sportswomen with children is the lack of childcare available. Sportswomen like Evonne Goolagong-Cawley and Lisa Curry are financially secure and able to travel with a nanny. Other women must become supermums. Perhaps Goolagong-Cawley learnt an early lesson from her junior rival in the country, Janine Murdock, whom she later remembered,

Janine Murdock, one of my big rivals — I lost only three singles matches between the ages of thirteen and seventeen, and two of them were to Janine — would be watching her kid sisters and brothers out of the corner of an eye while she played. I don't understand how she concentrated. She'd be yelling at them during a match — don't do this, or don't do that. She's probably got a family of her own now.

FROM GOLDEN GIRL TO GOLDEN GRANNY

Another hurdle awaits women in their sporting lives even after their children have grown up — the age hurdle. No longer able to be described as housewives, all older women are dubbed grandmothers. For decades the Australian media has insisted on categorising older women's sporting achievements according to totally irrelevant personal details. Here are a few examples from over the years, 'The Walking Grandmother', 'Grandmother on the Tennis Court', 'Australia's Amazing Grandmother', 'Grandmother in Crew', 'Grandma Wields a Nifty Bat', 'Golf Granny', 'Grannies on the Court at Kooyong', 'Cricket Granny Not Out'. All these headlines obscure the expert performances by many older women athletes who prove that age is no barrier to sporting success. The Walking Grandmother was actually a 52-year-old New Zealand woman who competed in Sydney in distance walks. Forty-five-year-old Nellie Walsh stroked the Victorian crew to victory in the 1940 four-oar championship of Australia. Eighty-one-year-old Kaye Kearney holed in one at the North Adelaide golf course in 1982. But in addition to these extraordinary achievements many older women regularly compete in sport and deserve recognition as sportswomen not grandmothers.

One of the most offensive headlines was from a July 1990 edition of the *Canberra Times* which described a new career as a sports lobbiest for Marjorie Jackson (no

Physical activity and motherhood, an easier mix in the 1980s. But for the athlete the unavailability of childcare still remains a major concern. Perisher, NSW, 1983.
OVERSEAS INFORMATION BRANCH

Age is no barrier to sporting success. Croquet players, Canberra, 1981
OVERSEAS INFORMATION BRANCH

When sport is promoted as weight reducing women are caught in a double bind. Should they exercise to lose weight or lose weight to exercise? Advertisement from *The Home*, November 1931.

longer the golden girl) as 'Granny Meeting Challenge'. The day Don Bradman is headlined 'Australia's Amazing Grandpa', I'll eat my cricket cap.

THE BODY BEAUTIFUL

One hurdle remains constant for all sportswomen throughout their lives no matter what their status or age. When 23 cars left Sydney in 1905 bound for Melbourne in a reliability trial there was one woman among the drivers. Five days and a lot of dust and dirt later only one driver who motored across the finish line was 'quite recognisable' — Mrs Thompson in her single-cylinder Wolseley. Not only had she completed the arduous trial she had overcome an obstacle no male driver had met, she had kept up appearances. It has always been regarded as unacceptable for women to compromise their public face in the name of sporting pursuits.

There are two contradictory attitudes in the relationship between a woman's body and physical activity. The first dictates that sport is unfeminine and not becoming to women's beauty. The second that exercise is essential for an attractive figure and good looks. Women must balance the two attitudes in their sporting lives. The middle ground of moderation compromises success at all levels.

Moderation has always been recommended to sportswomen. Since women first started exercising they have been subjected to warnings concerning the dangers to their beauty of participating in too much sport. In 1913 Jacqueline Gore writing for *Everylady's Journal* published *Good Looks and Long Life A Guide to Beauty and Health in Australasia* and counselled against 'violent or long-protracted exercises for women'. In 1924 the *Australian Women's Mirror* warned:

> The woman who goes in for sports generally does it so strenuously or it might be more correct to say stridently, that she becomes too muscular and ungainly to ever attain the grace, ease and smoothness requisite for the ideal of feminine loveliness. Yet moderate sports are the ideal mode for keeping fit and young, provided one eats judiciously and cares for the skin and hair at the same time.

In 1947 Hazel Rawson Cades, associate editor of the *Woman's Home Companion* published an Australian edition of *Good Looks For Girls*. Her chapter on exercise recommended swimming, skating, dancing, tennis, horseback riding and walking, but counselled against strenuousness:

> Any form of exercise, however, no matter how congenial, must not be overdone. It is not necessary to be excessive or violent in order to be healthy. In fact, it is often harmful. Competition as it enters into games is an amusing sauce to the dish. But competitive games should not be played too hard, and from the beauty as well as the

LISA CURRY

A feminist dichotomy — does the body image of the Boyd sculpture at the Australian Institute of Sport (left) insult the elite swimmer or encourage the average swimmer? Why doesn't the sculpture portray the body image of a Lisa Curry (above)?
NATIONAL SPORT INFORMATION CENTRE

health angle it seems to me that competitions of endurance or speed are not satisfactory.

Sportswomen also meet artificial beauty hurdles. As sports clothes became briefer and sport more vigorous, women faced new 'problems' with their bodies. A whole new range of toiletries specifically for the sportswoman was marketed. In the 1920s readers of women's magazines were encouraged to buy Veet Hair-Removing Cream which promised 'freedom of action without embarrassment' for those wearing sleeveless bathing suits and tennis clothes. Ten years later they had to remove hair not only from under their arms but from their legs as well. Veet promised to do this in three minutes, 'less time than it takes to slip into your bathing suit'. Golfers were induced to buy Ven-Yusa Oxygen Face Cream to enable them to 'face all weathers without fear of complexion worries' and tennis players could keep their schoolgirl complexions with Palmolive soap. Specific beauty hints appeared in women's magazines aimed at the sportsgirl who was thought to be particularly susceptible to blisters and mosquito bites. The greatest problem for the Australian sportswoman though, was never the climate, the flies or the mosquitoes, but underarm perspiration. In the 1920s Odorono could be dabbed under the arms with cotton wool to check the development of perspiration:

The tennis season — warm weather, strenuous exercise, light clothing — special care is needed to keep underarms dainty — to prevent unsightly perspiration stains, disagreeable odour!

Sportsmen, in contrast, have never had the additional worry of appearance. In fact the reverse is the case — the more dishevelled, dirtied and muddied their appearance the more gallant has been the contest. The women's supplement of the *Sydney Morning Herald* in 1938 queried male criticism of sportswomen's appearance:

how about the men who indulge in football and boxing who proudly reveal broken teeth, battered eyes, cauliflower ears, and twisted limbs 'gloriously' earned on the football field or in the prize ring? And is a sturdy male athlete appearing on the beach in brief trunks, more or less hirsute, red of nose, knotty of muscle, unbelievably bony of structure, and peeling haphazardly like a papery cover of a large onion, a thing of beauty?

Keeping up appearances nags at sportswomen, amateur or professional. Evonne Goolagong recalled her thoughts during her match with Margaret Court to decide the 1970 Wimbledon final:

My hair was matted with sweat, and I kept tugging at it, suspecting it looked awful. But it was no time for the beauty parlour. I needed two more games. Maybe I was worrying about how I looked for an instant because I skidded to 15-40, hardly realising the game had begun.

As women began to take up more intellectual space and started to assert themselves more in the world, there began to be a compensatory corresponding decrease in the physical space they took up. The 1930s witnessed the beginnings of the weight loss and diet fads or 'reducing' as it was then called. Women were actually being asked to reduce the amount of space they physically occupied.

Although the most effective and efficient way to lose weight is through physical activity, negative messages about exercise were propagated through advertisements and advice columns to women. The best form of exercise was passive exercise. Advertisements promised ways that exercise could be avoided. Dr Paul Bouchaud's Flesh Reducing Soap in 1926 was an 'easy, simple and harmless way of loosening and removing all congested fat which is quickly dissolved and washed away'. Youth-O-Form Tonic Reducing Capsules required no 'tedious exercise'. In an article 'Slimming is not dangerous', John Newman told readers of a Sydney newspaper in 1936 that film stars pursued a strict exercise regime, 'They all play tennis, not so much because they want to, but because it is one of the most pleasant ways of taking exercise.' He recommended diet and moderate exercise for slimming. Exercise, he told women,

keeps your figure trim. It is good for your muscles and for your circulation. It keeps you fit, and fitness is 90 per cent of the slimming battle. But moderation is essential. Too much exercise is as bad as too little. Never strain yourself is the motto to bear in mind.

Mr Newman didn't explain exactly why too much exercise was dangerous in slimming. In the 1930s Arnott's developed a new range of biscuits for women, shredded wheatmeal, with the slogan 'keep you fit, keep you slim'. In case women thought biscuits more likely to put on than take off weight, Arnott's had medical testimony that explained that the biscuits stimulated the reduction of fat. For those who consumed too many biscuits, Berlei had a foundation garment in the 1940s that 'hinders the accumulation of excess fat by exercising a gentle massage action'. If this failed a woman could lose weight by doing her housework in the American 'Hollywood Silhouette' reducing suit made of airtight plastic, 'the perfect answer to the average woman's worries about her weight'. Thus by the 1950s the plethora of ways women could reduce their weight relied less and less on physical activity and more on passive exercise. In the process exercise acquired tedious and negative overtones for women.

The motivation for women taking up sport often had something to do with weight loss. But weight loss presented a double bind to the sportswoman — you needed to exercise to lose weight and you needed to lose weight to exercise, which did you do first? When new sports were introduced to Australian women their highest recommendation was often that they were weight reducing. This claim was used by sport promoters as well as companies with a financial stake in women's sport. Jantzen, interested in selling their costumes, promoted the sport of swimming for the purposes of keeping fit and trim. 'Your weight is your size' they told women. Malvern Star emphasised the connection between cycling, health and beauty for women of all ages:

> *Sparkling eyes, clear skin, shapely limbs, typify the charm and beauty of the 'It' girl in an outdoor setting. Nor does the young matron lose her 'It' attributes after marriage. Cycling lessens the burden of messages, keeps overweight down.*

Sports as diverse as diving and billiards relied on slimming as their most attractive aspect. Diving was an effortless way to beauty and removal of 'superfluous avoirdupois':

> *If you are not one who is keen about strenuous games you can be lazy and still get enough exercise with diving to get trim and fit. Doing your exercise while enjoying an hour or two at the pool is a pleasant way to beauty.*

Mrs McConachy, a New Zealand billiards champion, on a visit to Australia in 1934 told readers of a women's magazine:

> *As a medium for slimming, billiards is perhaps the only indoor game that can be recommended as a weight reducer. The constant bending and the distance traversed round the table by the average billiard player is sufficient to substantiate these statements.*

Badminton was also described as 'wonderful for the figure'. New sports, especially fad sports like roller skating, jogging and aerobics, are usually based more on diet and beauty factors than enjoyment and skill.

If sportswomen didn't put on their make-up, the press did it for them. Women doing so-called men's jobs were more often than not portrayed in newsreels applying make-up. So too were sportswomen. The more traditionally male the sport, the more likely the press was to ask women to be photographed using their compact! But such an approach did not cease with the decline of the newsreel. In 1932 the *Adelaide Advertiser* reported a possible ban on women using cosmetics in cricket 'to take the shine off the ball as they do their noses'. In early 1970 the New South Wales women's cricket team was asked to line up and look in a make-up mirror for a press photographer. Decades of sportswomen, especially team players, were trivialised in this way. The presence of make-up was an obvious way that the press could reassure the public that these women were still feminine as well as less threatening to the male ego. One newspaper used a photograph of two swordswomen applying lipstick as preparation for their bout during the 1950 Women's Open Foil Championship of Australia, despite the fact, (or indeed probably because of the fact), that fencers fight with a full mask covering their faces. The same style of trivialising photograph was just as likely to have been used well into the 1970s and 1980s by any newspaper.

The shape of the ideal sportswoman's body changed considerably from the days of Annette Kellermann. Kellermann's figure was much rounder and fuller than that considered appropriate in later years. In 1934 George Zephirin Dupain, founder of the Dupain Institute of Physical Education and Medical Gymnastics in Sydney, published his *Diet and Physical Fitness*. His series of studies in human nutrition, which illustrated the book, featured women described as vigorous and robust with well-modelled limbs, neck and torso. The women, dressed in bathing costumes, were without exception stocky and devoid of any muscle tone. After 1945 women were encouraged to return to the domestic sphere and their waists were once again unnaturally pulled in. The shape of the ideal woman (or those not pregnant with the baby boomers) was now dictated by Hollywood. Dresses were high waisted and the hourglass figure became the sign of the times. The perfect measurements were defined as a waist that was ten inches smaller than the bust or hips.

In 1957 the *Medical Journal of Australia* published the results of an anthropometrical survey of 5000 Australian women. Although emanating from the School of Public Health at the University of Sydney, the survey had been sponsored by a manufacturer of foundation garments. The survey revealed the average height of Australian women had increased to 5 feet $3^1/2$ inches and the average weight was 9 stone $4^1/2$ pounds. They were both taller and heavier than their English counterparts. Using women between 15 and 65 years of age (but half of the total between 15 and 24) the survey claimed the average build of the Australian woman was $34^1/2$ -$28^1/2$ -39 (bust-waist-hips). This they compared to British screen actress Diana Dors 35-25-35 and Hollywood's Jayne Mansfield 42-18-35. Sydney's *Sun Herald* compared the shape of Australia's Olympians with the average. Sprinter Marlene Mathews was 5 feet 7 inches tall, weighed 9 stone 13 pounds and measured 34-23-35. Both Betty Cuthbert and Winsome Cripps were 5 feet 6 inches tall. Swimmer Lorraine Crapp was also 5 feet 6 inches with Dawn

Fraser slightly taller at 5 feet 7 inches. Fraser commented in her book *Gold Medal Girl* on her use of weights in her 1955 training programme:

> *By the time I reached my swimming prime, my north-south statistics were thirty-nine inches, twenty-seven and a half inches, thirty-eight inches — and this included some muscle. But despite the constant accent on building up strength, I don't think it's necessary at any stage for a girl athlete to lose femininity.*

So when Australian sportswomen entered the competitive field they carried with them negative messages regarding exercise, body image, femininity and appearance. They should be victorious and win gold medals, but they must retain their femininity, look calm and relaxed and not overstrained, and they must not sweat profusely. In short, the public wants the results without knowing the hard work that goes in to victory.

In the 1990s professional and amateur sportswomen train harder than ever. Many Australian women have been caught up in the fitness boom. Sportswomen come in all shapes and all sizes. At the Australian Institute of Sport in Canberra a bronze sculpture of a woman swimmer stands outside the swimming hall. The image is old fashioned to say the least, and more reminiscent of Annette Kellermann than Lisa Curry. The body is stocky and without muscle tone. The shoulders are a great deal narrower than the hips. The body image is not one of a fit athletic swimmer, but Australia's elite athletes must walk past this sculpture every day on their way to training. Negative body image is yet another hurdle for sportswomen to overcome.

APPROPRIATE ARENAS

1945-1970

BY 1945 NEARLY 45 000 AUSTRALIANS HAD LOST THEIR LIVES IN THE WAR. IT WAS TIME TO RESTOCK. EVERY ARM OF THE MEDIA WAS EMPLOYED TO ENCOURAGE WOMEN TO RETURN TO THE HOME AND PRODUCE BABIES. For 25 years women were relegated to the roles of housewives and mothers. During this time a number of Australian sportswomen, products of the boom in sport before the war, defied the odds and rose to national prominence. They became household names. The women were all swimmers, athletes, tennis players and golfers and for these years they crowded the pages of newspapers at the expense of men's football and men's cricket. Ironically it was the golden age of women's sport.

The years up to 1939 had seen a consolidation and growth of women's team and club sports. Although no diminution occurred after the war in the actual number of women playing sport, a shift took place in the public acceptance of which sports were most appropriate for women to play. This was in spite of the fact that the range of sports available actually expanded rapidly in response to immigration programmes and the general prosperity in the community. Women's sport remained largely self-funded and amateur.

After 1945 the increase in the Australian population brought about by widespread immigration programmes had a significant effect on the nature of women's sporting choices. Indoor and gymnasium-based sports like table tennis, fencing, boxing, billiards, badminton, jiu jitsu and gymnastics rapidly grew in popularity. Although table tennis had been played before the war, the influx of migrants into the sport brought about a revolution in the seriousness with which the game was taken in Australia. With the improved competition players now devoted a greater amount of time to practise and a higher standard of play resulted. Table tennis was regarded as an ideal factory and social sport in the cities and the first national championships were held in 1946. Three of the players who dominated this era were migrants. Dora Berger, one of the hardest hitters in the game and holder of the world championship doubles title, arrived from Hungary in 1950. Berger also brought out her own custom made bats. Two players to represent their adopted states at national championships were Mrs A. Zaminko who migrated from Czechoslovakia in 1951 and Aldona Snarskye from Lithuania, a medical student at the University of Adelaide. In 1958 and 1959 Hungarian-born Suzy Javor was Australian table tennis champion.

Although women had honed their skills with the foil before the war in such organisations as the Swords Club and YWCA, it was not until 1949 that the first Australian Fencing Championships were held. An individual foil event was introduced at the 1950 Empire Games in New Zealand where the three Australian representatives, Catherine Pym, Elizabeth Stokes and Mavis Wilson rated third, fourth and eighth respectively. The influx of 'New Australians' made a marked difference in the standard and popularity of the sport. The best results came from Czech-born Johanna Winter who migrated with her family in 1951. She represented Australia at the 1960 Rome Olympics and won silver at the 1962 Empire Games in Perth in the individual foil.

Gymnasium-based self-defence sports like jiu-jitsu and boxing also extended their appeal among women. Until the 1908 Burns-Johnson fight in Sydney, women had not even been allowed to officially attend boxing matches. Undoubtedly some had, disguised in male clothing. Male-impersonation, traditionally used by women to allow themselves greater social freedom of movement and protection from harassment, was not as widely practised in Australia as elsewhere. Severe penalties were in place as a residue from convict society for impersonation and masquerade balls were still prohibited at the end of the nineteenth century. Effie Fellows, a male impersonator, had been caught by police at a boxing match in Perth in the early 1900s and harshly dealt with by the courts. After the Second World War boxing promoters encouraged women to attend bouts and from 1949 women's sparring matches were held at the Bondi gymnasium in Sydney.

HERE WE SEE VIOLET DOING THE DIFFICULT MASSE SHOT . . . .

Violet Lindrum inaugurated moves to form an Australian billiards association among the several hundred women who regularly played in Sydney. Violet taught herself to play at her own billiards parlour by potting 1000 balls every day. *Argus*, 19 November 1947.
STATE LIBRARY OF VICTORIA

Badminton grew in popularity stimulated by the arrival of British-born migrants. To help social interaction, groups like the Canberra YWCA offered migrants a one year free membership to their badminton club. Australian women played their first international matches against New Zealand in 1953 and competed at the 1966 Jamaica Empire Games when the sport was introduced there. Another indoor sport with essentially British origins was billiards. Violet Lindrum, mother of Horace, had opened her first billiard parlour in 1941 in Pitt Street, Sydney. Violet, who both played billiards and provided radio commentary for the sport, insisted on strict rules at her parlours. In 1947 she inaugurated moves among the several hundred Sydney women who regularly played to have an Australian women's billiards association established. These efforts were continued by her English daughter-in-law who arrived in Australia in 1953 after re-establishing the Women's Billiards Association in Britain.

Gymnastics also received a boost from Australia's migrant population. A gymnastics team competition had been introduced to the Olympic Games in 1928 with individual medals first awarded in 1952. The Netherlands, Germany, Czechoslovakia and the Soviet Union dominated the teams event. Gymnastics was not included in the Commonwealth Games until 1978. In the late 1950s Australian gymnasts were coached by Nelleck Jol who had represented the Netherlands at the Olympics. As well as supplying competitors keen to continue their home-country sports, migration also provided women with the coaching and training expertise needed in fledgling sports for generations.

Not all influences from Europe were positive. The international Cold War had an effect on some Australian sportswomen. One of the taunts thrown at Shirley Strickland during her career claimed that she was a communist. Strickland, who took physical culture classes in Perth for the Eureka Youth League, was forced to issue a denial in 1949:

I wish to say that I am not a Communist, and never have been one, and that since 1945, when I relinquished my position as physical culture instructress with the club, I have not been associated with it and know nothing of any change in its policy or activities.

More controversy erupted a year after the 1956 Olympic Games when Strickland, Betty Cuthbert, Lorraine Crapp and Dawn Fraser were invited to Russia to compete in the Moscow games.

The increased prosperity Australia enjoyed in the 1950s and 1960s introduced many middle class women to the pleasures of sport. Women in Australia traditionally had less time available than males to indulge in recreation. The introduction of the 40-hour week in 1948 did not have the same effect on working class women's leisure as it did for men. Women's leisure was restricted by their

The Redex round-Australia reliability trial crew sponsored by the *Australian Women's Weekly*, 7 July 1954.
NATIONAL LIBRARY OF AUSTRALIA

THE AUSTRALIAN WOMEN'S WEEKLY Presents

February 7, 1962

Teenagers

WEEKLY

THREE SPORT CHAMPIONS—page 4

Beatrice Hayley — GOLF   Heather Blundell — SQUASH   Margaret Smith — TENNIS

Supplement to The Australian Women's Weekly

Not to be sold separately.

Appropriate sporting role models for sober young women, (l-r) Beatrice Hayley (golf), Heather Blundell (squash) and Margaret Smith (tennis). *Teenagers' Weekly*, 7 February 1962.

NATIONAL LIBRARY OF AUSTRALIA

social obligations, the end of their formal work commitments never meant the end of their work for the day.

The sport of fishing was popular among women in America. Dolly Dyer, of radio and later television Pick-a-Box fame, held many world and Australian big-game fishing titles set off the coast of Queensland. The sport was encouraged in 1949 with the visit to Australia of Chisie Farrington, 'an ace woman angler from America'. Farrington, wearing a cap studded with badges of her big-game fishing exploits, set new world marlin records while fishing at Bermagui, New South Wales. The largest fish Farrington had to her credit was a 720 pound tuna caught off Nova Scotia. Farrington was taken marlin fishing outside Sydney Heads on a boat owned and skippered by Win Gordon, Sydney's only woman big-game fishing boat operator. Newcastle schoolgirl Joan Watkins set an age world marlin record when she landed a 213 pounder in 1948. The press reported her father's conversion. Claiming he had always wanted a son, he told Joan, 'if you can catch a marlin at 15 years of age, I guess it doesn't matter any more'. Big-game fishing was only the tip of women's fishing. Many joined amateur fishing associations and in 1952 women formed an 'auxiliary' branch of the New South Wales Amateur Fishing Association, ending a 57- year ban on their membership.

Women also made inroads into the exclusive world of sailing. In 1946 over 150 women were foundation members of the Victorian Ladies Yacht Club. Of these, 12 members owned their own yachts with a further 30 being part owners. The club was formed in response to a ruling of the Victorian Amateur Yacht Racing Association prohibiting women from taking part in racing events. Elsewhere in Australia women sailing enthusiasts were restricted to racing on 'ladies days'. In 1951 two New Zealand women, Kit Wilson and Erica Wilson, were the first women to crew a yacht in the annual Trans-Tasman Auckland to Sydney race. Their yacht *Leda* was the first to cross the finish line.

Women who sailed yachts in summer probably headed to the snow for their winter recreation. The first women's national ski championships had been held in 1931 and in 1948 the newly formed Australian Women's Ski Club presented perpetual trophies to the Australian National Ski Federation bearing the names of all winners. The Australian women's skiing team regularly visited New Zealand for competition. From 1953 New Zealand women had the advantage of the experience of German woman ski champion Dr Hildesue Gaertner who was appointed coach to the New Zealand Olympic team. Women who were proficient on snow skis had no trouble adapting to the sport of water skiing which was introduced in 1948. Water skiing, which originated in the United States, had created interest in Australia after being featured in American newsreels during the war. In 1953 the Australian national water ski champion Betty Leighton competed in the world championships in Canada.

Women were just as likely to be behind the wheel of the speedboat as they were to ski behind them. Some went in for faster thrills than the usual speed of 40 kilometres an hour needed to tow a skier. Grace Walker, a member of the Royal Motor Yacht Club, was a speed-boat racing driver. In 1952 she was placed second in Australia's longest race, the 110 kilometres Hawkesbury River race, an event she won in 1957 clipping seven seconds off the record time by covering the distance in 53 minutes. Other speed enthusiasts formed the Women's Motor Cycle Club in 1949. Dressed in jodphurs, pull-on boots, goggles and gauntlets the members, ranging in age from 16 to 60, rode in club excursions or competed against men in motor cycle carnivals. Women's speedway driving received a boost in 1952 with the visit of the Dublin-born driver Fay Taylour. Taylour raced against local male speedcar drivers at the Sydney and Brisbane tracks owned by her promoters Empire Speedway Ltd. The only woman to race against her was Edna Wells, a Wynard Station ticket collector and part time racing driver. Wells broke the Sydney Sports Ground one-lap women's record in her first practice drive. In 1964 a special 'ladies invitation speedway race' at Melbourne's Calder raceway was won by 23-year-old 'secretary' Joyce Cooper from a field of ten local and interstate women drivers.

Readers of the *Australian Women's Weekly* were able to follow the fortunes of the *Weekly* sponsored all-women crew who competed in the round Australia Redex reliability trial in 1954. The white-overall clad crew, comprising staff reporter and captain-navigator Helen Frizell and drivers and mechanics Nan Broughton and Enid Nunn, drove a Humber Super Snipe. Four other women had entered the 15 500 kilometre trial which featured 263 entrants and carried prizemoney of £10 000. The women were ineligible for £200 of that money, allocated for beards shaved into intricate designs during the race, 'we're tough, but we're not as tough as that', they joked.

Polocrosse had first been played by women in Australia at Ingleburn, New South Wales during the war. The standard of riding improved rapidly and the Australian women's polocrosse championships were held annually from 1952. Although women were barred from being jockeys until 1979 several worked as trotting drivers. The first was established English driver Mary Barden who migrated from England in 1950 and took out a licence in Brisbane. Women were unable to race in Victoria and New South Wales. Ira Edwards drove trotters in track work (a practice banned in Sydney) in Newcastle, New South Wales, from 1951.

The ban put in place in 1936 to restrict the new membership of rifle clubs to men was not rescinded after the war. Consequently only women who had joined before 1936 were eligible to compete and their numbers dwindled to a handful. By 1950, although women could shoot on the ranges unofficially, only five were eligible to

TOSS IN for polo crosse practice match at Ingleburn (N.S.W.) Horse and Pony Club. Enthusiastic members of club are Mesdames T. H. Kelly, jun. (captain), Ernest Hirst (president), her daughter, Margot, Mrs. Albert Wood, Misses Jeanette Klegg, Barbara Drew, Monica Krippner, Noreen Moore.

New sport improves standard of horsemanship

Girls ploughed, planted own polo crosse field

By JOAN POWE

An up-and-coming game among horse-women in Australia with plenty of opportunity for riding skill is polo crosse, English combination of polo and lacrosse first introduced here by the Ingleburn (N.S.W.) Horse and Pony Club.

Sportsmen and women at Ingleburn have been polo crosse enthusiasts since 1940, but since war ended the game has spread to other country centres.

ON CREAM MARE, Jane, Miss Jeanette Klegg. Chukker lasts eight minutes; game is fast.

WE visited the Ingleburn team recently on their 18-acre playing field to watch a practice match.

President of the club, Mrs. Ernest Hirst, of "Springmead," Denham Court, Ingleburn, got the idea for starting polo crosse here when she was in England with her husband in 1938.

In England it was played mainly under marquees, but the Ingleburn Club has adapted it to outdoors, and has drawn up a set of revised rules.

They also have their own club uniform of white helmet, red puggaree, blue sleeveless sweater, and yellow shirt, worn with riding breeches.

Interest in the game is so high that several players travel 30 to 50 miles from other country districts and city suburbs to Ingleburn twice a week for practice.

"It's been called 'a poor man's polo,' having all the thrills of polo without necessitating players keeping a whole stable of horses," Mrs. Hirst said.

"When we started playing polo crosse we just used ordinary ponies, but now we find we want better and better polo ponies as we become expert at the game."

When they first began playing polo crosse in 1940, girls in the club hand-planted the field with Kikuyu grass, doing the ploughing themselves.

"We had drought after drought, but we managed to keep the grounds in fair order and the fields clearly marked out," Mrs. Hirst said.

Polo crosse is played with sticks similar to the netted lacrosse stick, and the ball is of soft white sponge rubber.

Coach Mr. A. S. Pilty, of Campbelltown, who played in the Goulburn polo team which won the Dudley Cup about 12 years ago, considers there is just as much skill involved in polo crosse, without many of the dangers of polo.

Up to date the club has had no more serious accident than a

sprained ankle, and no injuries at all to ponies, which wear special polo boots.

"In the tackling there've been quite a few spills, however, and we've formed our own Caterpillar Club, similar to the Air Force's idea," Mrs. Hirst's daughter, Margot, said.

"Those who've had to ball out from their mounts during a game get a stripe, and nearly all the old hands have one or two stripes up for past spills."

Ingleburn Horse and Pony Club has been in existence for many years, and stages bunts and gymkhanas regularly.

"One of our aims is to improve the riding standard among young people particularly, and we've found polo crosse the best training," Mrs. Hirst said.

"We're hoping to have our own club house on the grounds shortly, where horses can be kept to enable more city people to take part in the game."

BATTLE FOR THE BALL between Mrs. Tom Kelly, jun. (left), and Mrs. E. Hirst. Limit is placed on time a player can carry the ball on her stick before throwing.

SCENE DURING PLAY. Monica Krippner takes the ball. Players, three on each side, are changed after each chukker of eight minutes. Timing and skilful wristwork are features of play.

GALLOPING down field, Jeanette Klegg takes the ball from Margot Hirst. Field, 160 yards long, is about half the size of a polo field.

The Australian Women's Weekly — July 20, 1946

Page 11

Polocrosse — a combination of polo and lacrosse — was first played by women at Ingleburn, NSW. *Australian Women's Weekly*, 20 July 1946.

enter the King's Prize. At this time Australia's most successful shooter was Bathurst-born Florrie Fergusson who had been placed 22 out of 1440 competitors at the 1938 English King's Cup, making her only the second woman to ever win the coveted King's Hundred Medal. During the war she had instructed over 400 women to shoot and lobbied for women to be able to compete in the sport. Her lobbying paid dividends. In 1961 regulations were amended to re-admit women as members of rifle clubs. In 1970 Narrandera-born Judy Trim shocked the shooting community by winning the world pistol-shooting championships at Phoenix, Arizona. Trim had travelled at her own expense after being named a reserve in the male-dominated team. She became the first Australian to win such a prestigious title.

A number of other women's club sports grew, unhindered by prerequisites of class or money, but often hampered by male prejudice. Women lifesavers spent more time battling the men than the breakers. After women had been responsible for rescue, resuscitation and general duties at many surf beaches during the Second World War, the Surf Life Saving Association of Australia prohibited them from surf competitions in 1947. Women were restricted to march past events, which in some instances were only allowed if completed well before the start of the official programme. Some clubs banned women from march pasts claiming the weight of the reel carried by the women was too heavy. Within the ranks, some women's clubs refused to participate in the march pasts believing they were 'glamour' rather than competitive events. New South Wales women's teams competed in a range of activities at the 1949 Terrigal Beach carnival, including open surf, surf relay and surf ski. By 1953, 20 women's teams were competing annually in their own organised events with equipment borrowed from some men's clubs, but not with official approval.

Marching as a sport was introduced from New Zealand in 1946. The first team was formed in Tamworth, New South Wales, and soon spread to other New South Wales country towns as well as Perth, Adelaide and Melbourne. In 1947 a team was sent to New Zealand which won the Australasian championship. Each team consisting of 11 young women, including a drum major and pennant bearer. They performed military drill with 14 basic turns and movements. Competition marching was described as 'clean, colourful, attractive to watch and physically beneficial', but one Newcastle team ran foul of the local cricket team in 1954 who accused them of causing wear and tear on their grass. By 1970 approximately 10 000 young women belonged to marching teams.

Women's bowls pennant games and country week competitions were resumed in 1945. The first Australian women's bowls carnival was held in 1949. Women still faced opposition from male bowlers who either restricted the times women

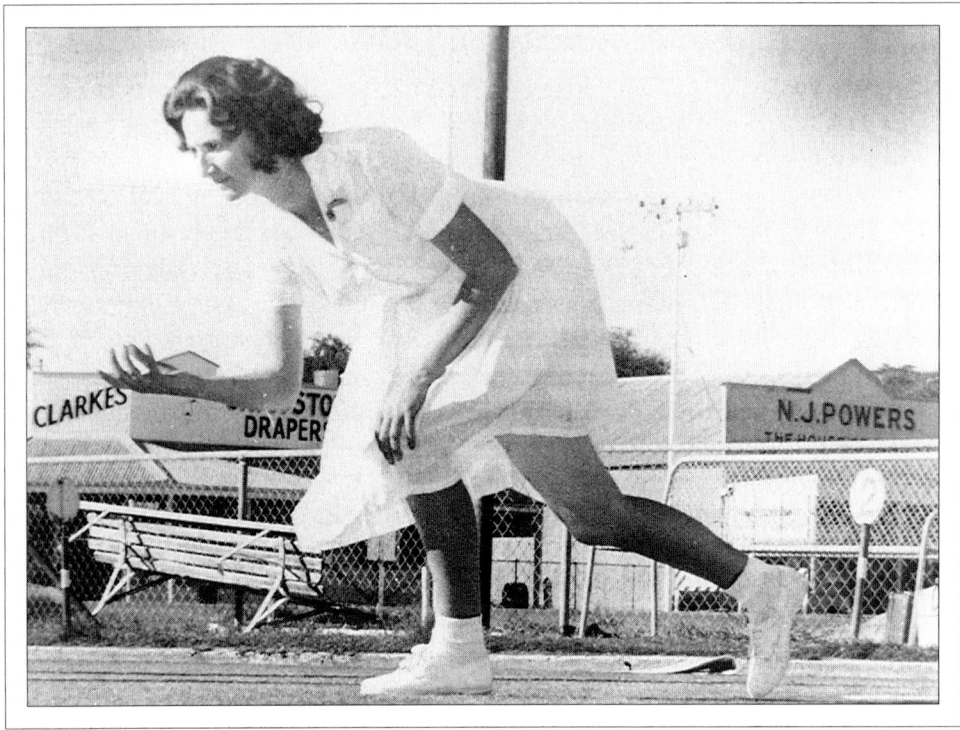

Women's pennant bowls resumed after the war but males continued to restrict women's playing hours at many clubs. Cloncurry, Qld, c. 1968

could spend on the greens or refused to grant them membership. By the 1970s over 120 000 women bowlers, representing 1825 clubs, were registered in Australia.

This era saw the start of marathon and endurance challenges among women who proved themselves game to take on anything. The easing of the old social chaperon restrictions after the war meant that many women had greater freedom to take on the challenges of the countryside. In 1945 six members of the Sydney Bush Walkers' Club performed an 'extraordinary test' by competing in a 16 kilometre competition walk. Walkers everywhere were inspired by the feats of Russian-born marathon walker Dr Barbara Moore. Moore had captured world attention in February 1960 by a marathon walk in Britain where she covered the length of the country (1650 kilometres) to Lands End in 23 days. Two months later she walked across America in 85 days. In July the Blacktown Railway Centenary Committee invited the human train to Australia. Dr Moore originally intended to walk from Adelaide to Blacktown in Sydney, but as she was still recovering from an ankle injury (acquired when she was struck by a car during her trans-America hike) she set out for a mere constitutional from Albury to Blacktown. She covered the 640 kilometres in a fortnight, fuelled only by her strict vegetarian diet. Moore made headlines in Australia claiming she would live to 200 and have a child at 100 years of age. She sparked a craze of endurance test walking in Australia.

Women also took on distance cycling challenges, though nobody seemed keen to try for the one-year distance cycling record that Pat Hawkins had attempted in 1941–1942. Cycling was also incorporated into women's holidays. In 1947 three former AWAS cycled from Melbourne to Sydney in three weeks. Cycle racing was revived and many new clubs were formed to contest the 1947 Australian cycle championships.

The first Australian marathon canoe race was held in 1951 down the Hawkesbury River. The 160 kilometres race included 20 kilometres of rapids. Male officials baulked at the entry forms submitted by two crews of women for the marathon in 1952, but allowed them to race as a trial. The four women were all experienced members of the Youth Hostel Association canoe club, and included twin sisters Joyce and Lillian McCallum who had emigrated from Lancashire in 1948. Both women's crews completed the course in under 24 hours to rank among the first eight crews (of a total of 19) that finished within the time. One of the women took on the rapids again in 1954, ten months after the birth of her daughter.

Perhaps the greatest marathoner of all from this period was swimmer Linda McGill. A strong medley swimmer, McGill had competed at the 1962 Commonwealth Games where she won three medals. She was selected for the 1964 Tokyo Olympics but clashed with swimming officials over their ban on swimmers attending the opening ceremony and her refusal to wear the official Australian swimming costume, which did not fit her properly. She was one of four women swimmers to be banned from competitive swimming after the Games (another was Dawn Fraser who received a ten year sentence). Holidaying in Europe 19-year-old McGill learnt that the Australian Swimming Union had banned her for four years, effectively ending her swimming career. In defiance, she immediately turned professional and set out to swim the English channel. Relying only on her fitness acquired for her Olympic swims (the 440 yards individual medley was her specialty), she completed the crossing on 7 August 1965 in 11 hours, 12 minutes. In September 1967 she made two more channel swims. The first, in unfavourable conditions, took 13 hours, 2 minutes. The second set a new women's record and made her the first woman to go under the ten hour barrier when she completed the swim in 9 hours, 59 minutes. But the channel swims were only the start of McGill's marathon swimming. In the following years she proved herself in the waters of the Dead Sea, the Black Sea, Loch Ness, around

SOFTBALL PLAYERS WILL MEET N.Z. TEAM

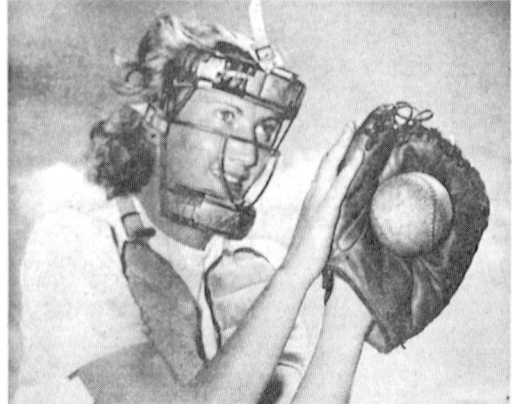

WITH BAT in position for a "bunt" is Royce Jackson (right). A bunt is a stroke made by allowing bat and ball to meet, without making a hit. The catcher here is Dot Lumsden.

CATCHER Dot Lumsden, of Melbourne "Rebels" team, is a foundation member of Victorian Women's Softball Association. In trial game she is wearing standard padded wire mask, catcher's mitt, and padded body protector. The association was founded during the war.

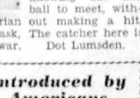
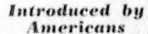

Introduced by Americans

FIRST international women's softball championships in Australia will be held in Melbourne from March 30 to April 3, when Australian teams will play New Zealand. The international Australian team will be selected after interstate championships have been decided at the softball carnival in Melbourne on March 19. Softball was introduced to Australia by American servicemen and nurses. It made its debut in Melbourne in 1942, and now has keen followers in all States. The game is played with a leather-covered ball about the size of a grapefruit. It is fast-moving, and closely resembles baseball. Team is composed of nine players. Matches, which have seven innings, usually last an hour and a half.

SPECTACULAR SLIDE is made by Leila Jones, often called the "Babe Ruth" of women's softball, as she attempts to reach home base and score. Catcher Barbara Porter attempts to put her out. Home base must be touched to score run.

PITCHER and captain of Victorian State team, Myrtle Edwards, is about to deliver ball. She is an international cricketer.

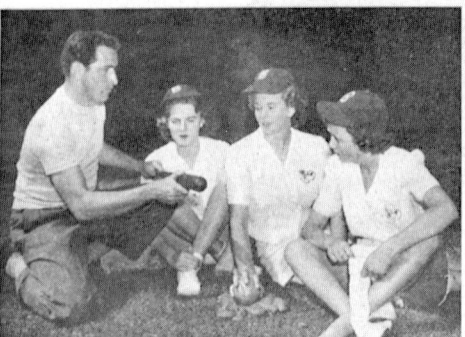

FORMER AMERICAN G.I. George Reday, living in Melbourne, shows Maureen Cunningham, catcher, Gloria Allardyce, first base, and Aileen Mumford, centre field, of "The Bears," a junior team, how to "bunt." George is a coach.

BENDIGO TEAM, led by catcher Val Collins and captain Betty Collins. Val and Betty have been chosen to play in Victorian team at interstate championships in Melbourne on March 19 before international matches.

The Australian Women's Weekly — March 5, 1949

Page 25

Softball was first played in Melbourne by American nurses in 1942 and rapidly grew in popularity. *Australian Women's Weekly*, 5 March 1949.

NATIONAL LIBRARY OF AUSTRALIA

Hong Kong and Manhattan Island after surviving a serious car crash in 1976. In 1968 she became the first person to complete the 40 kilometre crossing of Port Phillip Bay from Port Arlington to Frankston. She won the race, against eight male competitors including Des Renford, in just under 13 hours.

Alongside the introduction of new sports and new challenges, women continued to play team sports in ever increasing numbers, although the glare of publicity was usually directed elsewhere. Australia's main rivals in the international arena in team sports continued to be England and New Zealand. The availability of air travel increased the frequency with which international tournaments could be held. This gave women greater opportunity to continue both a career and family while pursuing their sporting interests at a representative level. Some women still spent as much time fund raising as they did actually playing their sport!

Softball had made its debut in Melbourne in 1942, introduced by American army nurses. The sport spread to all states and after the war national championships were contested. In 1949 Australia played its first international series, defeating New Zealand two tests to one before a crowd of 10 000 spectators at St Kilda Cricket Ground. The national team first toured overseas when they visited New Zealand in 1951. Australia continued to play international softball and hosted many overseas teams including South Africa in 1960.

Despite the pronouncement by an English headmistress in 1953 that her charges seemed more interested in sex than hockey, young women in Australia continued to bully their way through this era. In South Australia, for example, the number of women hockey players between 1946 and 1965 nearly doubled. Spurred on by Dr Marie Hamilton, president of the Australian Women's Hockey Association from 1946–1954, appeals were launched in 1951 to provide multi-purpose playing fields for women as a memorial to women war workers and servicewomen. The first hockey national championships after the war were played in 1946. In 1948 the Australian team resumed its international touring when a side was sent to New Zealand. Players were required to pay their own fares which were £70 each, but for the first time the team travelled by air. In 1953 Australia secured the coaching services of the former English women's coach, Eileen Taylor, who prepared the team for their 1953 tour to England (by boat) where an international series was to be played. In 1956 Australian hockey received a further boost when the international series, featuring teams from America, Scotland, Canada, India, South Africa, England, Ireland, New Zealand and Holland, was played in Australia. After the tournament teams travelled to various parts of the country playing matches. Over £30 000 was raised by hockey players in Australia to finance the tournament costs — a great proportion of it by selling cups of tea at sixpence a cup after club matches!

One woman prominent in both hockey and cricket was Mollie Dive. She captained Australia in cricket tests against England in 1949 and 1951 during which Australia won and retained the 'Ashes', as well as managing the New South Wales hockey team. She was honoured by the naming of the Mollie Dive Stand at the North Sydney Oval — one of the few women in the world to have a football stand named in her honour.

It had taken until 1949 for the English women's cricket team to make the tour to Australia that had been planned for 1939. The year 1949 also saw the first testimonial match played in women's cricket — for former Australian fast bowler Nell McLarty who had been seriously ill since 1940. Undeterred by illness, McLarty had an enormous influence on women's cricket coaching many players. In 1990, at the age of 78, she was still one of cricket's most respected active coaches. One of McLarty's prodigees was spin bowler Betty Wilson, by far the best all-rounder in women's cricket. Wilson took 7 for 7, including the first hat-trick in women's test cricket, as well as scoring a century with the bat in the second test against England in 1958. For her extraordinary ten-year test career batting average of 57.46 and bowling average of 11.8, Wilson was elected to the Australian Sports Hall of Fame in 1985. Australia played tests against both England and New Zealand during this period at regular intervals, and although the numbers were temporarily threatened by a move to softball, cricket maintained its popularity among women. The game of vigoro continued to be played but never again reached its pre-war popularity, overtaken by both cricket and another modified game, cricko.

Women's basketball (renamed netball in 1970) continued its status as one of the most popular winter team games for women. In 1956 Australia made their first tour to England winning the series convincingly. International tournaments with New Zealand remained a difficulty because of the seven-a-side versus nine-a-side controversy. The inauguration of the International Federation in 1960 finally codified the rules and official world tournaments were contested every four years beginning in 1963. Australia won the inaugural World Cup.

Both codes of football flourished among women immediately after the war. An Australian Rules match in Melbourne in 1947 drew a crowd of 25 000 and was cited as a source of alarm by clergymen attempting to have Sunday sport prohibited. Women's teams from South Melbourne, St Kilda, Footscray and Carlton played a series of matches in 1947 on Sunday afternoons, the only time they had access to football grounds. Women also played rugby league in New South Wales, but no formal competition existed and matches were often played as fund raising games for local war memorials. Women's rowing also expanded in this period with sculling being added to the programme, along with the fours and

Page 76 — Teenagers' Weekly

MARGARET SMITH

Supplement to The Australian Women's Weekly — March 16, 1960

Margaret Smith (later Margaret Court) from Albury, NSW, went on to win the Wimbledon tennis championship three times and was the second woman in history to win the tennis Grand Slam. *Teenagers' Weekly*, 16 March 1960.

eights event, at the 1947 national regatta. Other team sports such as waterpolo and volleyball also attracted a committed following of women after the war.

Women's athletic and swimming championships recommenced soon after the war with competitors aiming for the 1948 Olympics. Swimming officials are perhaps best remembered for their bans rather than their encouragement of women swimmers in this period. The most successful swimmers were Dawn Fraser, Lorraine Crapp, Marjorie McQuade, Karen Moras, Beverley Whitfield and Latvian emigrant Ilsa Konrads. Behind them thousands upon thousands of young Australian women got up at the crack of dawn to religiously plough up and down swimming pools throughout Australia. Their training schedules were now year-round with an emphasis on endurance and fitness work. Extra swimming events made their way into the Olympic programme and by 1968 women could also contest 200 metre and 800 metre events as well as 100 and 200 metre backstroke, breaststroke and butterfly and medley events.

Tougher events for women were also introduced on the track with separate cross-country, road relay and road walking championships held under the auspices of the Australian Women's Amateur Athletic Union from the early 1960s. National athletic championships were held biennially until 1962, then annually. Junior championships were introduced in 1963. The top athletes Shirley Strickland, Marjorie Jackson, Betty Cuthbert, Charlotte McGibbon-Weekes, Norma Thrower, Marlene Mathews, Michele Mason, Pam Kilborn and Maureen Caird were backed by a host of dedicated managers and administrators. Both Strickland and Mathews later turned to coaching.

Despite the unparalleled success of women athletes in this period, women's athletics never received the facilities or funding it deserved. In 1951 women competing in amateur athletics had to alternate their races with those of the professional speedway drivers who shared the Sydney Sports Ground on Saturday afternoons. In preparation for the 1958 Empire Games in Cardiff, Betty Cuthbert competed in races held during the half-time break in rugby league matches at the Sydney Cricket Ground each Saturday afternoon:

> We'd warm up outside the ground and as soon as the half-time whistle sounded we'd scamper on to the track, have our race and rush off again. All the time the officials were anxiously shouting: 'Hurry up now, girls, we haven't got much time . . . ' The crowd wasn't exactly the best to compete in front of. They didn't know much about athletics so weren't very receptive and, of course, there was the usual ragging and catcalls from the drunks . . . Apart from this, we had to go to fund-raising campaigns all the time to raise money to send the Australian team away.

While women's sports maintained a regular and ever growing number of players, the major growth areas for women between 1945 and 1970 were tennis and golf. These sports were considered by many to be the most 'ladylike' of all sports available to women and it was no coincidence that both retained the title 'Ladies' rather than 'Womens' for their organisations. Along with the amateur Olympic sports of swimming and athletics, golf and tennis were regarded as the most appropriate arenas for women to compete in. Tennis and golf allowed women in sport to be seen by the press and by the public as still retaining so-called 'femininity' and grace. They fitted better than team games with women's proposed roles in life and required no compromises to be made to femininity. In neither sport were women required to wear a uniform and individual taste in fashion could be picked up by the media. Both sports had been the preserve of the upper, then middle class women. Both sports had modified rules for women emphasising women's comparative frailty — a maximum of three sets in tennis and a shorter women's tee in golf. With one exception the only sportswomen to be accorded star status and to be promoted or even noticed by the press in this period were athletes, swimmers, golfers and tennis players.

Although regarded as a more appropriate sport, the road to the acceptance of national and international tennis for women was just as rocky as for other sports. The administrator who did the most to put women's tennis on the map in Australia was Nell Hopman. She was described, on her death in 1968, as a tennis suffragette. As a player Hopman had reached the finals of the Australian championship in 1939 and, after the war, she combined administration with tennis. She was elected in 1946 as the first woman council member of the Lawn Tennis Association of Victoria. She fought long and hard for women's tournaments to be staged in Australia and for women to gain overseas experience. She campaigned relentlessly to have a women's equivalent of the Davis Cup and in 1963 her dream was realised with the staging of the first Federation Cup in London. Her achievements were crowned when Australia was the host country to the Federation Cup in 1965.

Ironically the player to have the most success, and who played the largest part in Australian Federation Cup team wins for many years, was a confirmed Hopman critic. But the name Margaret Smith (later Court) was to emerge as the most memorable in women's tennis. As a 19-year-old and recent winner of the Australian championship Smith toured overseas in 1961–1962 under the management of Nell Hopman. On their return Smith severely criticised Hopman for her disciplinary actions and for the standard of motels and food provided for the players.

Margaret Smith was born in 1942 and grew up in Albury, New South Wales, where she learnt her strong serve and volley game. In 1960 she won the first of her Australian single titles, a feat she repeated another ten times. In all she won a massive 67 Grand Slam events during her career (Australia, French, Wimbledon and US titles) raising the winners plate at Wimbledon three times above her head.

In 1970 she became the second woman in history to win the Grand Slam — the four titles in one year. She was never beaten in a Federation Cup singles match guiding Australia to victory in 1963, 1964, 1965, 1968 and 1971. Despite being dubbed the 'Aussie Amazon' by the American press and sensibly declining to wear the new tennis fashions that restricted her play, Margaret Court was always careful to stay within the bounds of accepted female behaviour. In her autobiography she stated:

> *Certainly I try to hit a tennis ball as hard as I can and if I have trained myself close to a masculine degree of efficiency in this respect, it does not mean that I have forsaken any of my femininity or gathered any of the attributes of an Amazon.*

Other women of the period who were forced to play tennis in the shadow of Margaret Court were Leslie Bowrey-Turner and Judy Tegart, both relegated to doubles titles by Court, and two champions who bridged the war years — Thelma Long and Nancye Wynne-Bolton.

Women's golf also had its fair share of committed administrators , many of them making the transition from player to administrator successfully. After the war women's golf already had an international event — the Tasman Cup — on which to build the futures of up and coming players. This tournament, between Australia and New Zealand, was revived in 1949 and from that year held annually until 1954 when it was staged every two years. The first women's team to compete in the British Women's Championships left in 1950 and included Queenslander Joan Fletcher, Sydney-born Pat Borthwick and Western Australian Maxine Bishop. Former Australian champion Leonora Wray captained and managed the team. Wray, born in 1886, had won the Australian amateur championship in 1907 and 1908. Struck down by typhoid fever she made a comeback and won the championship again in 1929. She was elected president of the Australian Ladies Golf Union in 1954. Pat Borthwick dominated Australian golf between 1947 and 1957, winning the Australian amateur championship four times. From 1964 an Australian team competed in the Espirito Santo Trophy, the women's world amateur golf team championship, an event held every two years. There were scores of other great golfers and administrators among the thousands of women who belted the ball around fairways across Australia. Gertrude McLeod, the president of the Queensland Ladies Golf Union for 30 years and national president between 1949 and 1954, has the honour of having Australia's first women-run golf club named for her — the McLeod Country Club located in the western suburbs of Brisbane.

The only Australian sportswoman not an athlete, swimmer, tennis player or golfer to gain national and international attention in this period was the phenomenal squash player Heather Blundell-McKay. Australian squash and McKay have become synonymous. Born in Queanbeyan, New South Wales, the year before Margaret Court, McKay was a top hockey player before concentrating her attentions on squash. Like Court, she won her first Australian championship in 1960, but did not relinquish the title until 1973. She won the British championships (regarded as the world title) from 1962 until 1977, an incredible 16 consecutive titles. Remarkably though, McKay was rarely accorded the media attention she deserved in Australia, usually rating only a few cursory paragraphs. After a brief retirement she returned to competition squash in 1979 and took out the world championship at the age of forty. Playing with faultless technical ability and a strong determination, during her entire career she lost only a sprinkling of games and two matches.

The unrivalled success of Australian sportswomen in this era belies the title of an Australian book on sport in the 1950s — *Young Men in A Hurry. The Story of Australia's Fastest Decade*, published in 1961. Not only does the title insult the women who achieved so much, individual chapters in the book are only accorded to two women, Dawn Fraser and Ilsa Konrads. The depth of talent among Australian sportswomen deserved much more. Throughout this period the grass roots of Australian women's sport were just as strong as the blossoms. By 1970 millions of Australian women enjoyed sport as part of their recreation and leisure.

SHOESTRING SPORTS

AND THE
ADVERTISING DOLLAR

SPORT, MONEY AND ADVERTISING ARE INEXTRICABLY LINKED IN A COUNTRY WHERE DISTANCE TYRANNISES EVEN THE MOST STOUT-HEARTED SPORTS ADMINISTRATOR. Women's sport has always been played in a state of near poverty as the corporate and sponsorship dollar is directed elsewhere. Undaunted and perhaps even accustomed to an impecunious existence, women have banded together without financial backers to run their sporting associations on a shoestring budget. Sportswomen have traditionally needed fund raising skills as well as sport skills. Ironically, while offering little in return, corporate Australia has never been averse to employing the image of the sportswoman to help them reap the benefits of consumer profit. In the process, the advertising world exerts an enormous influence over the public face of women's sport.

In the 1920s businesses began to take an interest in women's sport, but their motivation was based less on philanthropy than on greed. Sport for women workers was organised by welfare superintendents employed by large retail and industrial establishments. If employers needed convincing that their extra expenditure on sport was profitable, the new scientific studies allayed their economic fears. A test conducted at a Sydney chocolate factory found that women packers, after three months of playing tennis in their spare time, increased their working rate by ten per cent. Not only could they personally earn four shillings a week more on piece work, they were less fatigued at the end of the day. Their work demanded a high degree of precision and quickness of hand and fast games of any sort — especially tennis, table tennis, cricket and badminton — were found to improve their hand-eye co-ordination and their quick decision making ability. Waitresses with tired and aching feet were recommended hockey, lacrosse and athletics to develop the leg muscles and strengthen the back. Office workers were encouraged to take up any form of strenuous exercise to counter sluggishness and restricted blood circulation caused by many hours spent at an office desk.

Physical fitness became the basis of industry efficiency. In Sydney the firms Hardies, Fostars and Peek Freans sponsored their employees in basketball, hockey, tennis and vigoro teams as well as physical culture classes. The firms purchased all sporting materials and provided other assistance to players. A glance at the 1936 draw of women's basketball teams in Melbourne reveals the team names Prestige, AMP, Pelaco, Semco, Holeproof, Hoadley's and Myer's. Companies like Shell formed their own athletics clubs and Angus and Coote donated trophies for women's amateur athletics. In 1933 the directors of Arnott's presented the workers with two tennis courts, a practice court and a new clubhouse after the Arnott's A-grade women's tennis team reached the finals of the local Homebush competition in Sydney. This was in addition to the baseball and cricket fields provided after two women baseballers were selected in the New South Wales side.

So successful was this fledgling sponsorship that private employers began to experience a shortage of female domestic workers. In examining the 'steady exodus from kitchen to factory' the magazine *The Home* asked in 1926 'What moves have mistresses made to the same end? What counter-attractions have they to offer? The answer is: Practically none.' In addition the domestic worker did not have their Saturdays free for sport as the factory or office worker did.

But employers' support of sportswomen was usually terminated as soon as the sport began to intrude on working hours or profits. Women from all sports were forced to resign their jobs once selected for state or national teams, the more fortunate were allowed leave without pay. In the 1930s an overseas tour meant an absence of up to nine months as players travelled by boat and few jobs for women were held over for this length of time. The most support employers gave was moral support. The owners of the Melbourne exclusive clothing store Henry Bucks, where Australian cricketer Nell McLarty worked as a machinist, still displayed in 1990 a photo of McLarty's spectacular catch at the Oval in 1937.

The twentieth century had brought a new range of magazines and periodicals directed specifically at women. Hand in hand were advertisers anxious to associate their products with the lifestyle of the women who bought the literature. As women's interest in sporting pursuits developed so too did the advertisers' interest in sportswomen, both as a potential market and as a source of new advertising copy. But even in eras when individual sportswomen have enjoyed considerable success, advertisers have been more likely to feature anonymous sportswomen. A variety of areas exist where active women became the prime advertising targets.

The entire campaign to market various brands of 'sanitary protection' was based on their appeal to the sportswoman though a named sportswoman has never been associated with a particular brand. (In the late 1980s, before confirming her Blackmores' sponsorship, Kay Cottee had preliminary discussions with the marketing manager of the tampons division of a pharmaceutical manufacturer. The manager informed Cottee that the amount of money she needed was too much for one product to absorb!) In the 1920s and 1930s brands such as the American Kotex and the British Menex pads most often featured golfers in their advertisements. One Kotex advertisement offered advice from an unnamed woman athlete. As women's sporting clothes grew briefer a need for absolute secrecy was perceived as the most essential ingredient for the menstruating sportswoman. The new Wondersoft Kotex, worn with the Wonderform Belt, was able to promise success at tennis, as well as showing no 'tell-tale lines'. After the Second World War the Meds tampon, made by Johnson & Johnson, became available in Australia. Although pads, or sanitary napkins as they were now called, continued to be marketed for the active woman it was the tampon which came to be associated with the 'absolute freedom' of the sportswoman and promised her 'five days of new freedom'.

In the 1920s other advertising that featured sportswomen promoted women's increasing social and financial independence. Advertisers were not averse to employing images of active women in their search for consumer support. The Ford Motor company went one step further and claimed in 1925,

A Ford car has been the stimulus to thousands of women to lead happier, healthier, and more active lives. It enables them now to do things and to go places that hitherto had seemed out of the question.

Ford's newly mobile golfer could fuel herself on Uncle Toby's Oats, the chosen breakfast of women golfers who wanted to excel. The active middle class woman could take along a Kodak camera on her annual skiing holidays to Kosciusko or

Mount Buffalo and either take snapshots with the standard Kodak or become a movie maker with the Cine-Kodak. For those women who couldn't afford a trip away Ovaltine food beverage was 'as good as a summer holiday for building up a store of vitality and health'. The Dunlop Rubber Company provided their own brand of golf balls, tennis balls and bicycle tyres for the active woman. When Gladys Hay won the 1921 Victorian Ladies Golf Championship she did so using and endorsing the new 'Why Not' golf ball manufactured by W.T. Henley's Telegraph Works.

A sportswoman's buying power may have decreased in the 1930s but her bombardment by advertisers continued to grow. While beer was marketed for the male consumer as a man's drink, stout was promoted as a woman's drink. In 1936 Tooheys Oatmeal Stout promised to build beautiful bodies for women. The type of beauty the advertisements had in mind belonged to the fit woman — the athlete, hurdler, golfer, runner and hockey player. Cigarette companies also sought to entrap women in a new sophisticated sporting image. As well as advertising

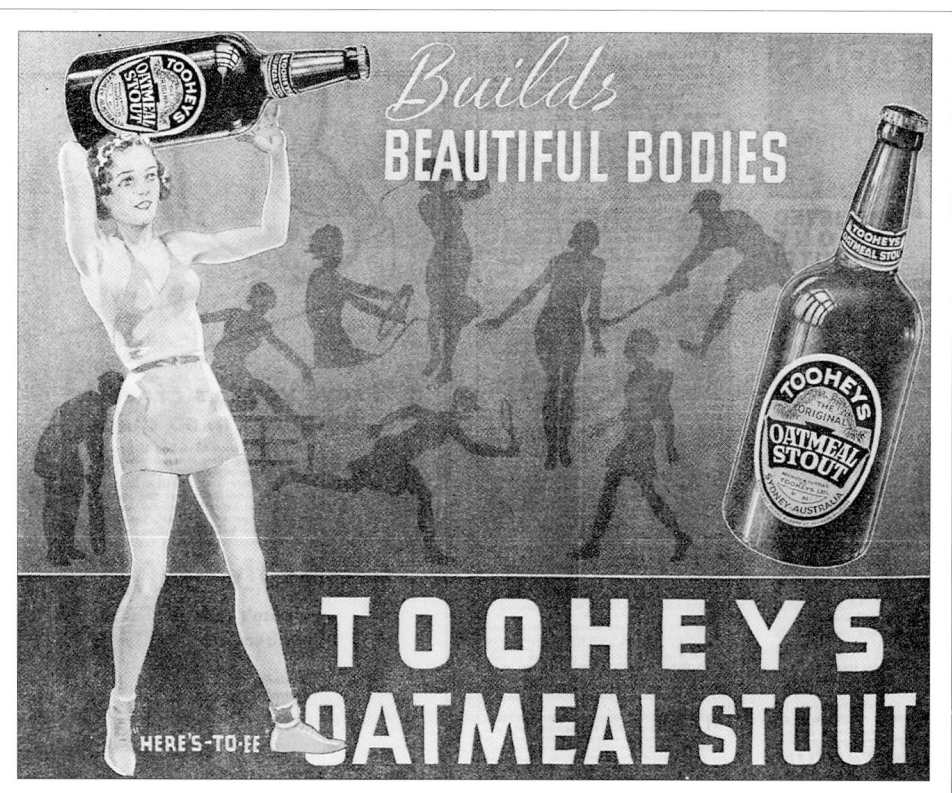

One of the many companies to directly link their product with sportswomen. Advertisement from the *Sydney Morning Herald*, 21 April 1936.

cigarettes as a remedy for sore throats (!) and nerves, the latter said to be caused by staying up late dancing or playing too much tennis, they featured advertisements with horsewomen, and pool and beach swimmers.

The connections between sport and smoking and drinking were not accepted blindly by all women who belonged to an organised sporting association. While male cricketers were featured on cigarette cards, women who smoked were excluded from selection in the 1937 cricket team that toured England. The contract that players signed stated 'no member shall drink, smoke or gamble while on tour'. In previous seasons a number of players had been dropped from the Victorian team for smoking at a cricket match. Women administrators were keen to have cricket accepted as a suitable sport for women and shied away from associating players with a racier and socially threatening image.

The serious sportswoman as well as the holidaymaker needed her own sports equipment in the 1930s. Anthony Hordern's catered to both and marketed women's golf clubs, tennis racquets and the latest beach craze the aero-wheel. The Sydney sportstore owned and run by Australian men's wicket keeper Bert Oldfield sponsored their own women's cricket team, Oldfield's, in the local Sydney competition. One of the most expensive and most common pieces of equipment was the bicycle. When Joyce Barry set the Newcastle to Sydney cycling record of just over six and a half hours in July 1937 the manufacturers boasted she used a Malvern Star. But the bicycle didn't even belong to Joyce Barry, she had borrowed it from Hubert Opperman, a fact that wasn't allowed to get in the way of good advertising copy,

Three years ago a weakling ordered by her doctor to take up cycling for health, to-day a splendid specimen of Australian girlhood, Joyce Barry is the holder of the Newcastle to Sydney Women's Unpaced Cycling Record. Another triumph for Malvern Star! Joyce chose her mount with the greatest of wisdom.

Riding Opperman's 'three speed geared bicycle' with tubular tyres and wearing 'regulation racing costume' Barry reportedly drank milk and ate several oranges during the ride. The Milk Board jumped aboard the Joyce Barry bandwagon and featured the 18-year-old cyclist in their November 1937 'Health and Milk Week' advertisements. Barry obligingly endorsed milk as 'the best food to keep fit on':

I cannot stress too much the importance of including milk as the chief food in my training diet, the truth of this being proved by the absence of any feeling of strain in my recent ride from Sydney to Melbourne.

Named sportswomen rarely endorsed sporting products. Advertisement from *The Home*, June 1923.
NATIONAL LIBRARY OF AUSTRALIA

Mrs E.M. Stace and 'Desmond' held numerous side-saddle jumping world records between the years 1907 and 1914. The horse, but not the rider, was identified in the Tooheys pub painting. Courtesy of J.W. and M.J. Blackford.
POWERHOUSE MUSEUM

Joyce Barry, if not the recipient of a Malvern Star bicycle, may have at least received some free milk.

The late 1930s to the 1950s was the era of concern over the general decline in the health of the population. Modern city life was named as the cause. It was beginning to take its toll and nervous disorders afflicted people as never before — even women who did not yet know it were starting to look nervous, listless, tired and lacking in vitality! National fitness movements were one solution, self-drugging was another. A range of products was marketed to combat the ills caused by modern life, all claiming to calm the nerves. The products included cigarettes, tea, chewing gum, assorted tonics and the cure-all aspirin. By the late 1930s Australian women had been convinced to swallow on average 300 aspirin tablets per year, nearly one tablet each every day. And who better to use in advertisements to demonstrate the stress of a busy life than the listless sportswoman:

Enjoy winter fun! Race over the snowy slopes on the skiing run! Glide across the skating rink and thrill to the zip of the flashing blades cutting the ice in a burst of speed! On the golf course, step up, tee up, and drive off with confidence! Let Vincent's A.P.C. help you keep fit this winter!

Take a Kodak with you

Days at Kosciusko and Buffalo will be the merrier if there's a Kodak or Ciné-Kodak in the party.

Then, when you're home again you'll have all the fun and excitement safely caught for all the days to come.

The Ciné-Kodak is a wonderful companion at holiday time. It's just as easy to make your own movies as ordinary snapshots—but what a difference when you see them, with all the life and action of the original, on the screen in your own home! Ciné-Kodak prices range from £16/16/-, and deferred payments may be arranged. Other Kodaks from 27/6.

Of all Kodak Dealers, and

KODAK Australasia) Pty Ltd.

379 George Street and 108 Market Street, Sydney.
"The Block," 284 Collins Street, and 161 Swanston Street, Melbourne C.1.
And all States and N.Z.

A new range of women's magazines brought advertisers ready to associate their products with the lifestyles of the readers. Advertisement from *The Home*, July 1928.
NATIONAL LIBRARY OF AUSTRALIA

Seventeen-year-old champion Victorian professional cyclist Iris Bent rode to victory in 1948 not on milk but on Aspro. 'There is plenty of nerve strain and

Even aspirin companies employed the image of the active woman to sell their product. Advertisement from *Australian Women's Weekly*, 10 April 1948.

tension in cycle racing and I find Aspro definitely soothes and calms me', her advertisement said.

Less sinister were the range of milk-based tonics recommended to improve health. The Milk Board targeted young active women with the slogan 'A quart a day is the healthy way' and claimed 'Milk — Nature's own tonic, is the finest food to supply the energy and stamina necessary to win the hardest game'. For a girl who was too quiet and had 'outgrown her strength' several weeks of milk-based Horlick's recommended by a neighbour would soon get her back into a game of rounders and make her 'sturdy and high-spirited'. By the late 1940s white coated doctors, rather than informed neighbours, were promoting Horlick's to prevent your Jill from being 'a dud'. Six 'interesting women', (one of them a swimmer fortuitously named Dorn Fraser), recommended Bonox in 1946 to improve physical fitness and stamina. Cadbury's Bourneville Cocoa promised 'Food for fitness' and their Bourn-Vita 'Energy to spare'. Nestle's Milo, 'the tonic for the times', helped 'to soothe the nerves, banish fatigue and relax the body' as well as providing healthy energy.

A range of food, other than the tonics, was recommended for fitness. For the tennis player the 1934 active breakfast was provided by the energy giving Kellogg's Corn Flakes — the reason, according to their advertisement, for the improved standard of women players from 1884 to 1934. The older woman could keep herself on the 'sunny side of life' (and retain her hockey prowess) by eating Kellogg's All-Bran twice a day. The cereal elixir of youth promised, 'No one would ever guess she was over forty. With her fresh complexion, clear eyes and bounding health she seems more like a girl in her twenties.' For tennis players who were nervous, fatigued or thirsty, Wrigley's chewing sweet provided relief. During an adjournment in a hard fought tennis match, women were encouraged by 'the Lipton Man' to drink his tea.

When Patsy Byrd, 'popular ski instructress at Kosciusko' stated in 1950 that 'it snaps louder than ever at Kosciusko' she was not referring to her pupil's limbs but to Small's Club chocolate, which Patsy took with her when skiing for 'quick nourishment'. (Advertisers in 1990 persist in trying to promote chocolate as the ideal quick energy boost when in fact it raises blood sugar and makes you feel shaky and weak.) Tennis players served snappy salads and skiers had balanced flavour when they ate Maxam processed cheese. Arnott's associated their milk arrowroot biscuits with the schoolgirls' sporting prowess and shredded wheatmeal with the health and fitness plan of the adult woman. If your diet was insufficient for sport you could add vitamins and help yourself to sparkling health with 'Vit-o-Fruits'.

Australian food was characterised in the 1950s by stodge. No wonder the sportswoman needed laxative help. Swimmers, golfers and tennis players could all be helped back to vitality by Andrews Liver Salts, Dr Morse's Indian Root Pills, Beecham's Pills and Eno's Fruit Salts. Even Barbara, 'based on a real-life story', could be first past the post in the under-nine 60 yards sprint if fed Laxettes.

The 1940s and 1950s witnessed a trend towards things white. White sports clothes, white sports shoes, white washing and white teeth. The tennis player, basketballer and cricketer could all achieve dazzling white shoes with Nugget White or Kromo White. Successful tennis players and exhilarated skiers could smile confidently with Ipana or Kolynos. From 1946 to 1949 Rinso ran an advertising campaign featuring a range of women's sports popular in the community at the time. Rinso women were on a good wicket, never stumped on washdays and topped the scores for whiter whites. In the advertisements women exclaimed 'ahoy there m'hearties' and 'fell hook line and sinker' for Rinso. Lux could be used to wash the knitted clothes of the outdoor girl who could write to Lux for her free pattern to knit an attractive jumper appropriately called Outdoor Girl. By the 1960s Rinso users still found it 'as easy as pie to get snappy tennis whites'.

Young women needed their Malvern Star bicycle to travel to their first job, go visiting, to tennis, weekend rambles or on holidays. The 1946 'ladies model' cost £13. 13 shillings and now came in 'duo-tone enamel to go with her smartest frocks' and a strong corded dress net. For £59. 10s a woman could purchase the Malvern Star Auto-Byke with a two stroke engine to enjoy 'travel and adventure in the great outdoors' like,

Pat Norton and Nan Watts attractive Melbourne girls who recently set a new fashion in Australia for inexpensive travel by touring Tasmania and making a trouble-free trip from Melbourne to Sydney and back.

The bike was economical but you needed plenty of time — top speed was 40 kilometres per hour.

In the 1960s many new labour saving devices and products — from saucepans to Dulux paint — promised the housewife extra time in which to play tennis and even go bowling. Spoil-sport headaches could still be cured by Vincents powders. But advertising was moving further and further away from the realities of women's sporting lives. Sportswomen were experiencing more problems than just headaches in their sports. Women's sport had been left behind in the television era. Despite their obvious success on the tennis court, in the pool, on the athletics track and golf course, the image of the world beating Australian sportswoman was not deemed as appropriate for the television screens as the Australian sportsman. To make matters worse a catch-22 situation developed where advertisers refused sponsorship to women who did not have television coverage and television refused airtime to women without sponsors. Individual sportswomen as well as teams played on without financial help, some relying on the generosity of others to enable them to compete interstate or overseas.

Women in professional sports, most notably tennis, fought for and won greater prize money. Women surfers received substantial prize money for the first time in 1988 due to the sponsorship of the Medical Benefits Fund. In November 1990 professional surfer Wendy Botha attacked the allocation of prize money in a world tour surf event in Newcastle, New South Wales. The winning woman received $4585 and the winning male $13 100. She said:

Ninety-nine per cent of the time we get a quarter of what men get . . . We surf the same waves and do the same training . . . The argument is that women aren't as good and that there are not as many women competing as men. But there are thousands of young girls who surf in Australia, and if there was more prize money more would compete. In one competition where we did get more money the men were up in arms. They went wild and threatened to stop women surfing.

In amateur sports women have had to rely on their own fund raising supplemented by a small amount of government assistance. The New South Wales state government has the best record of funding women's sport, and even in that state males receive twice the amount allocated for women. In Tasmania men's cricket receives ten times more than all women's sport per year.

In new sports such as triathlons some glaring disparities in sponsorship have occurred. In 1984 a triathlon held in Geelong, Victoria, offered prizes to both women and male competitors. The first woman home received a bicycle and the first male to finish received two return air tickets to Hawaii. In some sports, prizes for boys are worth more than those for adult women. Marathoner Tani Ruckle refused to run in events where women's prize money was less than men. Her co-marathoner, America-based Lisa Martin, had no such problems as US legislation prevented unequal allocation of prize money.

Only in recent times have corporate sponsors started to come to the party regarding women's sports and usually only after the Australian team has earned world honours on their own fund raising. Netball, the largest women's sport with one in seven Australian women playing regularly in 1990, struggled to attract the corporate dollar. The high profile of the articulate Australian captain Anne Sargeant helped the cause and from the mid 1980s Johnson & Johnson and Dunlop shoes sponsored the world championships and Esso sponsored the superleague. In 1988 Shell Australia sponsored the women's world cup cricket competition in

Australia. Before the victory of the women's hockey team in Seoul in 1988 organisers of the 1990 world hockey cup were told that the asking price of $350 000 to stage the tournament in Australia was absurd. With the glint of Olympic gold still in their eye, Telecom offered $500 000 sponsorship to stage the world cup.

In the last couple of years sportswomen have increasingly invaded advertising screens. Lisa Curry promotes Uncle Toby's; Lisa Forrest, Sebel's; Lisa Martin, Rexona; Jane Flemming, the Meat and Livestock Corporation; Kerry Saxby, Bega Cheese; and Kay Cottee, Blackmores and Duracell. Perhaps it is just a coincidence that the majority of sportswomen used in endorsement advertisements are blond. With decades of advertising which has exploited the image of the active woman, corporate Australia owes it to all Australian sportswomen to substantially upgrade and extend their level of sponsorship.

PLAYING WITH THE PRESS

IN 1984 A SURVEY OF AUSTRALIAN CAPITAL CITY NEWSPAPERS REVEALED THAT ON AVERAGE 1.3 PER CENT OF AVAILABLE SPACE IN SPORTS SECTIONS WAS DEVOTED TO WOMEN IN SPORT! What information that did appear was certain to be swamped among a massive 98.7 per cent of column space devoted to male sporting culture. Sport played by schoolboys and animals rated more mention. How had women, brought up on the deeds of the Stricklands, Frasers, Cuthberts and Courts, come to be so cut off from information and how had their sports been relegated to such an inferior position?

When women moved into the administration and control of their own sports from the 1920s, they also moved into one very significant area for the first time — sports journalism. This served several important purposes. It heightened the public awareness of women's sport and thereby created a more effective base from which to lobby, it provoked interest and drew record numbers of spectators to their sports, it served as an effective recruiting and coaching medium and it provided women with their own sporting heroes and role models.

The coverage of women's sport started in a small way with sportswomen providing results to newspapers on linage fees. As national and international

Journalist Ruth Preddey not only reported women's
sport but regularly canvassed issues of concern to the
growing number of sportswomen in the 1930s.
ABC ARCHIVES

tours got under way a need was seen to expand the coverage and women journalists, usually with strong links to several sporting organisations, were employed on a regular basis. When the first issue of the *Australian Women's Weekly* was published on 10 June 1933 it contained two full pages devoted to women's sport. This format continued for several years under the guidance of the *Weekly's* leading sports writer Ruth Preddey. Preddey was a foundation member of the New South Wales and Australian Women's Cricket Council and had played in the 1912 New South Wales cricket team. In 1933 she was an Australian cricket selector, an A-grade hockey and tennis player and a keen golfer. Preddey not only reported women's sport in great detail she used the pages of the *Weekly* to canvas issues she considered important to the development of women's sport. Her main concerns were that women should control their own sports, and that regular state, national and international competition was the road to sporting excellence. Her pages catered to all women, from the international through to the club player. They placed sport as an issue central to women's lives for the first time. In addition, other sportswomen contributed articles or were employed by the *Weekly* to cover major events including Dorothy Kearney on golf and Joan Hartigan on tennis. The *Weekly* also featured regular 'How to Play' hints for all women's sports.

The pages proved so popular with women that when the *Sydney Morning Herald* started its separate women's supplement in November 1933 they employed Kathleen Commins as a women's sports journalist. Commins, a keen tennis player and cricketer, was studying part time for an economics degree at the University of Sydney and had been the first woman to edit *Hermes*, the student newspaper. She was introduced to the *Herald* by Sydney *Sun* sports journalist Pat Hansen and asked to provide hockey and cricket scores. Commins's initiative to provide more than the bare bone results coincided with the *Herald's* desire to include a regular feature on sport in their supplement. She contributed leading articles as well as results in a regular segment 'Jottings on Sport'. After six months she was employed full time and wrote on women's sport for the *Herald* as well as other Fairfax owned publications like *The Home*.

Pat Hansen, in addition to writing on women's sport for the *Sydney Sun*, provided regular articles in the journal the *Woman's Budget*.   In Melbourne Pat Jarrett wrote on women's sport for the *Melbourne Herald* and Dot Debnam wrote for the *Sporting Globe*. Jarrett even accompanied the Australian women's cricket team on their 1937 tour to England and Holland providing regular copy for Australian newspapers. In Melbourne a separate monthly newspaper devoted entirely to women's sport, *The Sportswoman*, was published from the mid 1930s. Its journalists were mostly state representatives 'approved and nominated by the associations they represent' and included Valda Unthank on cycling, Dot Debnam on cricket, Marjorie Beaumont on basketball, Sybil Taggart on hockey and Maisie McDiarmed on baseball. As a consequence of this across-the-board coverage, some sportswomen from the 1930s era possess a staggering wealth of newspaper clippings covering their careers. Local as well as interstate and international events were widely covered and the public got to know the players and their sports. Spectators regularly numbered in the thousands at local club games. The deeds and faces of the sportswomen stood out in the sports sections of newspapers until the beginning of the Second World War.

In addition to the newspaper coverage, women's sport segments were introduced on radio with results, interviews and match summaries being regularly broadcast to women listeners. Radio stations began sponsoring women's sporting events like golf tournaments. Gwen Varley, Melbourne radio station 3AW 'Sports Organiser' and reporter, invited day-time listeners in 1935 to join the 3AW Women's Golf Club. Interstate matches were contested with the Sydney 2CH Women's Golf Club.

Kathleen Commins, Ruth Preddey and the other professional women's sports journalists and radio announcers kept the issues of women's sport constantly before their readers and listeners, never missing an opportunity to promote their cause. They treated their sport in a serious fashion. Women's sport was reported by women and men's sport by men. But there were still two areas where women did not control what was said about women's sport — the newsreel and the cartoon. Both were under the jurisdiction of men and both were receptacles for derogatory remarks on sportswomen. In a pre-television era the newsreel was an important source of information on current events and they were screened regularly at local cinemas. While not all footage of sportswomen was demeaning, the voice over commentary always was. As women 'invaded' male territory in all realms of life the newsreel was one medium where women could be smartly put back in their 'proper' place. The newsreel remained a powerful tool for trivialising women's achievements for several decades. The power of the newsreel did not go unnoticed by those fighting to have women's sport accepted on its merits within the community. In 1935 Ruth Preddey writing in the *Australian Women's Weekly* issued an attack on male newsreel commentators who made 'unchivalrous and belittling' remarks about sportswomen:

> *Women are puting good work into the organisation of good, clean, wholesome sport, and it is most disheartening to have their efforts ridiculed, and have facetious remarks made about the players when their game is shown on the screen.*

Everything was not smooth sailing at the newspapers either. Kathleen Commins at the *Sydney Morning Herald* was summoned by the assistant general manager, Rupert Henderson, just before the tour by the English women's cricket team in 1934, and told she was writing too much about cricket. Trouble was also brewing at the *Australian Women's Weekly*. Following an overseas trip by the editor-in-chief George Warnecke in late 1935, the women's sport section was reduced from two pages to one page an issue. On his return Warnecke promised his 290 000 readers 'grand new features' and by early 1937 they got them — and women's sport was slowly sacrificed on the altar of Hollywood, movie stars, and imported American culture.

During the Second World War newspapers were greatly reduced in size and some even temporarily amalgamated. Supplements and women's sections were suspended. When the newspapers returned to normal after the war a new agenda was operating for women. It was women's duty to restock the population and the emphasis now was on motherhood, homemaking and domesticity, not sporting teams and international tours. The newspapers were full of advice for the mothers of the baby boomers. The only fitness women needed in post-war Australia was the fitness required to produce healthy babies.

Except at times of Empire, Commonwealth and Olympic Games, Wimbledon or golf championships (when the deeds of swimmers, athletes, tennis players and golfers were just too difficult to ignore) women disappeared from the sporting pages. The coinciding new emphasis on fashion ensured that when women were mentioned, what they wore and what they looked like when they played sport was deemed to be of more importance than what they achieved. Women's sport was taken off the sport pages and placed firmly in the women's section, thus relegating the reporting to fashion, gossip and socialising. Journalists like Ruth Preddey continued to write sport for the major dailies, and Preddey was sent by the ABC to cover the 1948 and 1956 Olympic Games (she was eventually awarded an MBE for her services to sport, broadcasting and journalism). But on the whole, women journalists were relegated to a small weekly column tucked away in the women's section.

Women sports journalists like Doris Magee, manager of the women's section of several Australian Olympic contingents in the 1950s, June Bartlett, Heather

McCulloch, Rosemary Munday, Pat Borthwick the golfer and Helen Stockman on 2UE, no longer had the column space or airtime in which to canvas issues relating to women's sport. In newspapers they were relegated to a weekly round up occupying no more than a couple of half columns. When injustices occurred in selection or funding or grounds or equipment allocation there were insufficient women's voices with media clout to lobby for improvements. The overwhelming success of sportswomen in the four arenas deemed most appropriate for women's sporting ambitions saw all other women's sports, especially team sports, conveniently relegated even further into media oblivion.

With the introduction of television in 1956, television announcers took over where newsreel commentators had left off and women's sport was trivialised, if reported at all. Only individual sportswomen received coverage and the press was saturated not with their deeds, but with the details of their personal lives. This practice spread to all media and the public learnt the engagement, wedding and motherhood plans of sportswomen like Dawn Fraser, Lorraine Crapp, Betty Cuthbert, Shirley Strickland and Margaret Court. The *Australian Women's Weekly* now thought it more appropriate for their readers to see Marjorie Jackson, not in full running stride, but photographed with the Sara quads.

As men took over the commentary of women's sport it became increasingly sexist (and in Evonne Goolagong's case racist as well) referring more to their attractiveness as women than to their sporting prowess. Other men moved to exclude such trivial and irrelevant comments on women's sport from the sporting pages and in doing so removed all mention of women's sport, leaving the pages free for the exploits of men and animals. By the time that the dollar entered sport, women had been relegated to second class sporting citizens. Without a media profile women had no chance of enticing sponsorship and without a sponsor women's sport now had no hope of attracting media coverage.

By the 1970s sponsors had pulled out of women's golf leaving only three appropriate arenas — tennis, athletics and swimming. Each of these sports had a predetermined and specific timetable — they were not ongoing as was the case in team sports. Media coverage of any women in sport became sporadic and temporary. Even the team based Federation Cup tennis tournament never received the media exposure of the men's equivalent, the Davis Cup. In the public eye team sport was the male domain.

But the 1980s witnessed the impact of feminism on women's sporting lives and, just as importantly, the beginning of anti-discrimination legislation. Individual women, after a 40 year absence, began to knock again on the doors of serious sports journalism. The entrance of women to sports journalism in the 1980s was called an attack on the last male bastion. But this so-called last bastion had in fact crumbled in the 1930s and had since been propped up bigger and better than ever.

Raelene Boyle provided guest commentary on athletics
in an era when women
sports journalists were not often employed.
ABC ARCHIVES

It proved more defiant the second time round. In 1980 no women sports journalists and reporters worked in radio or television. By 1984 two worked in radio and by 1988 eight worked in radio and ten on television. Debbie Spillane, a Sydney grade cricket umpire and accredited rugby league coach, began her sports commentary career with radio station 2GB after entering a sports commentator competition. Once employed, Spillane immediately rebelled against the notion that she should give the radio listeners the 'woman's point of view' on sport and instead insisted that she was a journalist reporting sport and need not necessarily have a different angle or viewpoint. From 2GB she moved to the ABC in 1984 and was sent to the Los Angeles Olympics to provide commentary on swimming and diving. Back in Australia she slowly moved towards commentating the two loves of her life, cricket and rugby league. In 1984 Melbourne ABC television employed lawyer Elaine Canty as a sports broadcaster. Anne Fulwood became the first woman to read the television sporting news when she was employed by Channel Seven in 1983 and Jeanette Fulford anchored the SBS sports programme.

As in the 1930s many women who broke into sports journalism were sportswomen themselves. In 1984 Channel Seven hired ex-professional tennis player Kerryn Pratt who later continued her career with Channel Nine. In 1984 Channel Seven also hired ex-Olympic swimmer Lisa Forrest who had trained in sports broadcasting at radio station 2GO in Gosford. A temporary setback to women's sport journalism occurred when Channel Nine hired actress and cricket follower Kate Fitzpatrick to commentate test cricket. The plan was ambitious. Cricket commentators traditionally cut their teeth on Sheffield Shield before moving on to test cricket. Fitzpatrick didn't have a practice call or even a trial run. She was thrown in at the deep end of test cricket and floundered. It was not until 1990 that Channel Nine again risked employing a woman sports commentator when they hired proven sports authority Lisa Curry to front a national sports show. Other sportswomen have appeared sporadically on the screens. Former sprinter and Olympic silver medallist Raelene Boyle was a guest commentator at the 1988 Olympics telecast by Channel Ten. Olympic gold medallist and retired hockey goalkeeper Kathleen Partridge provided regular commentary for the ABC during the 1990 hockey world cup held in Sydney.

By 1980 only three Australian newspapers employed a woman sports journalist. By 1984 the number had grown to ten and by 1988 to seventeen. Louise Evans took over at the *Sydney Morning Herald* where Kathleen Commins had left off 40 years before. She was joined by Heather Smith and both women worked to gradually expand the range of sport in the paper as well as canvas issues relevant to women's sport. Nicole Jeffreys was employed by the *Australian* to cover rugby league and rugby union. Some specialist commercial publications and journals catering to women's sport appeared, including *Woman Golfer*. In the first edition in 1990 the male editor (perhaps forgetting that the magazine was produced by the *Australian Golf Digest*) remarked, 'Our golfing girls have been patient and long-suffering, content to devour the crumbs left from the many male-orientated publications'.

In 1985 the extent to which media bias affected women's sport was highlighted by the findings of the Working Group on Women in Sport established by the Office of the Status of Women and the Australian Sports Commission. Its report, *Women, Sport and the Media*, recommended a number of changes to media coverage most of which were to be monitored by a proposed Women's Sport Promotion Unit. But entrenched attitudes usually take more than just a government department to change, they need a full commitment from the people owning, operating and employed in media outlets.

Despite the influx of numbers of women into sports journalism and reporting in recent years, the media coverage of women's sport remains shockingly low and heavily patronising. Visual media continue to choose sexually exploitative images to present to the public and print media still provide irrelevant personal information. Few women's sports receive live television coverage — the best they can usually hope for is edited highlights screened outside peak viewing times. But the technical standard of the coverage of women's sport is also inferior. Some male commentators have complained that they find netball a dull television sport and women's cricket slow. But such charges have been answered by Australian netball captain-turned-commentator Anne Sargeant who believes that more cameras and basic training and education of camera operators in netball would automatically improve coverage. No research is put into netcams by television stations to improve the angles! Likewise women's cricket has never been afforded the multiple cameras and instant replays that turn the far-away game of cricket into a lounge room sport. Until women's sports are given down the line equality in technology, inferior television coverage will confirm rather than repudiate charges of second rate sports and sportswomen will continue to have to play against both their sporting opposition as well as the unsporting press.

DOUBLE DISCRIMINATION:
ABORIGINAL SPORTSWOMEN

IN THE CULTURAL PECKING ORDER OF AUSTRALIAN SPORT, WHITE MALES HAVE ALWAYS PLACED THEMSELVES AT THE TOP. They determine the order of those who follow: second are race horses, third Aboriginal males, fourth white women and fifth and last black women.

Aboriginal women, because of their imposed inferior social status, remained largely untouched by the sporting traditions developing through the private school and university system in late nineteenth century Australia. What exercise traditions they had within white society were discipline-based and centred around the calisthenic and physical culture movement.

If an individual Aboriginal woman champion was going to emerge in Australia, history would determine that she would most likely do so in the sport of swimming. Since the arrival of the invaders in 1788 Aboriginal women were noted as being strong swimmers. It was for this reason that they were used in Broome as divers for pearlshell. By a strange twist, swimming is the only one of the four sports deemed most appropriate for women (the others being tennis, golf and athletics) that Aboriginal women have not excelled in. They have had success in the sports most likely to be reserved for the middle classes — tennis and golf. Despite the amount of publicity given over the years to Aboriginal male cricketers, the only Aborigine to ever represent Australia in cricket is Faith Thomas.

The swimming tradition, in the cities at least, was not continued among Aboriginal women. Coaching and access to a pool for training costs money and requires a great deal of familial support. (Not surprisingly, the Aboriginal sportswoman who has achieved most in Australia — Evonne Goolagong — was removed from her home and brought up in a white family.) We can only speculate on how many potential swimming champions went unnoticed. The first Aboriginal golf champion was May Chalker, one of ten children. Her parents were farm workers at Wagin, a wheatbelt town in Western Australia 200 kilometres southeast of Perth. She took up golf, the only recreation available for women in her town, at the age of 23 and played on the local rough sand course for the four or five months of each year that the hot weather permitted. Chalker moved to Perth with a golf handicap of three and in 1979 won the state mixed foursomes championships teamed with her son. In 1982 she won the Western Australian women's amateur championship and was elected Western Australian team captain. In all she represented her state six times in golf. Her daughter Marion Chalker, born in 1961, played in the Western Australian junior state side until continual back trouble forced her retirement.

Also born in wheat country, but this time in the Riverina district of New South Wales, in 1951, was a young woman about whom the *Australian Women's Weekly* predicted in 1964,

within ten years the centre court at Wimbledon may feature 12-year-old Yvonne Goologong of Barellan, NSW. . . she is part aborigine, pretty and charming, and her tennis ability is already outstanding.

Evonne Goolagong, already a champion at twelve. Throughout her career, Goolagong was patronised with both racist and sexist descriptions by a white male-controlled media. *Teenagers' Weekly*, 1 April 1964.
NATIONAL LIBRARY OF AUSTRALIA

By the time she won Wimbledon for the first time in 1971 the *Weekly*, and every newspaper in Australia, had long since learnt to spell both her names correctly — Evonne Goolagong, but many of the sexist and racist descriptions persisted.

Goolagong had grown up in Barellan (which was basically an all-white town) where her father worked as a shearer; she was the third of eight children. As a child she played rugby, cricket and soccer and showed early promise as a sprinter at her school sports. Goolagong began her tennis career by hitting tennis balls with a broom handle, soon graduating to hitting them with a borrowed racket. Like thousands of other children she went through the visiting country tennis schools and at nine showed such promise that she was taken to Sydney to live with the family of her coach Vic Edwards during the school holidays, finally living permanently with them at the age of thirteen. At her first attempt at Wimbledon in 1970 she was eliminated in the second round. The following year she exceeded all expectations by defeating Margaret Court in the Wimbledon final. Serving to save the match, Court double faulted on match point. Goolagong went on to also win the French title in 1971, briefly earning her the number one ranking in the world. She won the Australian singles title in 1974, 1975 and 1976 before temporarily retiring to have her first child in 1977. She returned to tournament play, won the Australian open again in 1978 and reached the Wimbledon semi-finals in 1979. She won the championship for the second time in 1980 at the age of twenty-nine. She made another comeback in 1982 after the birth of her second child but was forced to retire in 1985 because of a recurrent foot injury.

She earned the ire of Aboriginal activist groups by playing in South Africa in 1971, 1972 and 1973 under the guidance of Vic Edwards, but refused to visit that country when approached again later in her career. Always subjected to racist slurs that she went 'walkabout' during tournaments, she was ironically accused of forgetting her Aboriginal heritage by some Aborigines in Australia. Goolagong-Cawley made a return to competition tennis in 1990 at the age of 38, in the first over-35s women's doubles event at Wimbledon.

Since her success every young Aboriginal woman who showed any potential at tennis received the 'new-Goolagong' tag. Among those compared with her were 13-year-old champion Natasha Khan from Mungindi, New South Wales, in 1985 and 11-year-old Catherine Hillard in 1987.

At the 1990 Commonwealth Games in Auckland, 16-year-old Queensland sprinter Cathy Freeman became the first Aboriginal woman to win a Commonwealth Games gold medal, and the first Aborigine to win a Commonwealth Games gold medal in track and field. She won her gold medal as part of the 4 x 100 metres sprint relay team. Unlike Goolagong a generation before, she was allowed to articulate her race pride, 'I have a lot to run for. I do it not just for myself, I run for my people', she proclaimed.

Aboriginal women have also represented Australia in cricket, softball, netball, volleyball and darts. Faith Thomas of South Australia is the only Aborigine to have played cricket for Australia. She played in test matches in the 1950s against both England and New Zealand. Jessie Boddington of Western Australia played cricket for her state against the visiting English team of 1948 at the WACA ground.

Netballer Marcia Ella, who grew up in La Perouse in Sydney, graduated from the Australian Institute of Sport in 1984. She toured England with the 1986 Australian netball squad and played in the tri-test series against New Zealand and Jamaica the same year. As centre or wing defence she played for Australia in the world netball tournament in Glasgow in 1987. Her inconsistent form (from absolutely brilliant to coasting) earned her racist slurs similiar to Evonne Goolagong and she bore the brunt of being labelled a token Aborigine in the Australian team. An outstanding netballer, she retired at the age of 25 to have a child. Dalma Smith played for Australia in the under-21 world volleyball championships in Italy in 1984-1985, and was voted best Australian player. In 1985 she was selected in the senior Australian volleyball team. Ivy Hampton of Alice Springs, represented Australia at darts in 1980 at the Pacific Cup held in Newcastle, New South Wales. Hampton also represented Australia as a veteran in the World Masters tournament several times. Joanne Lesiputty, born in 1966 in the South Coast region of New South Wales, played representative softball, basketball and netball before being selected in the senior Australian softball team in 1987. In 1989 she was awarded a special scholarship from the federal government for outstanding young Aboriginal sporting achievers.

Aboriginal women have represented their state in many other sports including hockey, soccer, basketball and badminton. Cheryl Mullett from Labertouche, 100 kilometres east of Melbourne, won the Australian under-19 badminton title when only 14 years of age. One of 12 children, Cheryl and the entire Mullett family were introduced to badminton via the local Methodist Badminton Club. A neighbour from her church provided the financial backing required to send her to championships in Perth, Sydney and Melbourne. Rose Damaso of the Northern Territory represented her state in softball, hockey, netball and basketball, an extraordinary achievement. In basketball Laura Agius represented South Australia and Leonie Dickson and Bobbie Dillon have both represented Tasmania.

In recognition of their vast achievements across many sports and the need for encouragement to help counter the double discrimination prevalent in our society, the annual National Aboriginal Sports Awards were inaugurated in 1986. The federal government also provided sporting scholarships for young achievers. But some Aboriginal women, mostly in the Northern Territory, have moved away from white dominated sporting culture and play in black only local competitions in a rejection of the European pattern of play and performance. In 1985 the federal government Working Group on Women in Sport reported:

we were told that often Aboriginal women displayed outstanding levels of talent and performance in a sport but, because they did not always conform to expected patterns of preparation and practice, did not receive the recognition they deserved.

EQUAL OR DIFFERENT?

THE READERS OF THE *AUSTRALIAN WOMEN'S WEEKLY* WERE TREATED TO THE SHORT STORY 'TOO GOOD AT GAMES' BY LOUIS ARTHUR CUNNINGHAM IN NOVEMBER 1934.

Sheila Craymer was thinking of how lonely and forlorn the house was with Doro and Chloe both gone, how dull and empty a house can be after a wedding — still, with ease and grace that had become second nature to her, she took her stance on the first tee, swung, and drove clean and true down the fairway. Old Aleck Drummond, pro. at the Riverside Club since Sheila was nine, was standing by the tee. He smiled and nodded — a smile of sixty wrinkles, a nod of sunburned sagacity.

'Ye'll be all alone now, Miss Sheila,' he said. 'With Miss Doro bein' married last year an' Miss Chloe this 'un.'

'Yes, it's pretty lonely, Aleck.' Sheila shaded deep blue eyes with a brown hand, gazing at her ball. She smiled at old Aleck. 'I'm the last of the Craymers. But nobody seems to want to marry me. Why, Aleck?'

'There's why.' Aleck waved a hand, gnarled and freckled at the little white pill, a lone white period on a vast page of green. 'Ye play too well, Miss Sheila.'

'You're telling me!'

'Aye. No man likes to take a beating from his wife, be it at golf or tennis or bridge. Ye're too good at games.'

In November 1934 Clare Dennis and Lesley Thompson had just returned from the Empire Games in London, the English women cricketers had arrived in Australia for their first series of test matches, three champion English women tennis players had just completed a tour of Australia and the Victorian centenary was in the process of being celebrated with specially organised sporting events for women.

A comparison of sportswomen's prowess with that of males serves two important functions in a male-dominated society — first it inhibits women from playing sports, and secondly it makes all males feel superior to all women regardless of their level of ability. As a result sport is left as a male-only preserve. The abilities of elite sportswomen and sportsmen actually resemble each other more closely than they do the rest of the population. The male obsession of comparing themselves with women reassures every male, regardless of his fitness or skills, that he is superior. Some male scientists have even made careers out of studying the differences! And for the women who persist in believing that they are equal at sport, an extra handicap is added — what you win on the sportsfield you lose at the registry door. Women must chose between being too good at games or married.

Women have always played against males in sport whether it be at a country picnic, in the playground of a small school or in the backyard of a suburban home. In the nineteenth century concessions were sometimes made to compensate for the handicap of women's restrictive clothing. The sexes competed against each other in handicapped colonial walking matches or pedestrianism and played bowls, archery, tennis, croquet and went shooting and hunting together.

When women began to move into sport in greater numbers in the 1920s and the 1930s they saw the need to organise their own sports, separate from males. The administrators from this period were treading on dangerous, sensitive sporting ground and they were careful not to put males offside. They co-opted them into charity matches where the result was less important (and less threatening) than the amount of money raised. This situation continued through to the Second World War when women organised mixed bowls and cricket matches to raise money for war loans. If asked, sportswomen agreed that males were physically stronger and that they had no desire to compete against them.

As a result women were, on the whole, left alone to play sport. Numbers of women, of course, had always been better at sport than males, but the latter had connived to keep women out of their swimming areas and away from their ovals. It was only when women began to enter sports that did not require physical strength that direct competition became a problem for men. In the 1950s a group of women entered a range of sports where an engine replaced the need for personal strength and power — motor cycles, motor boats, motor cars and aeroplanes. Those that did so proved themselves competent and their success rates were high.

Colonial women and men often competed against each other. Archery party at Yandilla, Qld, 1878.
JOHN OXLEY LIBRARY, BRISBANE

Because skill levels are equal, many sports can be played without a division of the sexes. But as women moved into sport in greater numbers, males restricted their access to facilities and membership and women foresaw the need to form their own sporting associations. Bowls at Maryborough, Qld, 1907.
JOHN OXLEY LIBRARY, BRISBANE

Grace Walker, a speed boat driver, won the Hawkesbury River Brooklyn Bridge to Windsor Bridge race in 1957. Dr Dorothy Rutherford established her aeronautical superiority over a field of male competitors in an aerobatic competition in 1957. Diana Marshal drove her outboard speed boat to over 30 wins in the 1950s, and won the New South Wales speed record for her class of craft. Women motor cycle riders tested their ability against males at organised motor cycle carnivals and sports days. Some women raced without official permission and, aided by a helmet and protective clothing, it is not known how many went undetected by race officials and the public. Speedcar driver Edna Wells recalled her experience in the 1950s:

I did race a motor bike under a foreign name on tracks outside the metropolitan area, but the officials had a fit when they found out I wasn't a man.

Males never relished the direct challenge of facing competent women in sport and the most common reason given was that men would be forced to change their competitive styles. This same excuse was used to try and exclude women from being jockeys in the other 'external engine' sport of horseracing. In their own eyes males had nothing to gain and everything to lose from competing against women. In the 1950s visiting Dublin-born race driver Fay Taylour had trouble finding male drivers to race against in Sydney. Women who were in sports that brought them into direct competition with males wanted to compete without fuss. The rest expressed no desire to compete against males in sport.

Trouble intensified at the 1956 Olympic Games when women stole the golden limelight. Women were not in direct competition with males but their medal tallies could be easily compared. Although a greater proportion of Australian women had traditionally been more successful at international competitions than male representatives, it was generally acknowledged that in 1956 women made the men look second rate. Newspapers searched for explanations:

At the Melbourne Games Betty Cuthbert, Marlene Mathews and Shirley Strickland have broken or equalled Olympic and world records for women. Yet on the same track in similar breezes Australia's swiftest men have gasped in to minor places.

Explanations citing favourable climate and better quality food as the basis for women's success were not convincing as boys were raised in exactly the same climate and reared on the same kind of food. Amid disturbing headlines like

'How strong is our weaker sex?' and 'Girls are leaving the men standing' the department of anatomy at the University of Sydney clutched at the explanation of gene fusion, 'A lot of lucky breeding must have been going on when the present generation of girls were born'.

Males began wondering if the elite women would soon catch up and outstrip the elite men in direct competition. Part of this fear came from the rapidity with which women were progressing in the Olympic sports. Discriminated against and barred from events for so long, women were quickly making up for lost time. When and where would it end? British women were already beating men in rifle shooting, cycling, and channel swimming and there were plenty of local examples to draw upon. When the feminist movement spread among women in Australia from the late 1960s, sportsmen, on behalf of all males, clung to their notion of physical superiority over women. Women may have been entering the work force, demanding equal pay, equal education and equal rights and they may have been able to match it with men intellectually but there remained one incontrovertable truth in society and that was that males were stronger than women. No equal opportunity legislation, no access to childcare, contraception or abortion could change men's superior brawn. Men knew that their superiority over women was natural, their bodies told them so.

It was no coincidence therefore that a number of direct competitions between sportswomen and sportsmen were staged in the 1970s. These were dubbed the battle of the sexes. In athletics and swimming women's times could be easily compared with those of males, but the comparison in such things as tennis and golf was more subjective. The first battle was when aging American tennis champion Bobby Riggs challenged Australian and Wimbledon champion Margaret Court to mixed singles in 1973. The match was held in California and Riggs easily outpsyched and outplayed Court. The return match however was a different story. Riggs took on American Billie-Jean King in a match that had all the hype of a title fight. It drew the largest tennis crowd ever and was televised world-wide. Billie-Jean King won and was able to use the occasion to push for greater prize money for all women tennis players. In 1968 former Olympic turned long distance swimmer Linda McGill had won the 40 kilometre swim across Port Phillip Bay against eight male competitors. In the field was the leading male endurance swimmer Des Renford who retired from the race about three kilometres from the finish. In 1973 an endurance swimming battle of the sexes was staged between McGill and Renford across Brisbane's Moreton Bay, but McGill withdrew about five kilometres from the end. In 1976 Australian Jan Stephenson played the Masters and World Open golf champion Ray Floyd in the Challenge of the Sexes golf match in California. The contest was played over nine holes, Jan Stephenson took 38 stokes to Ray Floyd's thirty-nine. In 1978 champion

In the 1970s top sportswomen were often treated as sex objects first and athletes second. It took a long time for the male-controlled media to use images of sportswomen that reflected their sporting ability. Dianna Thomas and Jan Thomas (later Jan Stephenson), 1972.
NATIONAL LIBRARY OF AUSTRALIA

squash player Heather McKay briefly turned professional and at the age of 38 was pitted against five professional male athletes in the promotional grand final of the All-Pro Racquetball Championship. McKay had played the sport for only two years and her male opponents had been narrowed down from a field of over 100 professional athletes from baseball, basketball, football and hockey leagues, but did not include any from racquet sports. McKay met the five men in turn and beat them all to collect the considerable $40 000 first prize. Such contests had no real meaning in the world of sport, irrespective of who won. They were the result of males' increasing frustration with women's competence not only on the sporting field, but in other areas of life.

By the 1980s the public had lost interest in head to head battles, but a new group of males rose to challenge sportswomen — the scientists. They became obsessed with measuring, quantifying, qualifying, computing, surveying, and evaluating sportswomen's performance, not for its own sake but in comparison with males. The justification for the invalid and inappropriate comparison was generally absent from the published papers or books but still the topic recurred at conferences and discussions on women and sport. In the press any achievement by an individual sportswoman over a sportsman was more often than not accompanied by a diagram or photograph clearly explaining the differences between the general physiques of the sexes. Such a comparison purposely invalidated the achievement of the individual, and made all men feel less threatened. One lengthy article on the topic (illustrated by a physique comparison photo) was published in 1980 in the *Sydney Morning Herald*. The article posed a series of dubious questions under the guise of serious, scientific research:

More general questions present themselves these days with the rush of women to athletic competition. Are women's bodies strong enough, tough enough to take the battles? And, one wonders, how good are women as athletes anyway? How do they compare with men? What are the differences and similarities, qualitatively as well as quantitatively? What are women's goals in sports, their goads, their expectations? And, incidentally, does any of this have a bearing on the battle of the sexes? . . . The answers must come . . . from the ordinary middle-class young women, the good athletes, but not necessarily the champions. Must they themselves not wonder at times what insanity has thrown them into these corridors, drenched in sweat, torn by mixed feelings of aggression and self-doubt, with prizefighter's cuts under the brows, tears in the eyes and, for God's sake, a dozen more of these foolish matches left before the end of the season?

With questions like those who needed answers?

But amid all the analysis, males misunderstood that their scientific data which proved that the performance of an elite sportsman was superior to an elite sportswoman did not mean that the same was true when it came to an individual level. Historically sportswomen have prevailed over all or the majority of their opposition in a number of sports including those requiring physical strength. Not all were elite athletes — many were just ordinary women of all ages and abilities beating ordinary men. The professional swimmer Annette Kellermann won races against males in Europe in the early 1900s. From her 1918 perspective she wrote:

A raw deal for women in sport

SIR: In a week which saw the launching of an inquiry into inequalities in prize money for men and women, I have been looking at the papers with an eye to determining how the media play a role. I have come to the conclusion that the media are collectively a male chauvinist pig which grudgingly reports women's sports results because he has been told to.

The *Herald* (November 26) was a prime example. The sports pages were dominated by men's sports almost to the exclusion of women's, even though the Australian women's netball team had just whitewashed the English team to a 3-nil defeat. This triumph was reported in barely 19 cm. And there was a one-sentence report of Newcastle surfer Michele Donoghoe winning the Women's Pro event at Newcastle. In four full pages of sport, this was the extent of coverage of women's sport.

There is an old saying that women have to do twice as well as men to be thought half as good. It goes on to say that luckily this is not difficult, but that is not true of sport. Sport these days is dominated by sponsorship, and is it any wonder that sponsors won't come across with money when the media do not give a damn about women in sport? When was the last time women's golf was covered by television cameras? What coverage do the women cricketers get? Indeed, how much coverage does any women's sport get — apart from the token netball — on television?

It is more than time for men to change their thinking about women in sport. What holds true for boys also holds true for girls, and that is if a kid has talent he or she should be encouraged equally. And the media coverage and sponsorship should be equal.

There is no longer any room for the attitudes engendered by the sort of remarks made by Pat Cash about women's tennis a couple of years ago. Women play sport with the same dedication and determination as men — witness the women's hockey team, but unless the media wake up to the wrong they are doing to women, this imbalance will continue to the detriment of all sport.

Denise Cumming,
Rockvale Road,
Armidale.

November 27

Men's natural gifts dominate

SIR: Denise Cummings's charge that "the media are collectively a male chauvinist pig" (*Herald*, December 8) is stronger on name-calling than common sense.

The media are simply reacting to public lack of interest in women's sport by not highlighting it. Should a grade cricketer be interested in women's Test cricket when he knows he could bowl the sides out cheaply? Can a weekend golfer be enthralled by women's golf when he could out-drive the board leader?

Women are perfectly entitled to enjoy their sport. But can they expect wide public interest when their achievements are equal to lower grade male sport?

Sadly, many women have been led to believe the things that they have traditionally done better than men — giving love and care to children, imaginative cuisine, embroidery, etc — are symbols of discrimination against them. So they have joined your correspondent in what is bound to be a futile quest for equality in areas that men, by their natural gifts, dominate.

Michael Edwards,
Chandos Street,
December 8 Ashfield.

From a time warp

SIR: The charge by Michael Edwards (Letters, December 15) that women should be content with the traditional roles of giving love and caring for children, creating imaginative cuisine and producing embroidery and not to expect a reasonable coverage of women's sport has me wondering whether this man has just stumbled out of some time warp or has spent a long time in isolation somewhere.

Mr Edwards asserts that males are superior in sports and therefore there is a public lack of interest in women's sport. Maybe it never occurred to your reader that a large percentage of the *Herald* readership may well be female and that that percentage is not reflected in coverage of female sport.

Men may very well wish to read about male sport, as you assert, but shouldn't women have the same opportunity to coverage of their sport? If you happen to be a woman golfer, cricketer, swimmer, cyclist, diver, rower, footballer, lawn bowler, runner and so on, shouldn't you be able to read about the events and people you aspire to rather than coverage that is unrelated to your ambitions?

Thomas Flannery,
Curlewis Street,
December 16 Bondi.

Such good sports

SIR: At the risk of being branded a traitor to my sex, I will comment on Ms Cumming's and Mr Edwards's sporting views (Letters, December 8 and 15).

The fact that a man of similar ranking will outdrive, outbowl and outplay a woman is indisputable. Also irrelevant.

What a treat it was to see (ABC-TV, December 14-16) professional golf played complete with impeccable manners, lovely smiles in triumph and in defeat, to listen to intelligent comments of the players during interviews. Compare that with the bored, wooden dials of the top male golfers and their "that stupid question again!" attitude.

Any Sheffield Shield team would have beaten the 11 Australian women who represented their country, the Test shown on TV years ago. So what? I'd gladly watch a replay of that exciting match again. Were Shield matches on TV, I'd probably read a book. The usual attendances to those may prove me no Robinson Crusoe.

Hockey played by top men or women ·is equally fast, furious and good to watch. Who won gold at the last Olympics, anyway?

Tennis, thankfully, receives near equal exposure and offers similar rewards. I'm yet to see an ugly American or an ugly Australian in women's games. I know which tennis I'd rather watch for pleasure and entertainment.

To cap it all, women have more sense than to seriously engage in any games involving that egg-shaped thing. While some aspects of feminists' aims continue to puzzle and, at times, trouble me, the score in this match is clear: Cumming 9, Edwards 1.

Ted Matulevicius,
James Road,
December 16 Gooseilabah.

Clubbed to death with a putter

SIR: I am delighted that Michael Edwards (*Herald*, December 15) feels I am perfectly entitled to enjoy my sport. Had this not been so, I would have been left to decide which piece of my numerous sporting equipment to select to finish my useless life as a woman with no children, and no skills in embroidery or imaginative cuisine.

Unfortunately, with no media support I will receive no sponsorship to enable me to enjoy my sport. Can anyone lend me an embroidery needle?

Mary R. Webster,
Yukka Road,
December 15 Regents Park.

An apt comparison

SIR: In reply to Michael Edwards's comparison of women's sport as being equal to lower grade male sport (Letters, December 15), I would like to say that while it is true a bantamweight boxer would not step into the ring against a heavyweight boxer just as many people flock along to watch a bantamweight fight as they do for the heavyweight variety.

Jan Hall,
Karingal Avenue,
December 15 Carlingford.

Media equity for women's sport is regularly debated in the letters pages of newspapers.
Sydney Morning Herald, 1990

247

I insist that swimming is not only a splendid sport for women but that it is the sport for women — the one sport, in fact, with the possible exception of dancing, in which she can fully compete with men. While it is true that men hold the actual racing records in swimming for both time and distance, yet, if we consider the more limited opportunity for women to swim and the small number of women who really master the art, and consider also the element of grace in swimming as well as the mere exhibition of strength, we must concede that women outrank men as swimmers. This is seen in the endurance competitions where the women swimmers, while lacking the speed which the strength of man may give, make a better average showing and show a smaller percentage of failures and quitters.

In 1938 the woman backstroke champion of Queensland M. Inwood won a five kilometres freestyle river swim against males by over six minutes, after being given a five-minute start. In the same year Jesse Sams of Milton, New South Wales, entered the sesquicentennial big-game fishing competition. She won the trophy by landing a 150 kilogram striped marlin off Ulladulla on the New South Wales South Coast, creating a new Australian record. The travel magazine *Walkabout* queried,

Who would have dared suggest at the beginning of the competition that the main trophy valued at £500 would be won by a woman angler? It was not that the women entrants lacked the necessary skill, endurance and experience, but rather that they were . . . probably outnumbered by male anglers by at least 50 to 1.

In 1972 Pamela Hudspeth of Sydney continued the tradition by beating over 1000 men in a big-game fishing competition to win a trip to the annual salmon derby in Vancouver, Canada. In 1988 Yvonne Geerts, a primary school teacher, won the Mallacoota Ironman championship on a two-kilometre run and swim course at Mallacoota Inlet in Victoria. In 1979 golfer and Macquarie University student Edwina Kennedy won her matches in the previously male-dominated Australian Inter-Varsity Golf Championships. In 1974 Elizabeth Felton of Subiaco, Western Australia became the first woman to win the Queens' prize in rifle shooting. In 1978 Barbara Kearney, Australia's top woman table tennis player, was barred from competing in her local inter-leagues club table tennis matches because she was winning 80 per cent of her matches against men. The disappointed Kearney claimed:

Champion fisher Jesse Sams. Historically women have achieved outstanding success in sports where they compete against men as equals.

I used to think all the grumbling was good-natured because on the surface anyway everything seemed friendly. But underneath they must have been feeling bad if they were prepared to go to all that trouble to have me barred from playing.

Jesse Sams won the NSW sesquicentennial big-game fishing competition in 1938.

In 1978 cross-country skier Colleen Bolton came ninth in a field of 302 in the Paddy Pallin cross-country 25 kilometre classic. In 1982 amateur cyclist Victoria Shand arrived at a Victorian race meeting too late for the women's race so entered a 22 kilometre marathon in which she was the only woman competitor; she won the race on her old upright bike. Later she took up cycle racing more seriously. In 1959 Phyllis Singelton, an axewoman and barmaid from Innisfail, Queensland, won the tree-felling championship at the local sports carnival. From 1987, Danielle Thomas won an Australian BMX title three years in succession. At the 1990 Commonwealth Games marathoner Lisa Martin posted a time better than Australia's third fastest male marathoner.

Athough some women have trained against male competitors (and some have refused to) sportswomen have rarely expressed a desire to compete against males in sports that require more than a modicum of strength. But it is perhaps not so much the issue of strength but the male ego that leads women to conclude that sport is more enjoyable and rewarding when played solely in the company of women. Hazel Hawke in 1990 knew something that the fictional Sheila Craymer had not known in 1934. When interviewed by the magazine *Woman Golfer* Hazel Hawke was asked how her golf game compared with that of the golf-dedicated Prime Minister:

'I don't play Bob,' she said with a twinkle. 'On handicap I've beaten him. I can tell you he's a good winner but he doesn't like losing.'

THE IMPACT OF FEMINISM

1970-1990

WHEN THE VICTORIAN LADIES CRICKET ASSOCIATION WAS FOUNDED IN 1905 FEMINIST VIDA GOLDSTEIN HEADED ITS LIST OF OFFICE BEARERS AS PRESIDENT, A POSITION SHE HELD UNTIL 1912. Goldstein was at the forefront of the suffrage movement and was the first woman in the British Empire to become a parliamentary candidate. Her support of the women's cricket association was mutually beneficial and it linked the feminist movement of the late nineteenth century with women's moves to control their own sports. Similarly, in New South Wales, feminist Jessie Street campaigned at the University of Sydney for women to have a separate and autonomous sports union. The perceived need for greater control of their own sports was consistent with the move to broaden women's political representation and with the call for women's lives to be enhanced and enriched.

When the second organised wave of feminism broke across Australia in the late 1960s, feminists were not, on the whole, at the forefront of attempts to broaden the sporting traditions of women. Feminism did not storm the bastions of male sporting supremacy either physically or intellectually. The reasons were simple. With their elementary political rights assured the agendas of feminism were devoted to demanding complete equality in employment, income and education, the right to child care and the right to control their own bodies through access to safe abortion and contraception. Once these things were won surely women's rights as human beings would be respected in all spheres. Also, sport seemed to many women to be closely linked with the male culture they were fighting against. The sportswomen themselves lacked a political analysis of their own oppression and the elite sportswomen in the public eye had little time or energy in reserve after the rigours of training and competition to devote to challenging the system. But nothing is won by women in a patriarchal society without a determined struggle. No flow-on effect occurs of women's rights. Nothing is ever conceded. For women to have equal access to the pleasures of sport and recreation they had to fight for it, and until the mid 1980s they had to fight small skirmishes in every sport alone and without the backing of legislation to help them.

In the 1970s women moved into an increasing number of sports requiring greater strength, endurance, exertion, elements of danger and increased physical contact. Robin Weckert,
1990 Australian weightlifting title holder, 75 k class.
THE AGE

The last 20 years has seen the introduction and growth of a number of sports which directly challenge the notions of what sports are appropriate for women to participate in. They involve sports requiring greater strength, endurance and exertion, elements of danger and increased physical contact and therefore potentially challenge concepts of correct body type and social behaviour for women. The most threatening are the sports of powerlifting, body building and associated power-based athletic events like shot put, discus and javelin, but also included are wrestling, kickboxing, motor racing, ice hockey, lacrosse, surfing, football, soccer, triathlons, parachuting, sailing, hang gliding and mountaineering.

English-born Jill Bamborough became the first Australian woman to set a world powerlifting record when she broke the dead lift in the bantamweight division in 1978. She lifted 147 kilograms, nearly three times her own body weight. Bamborough had taken up powerlifting (called weightlifting

Professional soccer player Julie Murray.
NATIONAL SPORT INFORMATION CENTRE

Formula-two racing driver Sue Ransom,1982.
OVERSEAS INFORMATION BRANCH

Australia-Japan golf tournament, 1980, featuring champions (l-r) Haruyo Miyazawa, Edwina Kennedy, Jane Lock and Toshie Matsubara.
OVERSEAS INFORMATION BRANCH

Wendy Turnbull at the Australian Open tennis championships in Melbourne, 1980.
OVERSEAS INFORMATION BRANCH

for men) as part of a personal fitness campaign after retiring from competitive athletes where she had won two medals (for England) at the 1966 Commonwealth Games as a 100 metres sprinter. The sport grew in popularity in Australia and more women incorporated a greater degree of resistance work into their training in all sports. In 1988 Heidi Wittisch became world champion in the 75 kilogram class, with Marilyn Waller (60kg) and Gael Martin (90kg) both gaining silver medals at the Women's World Powerlifting Championships in Belgium. Bodybuilding was introduced to Australia from America in 1981. Within a year over 800 women were members of the federation with Carole Bennett named the Australian bodybuilding champion. One woman to cross over between power-based sports was Victorian Bev Francis who represented Australia at the 1978 and 1982 Commonwealth Games in shot put and javelin. From 1980 Francis competed at the world powerlifting championships consistently winning gold in her class and setting numerous squat, bench press and dead lift world records. She had less success, however, in the more subjective bodybuilding contests often ironically being regarded as too muscle-bound, a situation she described as similar to saying to a woman you can't enter a sprint race because you're too fast. Francis was constantly taunted with claims that she was a freak.

Professional wrestling, boxing and martial arts contests have always attracted a keen following among women competitors, but plans in 1985 to stage a women's kickboxing match met with disapproval at a government level. The premier of New South Wales, Neville Wran, decreed that 'women punching and kicking each other is not acceptable to the community' and with the help of his sports minister Mike Cleary (an ex-rugby player!) made moves to outlaw the contest. In 1983 the Australian Ice Hockey Federation changed its constitution to prohibit women from playing the sport with men after Karen Sommerville played goalie for a team in the Sydney competition. The secretary claimed it was 'for the safety of someone like Karen . . . it has nothing to do with sexism or discrimination'.

Concerted pressure existed in Victoria for the re-formation of a Australian rules competition from the early 1960s, but it was not until 1981 that the Victorian Women's Football League was established and regular competition began. In 1986 football was included in the Aussie Sports programme which promoted equal opportunity in sport for all children under 12 years old, but drew criticism from the Queensland minister for education who claimed football (even for the under-12s) would 'downgrade womanhood'. Soccer for women began in Australia in the late 1960s and received its largest boost when it was introduced as a sport for schoolgirls in 1974. An estimated 60 000 women kicked off the 1978 season and by 1990, 20-year-old midfielder Julie Murray, veteran of four international tournaments, became the first professional player when she accepted a contract to play for the Fortuna club in Denmark. More acceptable than conventional football codes (for both women and men) is the sport of touch, originally called touch football, introduced to Australian women in 1976.

Hang gliding was introduced as a sport in Australia in the mid 1970s and by the 1980s about ten per cent of participants were women. Women parachutists make up a greater proportion of that sport with their 1000 members in 1986 being about a third of total numbers. The first representative women's team competed at the World Parachuting Championships in Czechoslovakia in 1982. Women's professional surfing received encouragement in the 1980s with the introduction of a separate women's world championship. On an individual level women surfers face harassment from male surfers as well as a smaller professional circuit and less prizemoney. Of the world's top ten women surfers five are Australian, including Pam Burridge the world champion, Pauline Menczer and Wendy Botha. Women broke into the male dominated world of surf lifesaving with the lifting of club bans across Australia in the 1980s. They went one step further and began competing in the range of endurance events including 'iron man' and triathlons. Maryanne Spiers became Australia's first woman professional lifeguard when employed by the Wollongong City Council, New South Wales, in 1980.

In 1973 the first all-women crew competed in the 18-footer yacht racing class. By the time Kay Cottee prepared for her round the world solo attempt by entering both the 1986 Two-Handed Trans-Tasman and Solo Trans-Tasman races, women's competitive sailing was more commonplace. In 1988 Cottee became the first woman to complete a solo, nonstop and unassisted voyage around the world. She covered more than 22 000 nautical miles during her 189 days at sea.

Speed attracted increasing numbers of women across Australia and in 1975, Formula Two driver Sue Ransom took out the Australian Women's Championship. Formerly a rallycross driver, Ransom was inspired by the visit to Australia in 1973 of Italian driver Lella Lombardi. In 1980 Alexandra Surplice entered the previously male dominated Hardie Ferodo 1000 at Bathurst, New South Wales, and in 1984 Margaret Halliday became the first woman in the world to win a national motor sport grand prix when she rode to victory in the 1000cc motor-cycle side-car Grand Prix at Bathurst.

But as compensation for their daring, skills and strength requirements Australian sportswomen developed a defensive attitude in the 1970s, unable to come to terms as individuals with society's pressures to conform to feminine roles. These attitudes gradually permeated all sports and women were constantly called upon to defend the juxtaposition of sport and femininity, and field constant innuendo regarding their sexuality. Racing driver Sue Ransom declared, 'Motor racing is a hard sport, but it's not a butch one. There's no reason why women should not compete, their reflexes are as good as men's . . . I've never had to sacrifice my femininity'.

Final of the 1987 Australian Netball Championship between NSW and Victoria. One in seven
Australian women play netball.
OVERSEAS INFORMATION BRANCH

Ransom removed her make-up before a race, 'If my mascara started running into my eyes when I was doing 160 km/h I could find myself in trouble', she patiently explained to the media.

A newspaper report in 1973 examined the problems of being a woman and a winner — the 'problem' being loss of femininity. Olympic swimmer Karen Moras, described as 'a girly sort of girl with blonde hair and penetrating blue eyes', was 'lucky to be able to stop doing muscle-building calisthenics when she was 12' the newspaper said. Regarding sprinter Raelene Boyle the paper claimed, 'unlike the women athletes who chop their hair short for extra speed, Raelene kept her hair long'. Penny Gillies, Australian hurdles champion, was also a normal woman:

every morning Penny gets up at 5.30 to cook breakfast for Les before he goes to work, and then gets ready for her teaching job. After school she goes home, does the shopping and housework, then when Les gets home they go jogging,

exercise that fortunately didn't build 'big bulky thighs'. In defending their right to play sport, and lacking a feminist analysis of their situation, some sportswomen were unconsciously trapped into emphasising conformity and femininity, the very things which were used by men to discourage women from playing sport.

Such attitudes spilled over even into the sports deemed appropriate for women. As competition got tougher and sportswomen needed to train harder, longer and with more emphasis on strength, so too did the pressure to conform to society's image of a real woman. Sportswomen did it tough — not only did they have to be world champions, gourmet chefs, selfless housewives and supermums they had to look like models in the process and conform to society's stereotypical feminine image at all times. The *Melbourne Herald* summed up Glynis Nunn's victory in the 1984 Olympic heptathlon:

Tears flowed like spring rain as the elfin Australian realised she had become her country's first track and field medallist for 16 years . . . there were women athletes at the Olympics who were distinguished by moustaches and physiques that would alarm Dean Lukin, and it is enough to say that Glynis Nunn was not one of them . . . Here was an athlete of undiminished femininity, who smiled warmly and spoke softly, who ran lightly and jumped and threw with grace, who triumphed with modesty and who accepted her hour of happiness in the time-honoured women's way. She cried that's why the world applauded.

Ironically since her victory Nunn has been in the forefront of moves to

Australian women's team sports have achieved an outstanding international record from foundations firmly established in the 1930s. Australia versus Germany, World Cup Hockey, Sydney 1990.
OVERSEAS INFORMATION BRANCH

The Australian women's basketball team scored a historic win over the Soviet Union in 1988.
NATIONAL SPORT INFORMATION CENTRE

In 1982 a women's volleyball national league was introduced providing players with a higher standard of regular competition. The Australian team training, 1985.

OVERSEAS INFORMATION BRANCH

encourage women to question the connections between femininity and sport through her Adelaide radio programme on 5DN.

When Evonne Goolagong defeated Margaret Court at Wimbledon in 1971 it was thought to be the triumph of grace over power. Unbeknown to the public Goolagong trained just as hard as Court, but her fluid, smooth 'natural' style of tennis didn't look like the hard work Court showed during a match. Goolagong put into words her own and the public's perception of her rival:

> *It hasn't been easy for Margaret Smith Court. She was no natural. She worked for her championships, drove herself through a training regimen that would make most male athletes faint away. She ran, did callisthenics and weight training, and practised . . . practised . . . practised . . .*

There are no apparent differences when compared to Goolagong's description of her own training:

> *To get ready for the overseas trips I ran for miles, sprinted, and jogged, spent time in the gym (Dupaine's Institute) doing callisthenics and medicine ball reflex-training . . . skipping rope — five hundred to a thousand skips at a time — and worked on my breathing. We'd go to the Edwards' beach home at Wamberal and run in the sand. That's work. . . [Edwards would] make sure I spent enough time on the court, hitting strokes over and over so that I could produce them automatically, and if I didn't, right back to the practice court we'd go.*

Although the country did not produce another Wimbledon champion (other than Goolagong-Cawley again in 1980) many women showed strong consistent play in winning Australian titles and grand slam doubles titles including Kerry Reid, Wendy Turnbull and Christine O'Neill. Women tennis players everywhere reaped the benefits of equal circuit prizemoney fought for by feminist tennis players like American Billie-Jean King in the 1970s.

In swimming and athletics women were also forced to train harder if they wished to remain competitive in world events. Many became professional sportswomen; gone were the amateur days and training schedules of Fanny Durack, replaced by the sheer hard work, constant dedication and single-mindedness of sportswomen like Lisa Martin, Debbie Flintoff-King and Lisa Curry. Athletics in particular witnessed a move towards greater endurance events. Recent research has proved beyond doubt that not only are women able to

Women's bowling clubs are flourishing in the harsher economic climate of the late twentieth century and have resisted takeover attempts by the male clubs who once spurned them. Canberra, 1987.
OVERSEAS INFORMATION BRANCH

Apprentice jockey Beverley Buckingham, the first woman to win an Australian jockey's premiership, 1982.
OVERSEAS INFORMATION BRANCH

In the 1980s efforts were made to involve more younger women in sports.
Little athletics championships, Melbourne, 1980.
OVERSEAS INFORMATION BRANCH

compete in more taxing sports, they are in fact physiologically better suited to them than males. The women's 10 kilometre walk will be finally introduced at the 1992 Olympics. Kerry Saxby, a walker from Ballina, New South Wales, holds the most number of world records by any athlete in Australia's history. Her success placed her walking style unfairly under great scrutiny as many overseas judges refused to believe her record-shattering times. She set the world's best times for 1500, 3000 and 5000 metres on the track and 3, 5, 10, 15 and 20 kilometres on the road as well as winning the gold medal at the 1990 Commonwealth Games for the 10 kilometre walk. Lisa Martin was the first Australian to ever win an Olympic marathon medal when she secured the silver at the 1988 Olympics. The marathon event was first introduced for women at the Olympics in 1984. Martin won the gold medal at the 1986 Commonwealth Games. At the 1990 Commonwealth Games she won the gold medal from co-Australian Tani Ruckle. Despite the inclusion of the marathon and 3000 metres event in the 1984 Olympics, followed by the 10 000 metres race in 1988, the competition has yet to see the 5000 metres.

The 1970s witnessed the rise and the decline of top level women's professional golf in Australia. Two professional tournaments were inaugurated for women golfers in 1974 — the Australian Women's Open and the Colgate sponsored Far East Women's Open. But the first only survived for five years before succumbing to disinterest from sponsors, followed by the cancellation of the Colgate tournament one year later. The fate of Australia's most successful, and most controversial, professional golfer was just as rocky. Balmain-born Jan Stephenson won the Australian Women's Open in 1977, five years after turning professional. Almost from the moment Stephenson stepped onto a golf course she caused controversy. As an 18-year-old amateur she was selected in Australia's 1970 Tasman Cup team to play New Zealand. She missed selection in another tournament the following year and responded by writing a magazine article strongly criticising the selectors. She also contravened the dress rules of women's golf by appearing in mini skirts. After turning professional in 1972 she won the US Rookie of the Year award in 1974. In 1982 she won the prestigious US PGA Ladies Championship and US Ladies Open Championship. But it was her posing for a series of soft-core porn calendars in the late 1970s and early 1980s which earned her the most criticism. A maturer Stephenson returned to top level golf after a car accident in 1987 had caused her to build up muscle during rehabilitation. Her increased strength ironically made her more successful on the golf circuit and she purposely set out to shed her pin-up image and be taken more seriously as a golfer. After the decline of the Australian circuit other golfers have been forced to pursue their careers elsewhere. Among the most successful are amateurs Lindy Goggin and Edwina Kennedy, and professionals Jane Lock,

Sandra McCaw, Nicole Lowein and Corinne Dibnah. Australian women's professional golf received a boost in the late 1980s by the staging of several lucrative tournaments both in Australia and Asia.

Women's team sports have enjoyed outstanding success in the last 20 years, but have suffered a corresponding inverse decline in publicity and media attention. Australian women's hockey, cricket, softball, netball, lacrosse and waterpolo teams have all been world champions. But in the competitive world of corporate sport, sponsorship and financial support have not been the automatic rewards for success.

The last two decades have seen the strengthening and expansion of all team sports in Australia. World tours or home series have been annual occurrences in almost all sports. The money needed to compete in such tournaments has been raised largely through personal contribution by team members and fund raising activities co-ordinated by individual associations. The investment paid dividends. Netball, a sport which one in seven Australian women play, has the largest following and for several years also had the woman with the highest profile in any team sport, Anne Sargeant who captained the team from 1983–1988. The Australian netball team won the world championships in 1963, 1971, 1975, 1979 and 1983. Netball was introduced as a sport to the Australian Institute of Sport (AIS), a situation also enjoyed by the hockey team but not the cricket team. When cricket was introduced in 1987 to the AIS Cricket Academy in Adelaide its 20 scholarships were restricted to males. The cricket team were also world champions winning the world cup (a competition first devised by women in 1973) in 1978, 1982 and 1988.

The hockey team gradually improved their international standing throughout this period and their victory at the Bicentennial Challenge in Perth in 1988 heralded a new stage of achievement. They successfully converted their hard work into a gold medal at the 1988 Seoul Olympics. With the staging of the 1990 World Cup in Sydney many thousands more women were attracted to the sport.

Australia's most outstanding achievement at international basketball (five-a-side) came with the women's team victory over the Soviet Union at the 1988 Olympics which put them through to the semi-finals. A national league competition had been inaugurated in Australia in the early 1980s giving players top line competition on a local level.

In 1982 women's volleyball also moved into a national competition. The national lacrosse team, a game played mostly in South Australia, won the 1986 World Cup held in Philadelphia. Another sport to miss out on AIS representation (and Olympic status) for women was waterpolo. Despite their inferior training facilities and constant struggle for financial support, the women won the 1986 World

Waterpolo Championships at Christchurch, New Zealand. All in all, an outstanding and enviable international record for Australian women's team sports.

Success has been no stranger to a host of other Australian sportswomen over the last 20 years. Sculler and former triathlete Adair Ferguson won a gold medal in the lightweight single sculls at the 1985 World Championships and the junior four-oar won the gold medal at the Junior World Championships in Hungary in 1989. Some other women's crews have never even been given the chance to compete overseas as controversy has constantly surrounded selection. The prejudices of the male-dominated Australian Rowing Council took over where the 'rowing is too strenuous for women brigade' left off. No Australian stepped into the giant squash shoes of the extraordinary Heather McKay, although in 1990 Australian women, headed by Danielle Drady, occupied five of the top ten squash rankings in the world. In 1990 Kirstie Marshall from Victoria became the first Australian woman to win an event at a World Cup skiing competition when she won the women's aerial event at Breckenridge, Colorado. In 1978 Colleen Bolton proved herself one of Australia's greatest cross-country skiers when she won the 32 kilometre Nordmarker Tour of Oslo, one of Europe's most prestigious events. Still on skis, although on the water, 15-year-old Megan Harrod of Wollongong, New South Wales, set a woman's speed record in 1979 on the Nerang River, Queensland, where she averaged 162.382 kilometres per hour over two runs. Other world champion water skiers include Tanya Williams and Deborah Pugh. In 1979 ice skater Robyn Burley won the World Ice Skating Championship at Jaca, Spain.

Australian women have moved into a wider variety of sports in the last 20 years and now participate in greater numbers in cycling, ten pin bowling, billiards, shooting, sailing, gymnastics, trampolining, sailboarding — the list could go on and on. Their path in all sports has not always been smooth but in the mid 1980s it was improved by the introduction of legislation giving some legal redress to their complaints of sexual discrimination in sport.

As a direct result of feminist efforts, the Commonwealth Sex Discrimination Act was passed in 1984, followed by several state Equal Opportunity Acts. The federal Act made it unlawful to discriminate against a person on the grounds of sex, marital status or pregnancy, or stereotyped views about those areas, but provided for exceptions for some types of single-sex sporting activity. Under this legislation damages of $7300 were awarded against the New South Wales Attorney-General and the Sydney City Council for cancelling the women's kickboxing competition in 1985. Sporting clubs were forced to open an option of full membership to women, a decision which has far reaching effects in bowling and golf clubs. Women had previously been restricted to associate membership and had access to the golf courses and bowling greens only during the week, times unsuitable for working women. In addition they had limited access to the facilities of clubs, often being restricted to certain areas and prohibited from playing billiards and snooker on the club's tables and they had no voting or decision making rights. The applications are not restricted to bowling and golf clubs as gymnasiums and squash courts have been found to discriminate against women seeking timeslots to play out of working hours. The drawback with most equal opportunity legislation, however, is that it is complaints-based. An individual must challenge the status quo, and is often reluctant to do so because of fear of reprisal or ignorance of their right to do so. Some clubs have charged women full membership without providing the extra benefits that go with that membership.

An ironic twist occurred in 1990 when the gentlemen of the male only Newport Bowling Club in Sydney invited women to join their club. Women had been excluded from the club for 26 years and in consequence had formed their own club in Newport. The men's belated invitation came not because of any altruistic notion, but because their club was in financial difficulty. The women's answer was simple — they declined the invitation. The men's president had claimed that it was 'just not economical to carry on with it as a men's club only. The ladies are going to find the same problems'. But the women's club was not facing similar financial difficulty because of the annual fund raising efforts of their members, a skill honed in women's sport from time immemorial.

One group who have provided the most vigorous opposition to women in sport are the gentlemen of the turf. After being rejected for a jockey's licence in the 1960s, Betty Lane became one of the first women to earn a living from racing as a trainer. In 1987 she had her hundredth winner at Randwick. Women jockeys mobilised in Australia after women in 16 countries including the United States, Canada and Ireland successfully fought to become jockeys in the early 1970s. The Australian Jockey Club (AJC) only permitted women to ride in all-women races at picnic meetings. At one meeting in 1974 Pam O'Neill had to overcome more than just the AJC and her co-jockeys, she had to deal with the trivialising press who wrote:

Attractive 28-year-old Brisbane jockette Pam O'Neill rode an immaculate race to win the $3000 Scarlet Novice Stakes, a feature race at Gosford yesterday. Mrs O'Neill . . . took the eye with her upswept silver-grey hairdo before the race. But she returned almost without a hair in place on the winner.

It wasn't until 19 May 1979 that Pam O'Neill became Australia's first woman to ride against men. To celebrate the day she rode three winners at a meeting in

Queensland. Earlier in 1979 the New Zealand jockey Linda Jones had won a race against men in Australia. Women have continued to enjoy outstanding success as jockeys simply because they have to be better than males to be given the chance in the first place. In 1981, 17-year-old Tasmanian Beverley Buckingham became the first woman to win an Australian jockey's premiership, and she did it as an apprentice.

It has been the area of schoolgirl sport that has attracted the recent interest of feminists. The playground is the origin of the most derogatory comment in sport, 'playing like a girl', and it has been here that efforts to involve more young women in physical activity have been directed. Throughout the mid 1980s a series of surveys revealed that schoolgirls were disadvantaged in sport classes. They lacked strong sporting role models as few sportswomen received sufficient media attention, they played sport under the constraints of femininity and they did not have equal access to the type and variety of sports. To compound this it was discovered that those schoolgirls who did not play sport were low achievers. As federal minister for education and youth affairs, Senator Susan Ryan launched a programme in 1984 to increase schoolgirls self-esteem through physical education in schools. She revealed that schoolgirls were discouraged from sport because of 'inaccurate and harmful myths' perpetrated by the general community, teachers and schools themselves. Schools of course were just a microcosm of society at large, but changes inaugurated in the playground had more chance of success. Efforts continued throughout the 1980s. In Tasmania a film entitled 'A Sporting Chance' was produced by the education department. In New South Wales a series of role-model days were held where schoolgirls could meet sportswomen. South Australia and the Northern Territory developed a 'Girls and Physical Activity' strategy. In Western Australia a Women in Sport Committee was established which produced a new coaching video, 'On Her Merit'.

The last five years have seen a blossoming of interest in the role of sport and physical activity in women's lives. A major initiative came with the establishment of the federal government working group on women in sport whose report in 1985 entitled *Women, Sport and the Media* proposed the establishment of the Women's Sport Promotion Unit attached to the Australian Sports Commission. The unit came into being in 1988 with Margaret Pewtress as chair and produced a national newsletter as well as a one-minute television community service announcement promoting the involvement of Australian women in sport. In 1990 it was renamed the Women and Sport Unit and relocated within the Australian Sports Commission itself to enable the unit to have a direct input into policy development. A series of conferences were held throughout Australia to highlight the state of women's sport and look towards the future. The largest of these, titled

'Levelling the Playing Field', was organised in 1991 by the Parliamentary Standing Committee on Legal and Constitutional Affairs investigating the status of women. In 1990 the federal minister for sport Ros Kelly (the first woman to hold that position) placed women's sport high on her agenda. She launched an initiative called the Sportswomen of Excellence Committee in an attempt to get more women off the sidelines and into sports. On the committee were athletes Jane Flemming and Debbie Flintoff-King, gymnast Monique Allen, netballer Anne Sargeant, skier Kirstie Marshall and basketball coach Jenny Cheeseman.

But government initiatives, legislation and press releases take a long time to filter through to the general community. The problems women face in sport are so entrenched and involve so many fundamental areas of life that positive change comes only slowly. In spite of this, sportswomen now have some basis and analysis which they can draw on to explain their discrimination even if they don't yet have the ability to solve it.

ENDNOTES

CHAPTER 1: COLONIAL PLAYERS, 1788-1900

The Parramatta sack race is from *Sydney Gazette*, 5 May 1810. For pedestrianism see *Hobart Town Gazette*, 25 October 1817. The Cow Pastures group is from J. Cumes, *Their Chastity Was Not Too Rigid*, Longman Cheshire, Melbourne 1979, p. 24. Baxter, Packer, Dixon, Eliza, and May are from Cumes, *Their Chastity*, p. 85, 96, 206, 212 and 247. For Denison see Maggie Weidenhofer, *Colonial Ladies*, Currey O'Neil, 1985, p. 42-3. See *Australian Etiquette or the Rules and Usages of the Best Society in the Australasian Colonies, Together With Their Sports, Pastimes, Games and Amusements*, People's Publishing Company Melbourne 1885, p. 563-74. For Aboriginal games see Constance Campbell Petrie, *Tom Petrie's Reminiscences of Early Queensland (Dating From 1837)*, Lloyd O'Neil, Melbourne 1975 (1904), p. 109-14. The advertisement is from Sydney Gazette, 24 January 1837, quoted in Cumes, *Their Chastity*, p 201.

For Peron see G. Dutton, *Sun, Sea, Surf and Sand, the Myth of the Beach*, OUP Melbourne, 1985, p. 9-10. The bombing quotation is from Petrie, *Reminiscences*, p. 111. For Aboriginal women and pearling see Susan Jane Hunt, *Spinifex and Hessian: Women's Lives in North-Western Australia 1860-1900*, University of WA Press, 1986, p. 102-3; J.S. Battye, The History of the North West of Australia, Perth 1915, p. 113. The Hobart bathing machine is from L. Robson, *A History of Tasmania*, Vol 1, OUP Melbourne 1983, p. 178. Bigge is from *Sydney Gazette*, 18 February 1834. The Adelaide and Glenelg baths are from J. Daly, Elysian Fields, Adelaide 1982, p. 73 and p. 75. For Newcastle see *Newcastle Herald*, 17 December 1884. For Deniliquin see G.L. Buxton, *The Riverina, 1861-1891*, MUP 1967, p. 96. Glenelg harrassment is from Daly, *Elysian Fields*, p. 76. For the Brighton flags see W. Bate, *A History of Brighton*, MUP 1962 (1983), p. 343.

For the Rockhampton Ladies Swimming Club see Lorna McDonald, *Rockhampton: A History of City and District*, UQP 1981, p. 115. The Newcastle tradeswomen's petition is from Newcastle Herald, 11 December 1894; the editorial is from 24 November 1898. For Albury see W.A. Bayley, *Border City. A History of Albury NSW*, Albury City Council 1976, p. 116. The swimming lesson is from *Illustrated Sydney News*, 3 March 1876. For Dick and Moon see *Argus*, 21 July 1902, *Australasian*, 26 July 1902; testimonial bracelet is from *Australasian Sketcher*, 11 May 1878. The Queen's Birthday tournament is from *Illustrated Sydney News*, 11 June 1881. For Cavill see *Australasian Sketcher*, 28 January 1882, and the *Bulletin*, 5 March 1881. For Bastard see Daly, *Elysian Fields*, p. 79. For Weigel see Marion Fletcher, *Costume in Australia 1788-1901*, OUP Melbourne, 1984, p. 163. The bondage quotation is from the *Illustrated Sydney News*, 29 October 1881. For Franklin see Robson, *History of Tasmania*, p. 359. For rowing see *Australian Etiquette*, p. 539. For rowing in Perth and Adelaide see M. Cannon, *The Long Last Summer*, Nelson 1985, p. 116. Boldt is from *Illustrated Australian News*, 19 January 1880. Elizabeth Macquarie is from Cumes, *Their Chastity*, p. 156-7. For fishing see *Illustrated Sydney News*, 9 December 1876, 12 June 1880.

The Sydney Hunt Hurdle Races are from Cumes, *Their Chastity*, p. 134. Riding habits are from Fletcher, Costume, p. 103-4. For Trollope see A. Trollope, *Australia and New Zealand*, Vol 3, Leipzig

1873, p. 136, 138–9. For kangarooing see *Australian Etiquette*, p. 465–9. For coursing see K. Dunstan, *Sports*, Sun Books Melbourne, 1973 (1981) p. 270; and *Australasian Sketcher*, 30 September 1876. Ambrose is from *Australasian Sketcher*, 21 September 1886. For Spencer see Weidenhofer, *Colonial Ladies*, p. 43–4. For Dixon see R. T. Wyatt, *The History of Goulburn*, Goulburn 1941, p. 439. For Hume quotation see Nancy Bonnin (ed), *Katie Hume on the Darling Downs, Letters of a Colonial Lady 1866–1871*, Darling Downs Institute Press 1985, p. 69.

Bowen and Rippon Lea archers are from *Illustrated Australian News*, 1 November 1895. For Daly see Daly, *Elysian Fields*, p. 132. For Queensland Marsupials Act see *Australasian Sketcher*, 21 September 1886. For Bowen opening rifle range see *Australasian Sketcher*, 31 August 1878. For ringoal see *Illustrated Sydney News*, 28 November 1889.

Jaques croquet advertisement is from *Illustrated Sydney News*, 13 May 1869. For Kapunda club see Cannon, *Long Last Summer*, p. 125. For Launceston see *Illustrated Sydney News*, 10 July 1871; for Brisbane see R. Lawson, *Brisbane in the 1890s*, UQP 1973, p. 210; for Ballarat see W. Bate, *Lucky City*, MUP 1978, p. 246. Lawn tennis is from *Australian Etiquette*, p. 535. Intercolonial matches are reported in *Illustrated Sydney News*, 6 June 1885, 22 November 1890, 6 December 1890, 25 October 1890. Tennis on board ship is from *Illustrated Australian News*, 1 October 1890 and at Quarantine Ground from *Australasian Sketcher*, 28 January 1882. The Clark letter is from *Illustrated Sydney News*, 8 February 1890. For football see C.T. Stannage (ed), *A New History of Western Australia*, UWA Press 1981, p. 669. For billiards see H. Alcock, *The Alcock Book of Billiards*, Melbourne 1901 (5th ed), p. 22–4. See NSW 'Act to Regulate the Keeping of Billiard Tables and Bagatelle Boards', Sydney 1881.

For cricket at Sofala and Bendigo see Betty Butcher, *The Sport of Grace*, Sports Federation of Victoria, Melbourne 1984. For Steiglitz game see *Australasian Sketcher*, 13 June 1874. For Deane see *Illustrated Sydney News*, 15 May 1886 and Butcher, *Sport of Grace*, p. 7. For Warrnambool cricket see Butcher, *Sport of Grace*, p.13–16; for Rockhampton see McDonald, *Rockhampton*, p. 552. For Australia v England match see *Illustrated Australian News*, 1 April 1895 and Butcher, *Sport of Grace*, p. 9-12. Rockley is from E. Lea-Scarlett, *Gundaroo*, Canberra 1972, p. 135–6 and SMH, 12 September 1935.

Roller skating in Newcastle is from *Newcastle Herald*, 5 July 1877. For the Elite Skating Ring see *Illustrated Sydney News*, 2 May 1889. For Bowen see *Australasian Sketcher*, 8 August 1874. For gymnastics and Dick and Moon see Roslyn Otzen, 'Recovering the Past for the Present: The History of Victorian Calisthenics', *Lilith*, No 5, Spring 1988. For massed displays see *Australasian Sketcher*, 23 July 1881, 19 November 1884. For Tasmania see 'Marie Bjelke Petersen' in Heather Radi (ed), *200 Australian Women*, Women's Redress Press, Sydney 1988, p. 97-9. For Foster see *Illustrated Sydney News*, 31 October 1889.

For the Argus picnic see *Australasian Sketcher*, 25 March 1882. For Queens Birthday and shipboard races see *Illustrated Sydney News*, 15 June 1878 and *Australasian Sketcher*, 26 August 1882. The go as you please contest is from the *Bulletin*, 8 October 1881. Azella is from Wyatt, *Goulburn*, p. 449. For Bendigo prize fight see *Australasian Sketcher*, 18 April 1874. For Castlemaine see *Australasian Sketcher*, 11 July 1874. For kickboxing see *National Times*, 16–22 August 1985, p. 50.

Golf at Moore Park is from *Australian Etiquette*, p. 531. For history of golf see J. Pollard, *Australian Golf: The Game and the Players*, Angus & Robertson, Sydney 1990, and *Woman Golfer*, No 1, 1990, p. 52–3. For bicycle performer Franzina see D. Whitelock, *Adelaide 1836–1976*, UQP 1977, p. 242. For tricycle race see Dunstan, *Sports*, p. 209. The Auburn race is from *Australian Encyclopedia*, Vol 3, p. 161. For the price of bicycles see J. Fitzpatrick, *The Bicycle and the Bush*, OUP Melbourne 1980, p. 40–1. For Brassey and Lamington see Dunstan, *Sports*, p. 209–10. Maddock is from *Australian Encyclopedia*, vol 3, p. 901.

McDonald is from Dunstan, *Sports*, p. 210. For the Van Tassells see *Newcastle Herald*, 10 February 1890, 17 February 1890 and Bate, *Lucky City*, p. 247–8.

The Gawler race is from Daly, *Elysian Fields*, p. 82. The tricycle race is quoted in Dunstan, *Sports*, p. 209. Serpolette is from J. Fitzpatrick, 'Australian "Cyclistes" in the Victorian Era', *Hemisphere*, Jan-Feb 1980, p. 16. The 1874 cricket match is from *Australasian Sketcher*, 16 May 1874. For satire see the *Bulletin*, 28 June 1884 and *Melbourne Punch*, 30 October 1884. The golf championship is quoted in Pollard, *Australian Golf*, p. 26. For tennis see *SMH*, 14 July 1936. For gymnastics see *Illustrated Sydney News*, 31 October 1889.

CHAPTER 2: LESSONS IN SPORT

The following sources were used to compile this chapter: *The Melbourne Church of England Girls' Grammar School (Merton Hall) Jubilee History*, 1953; Evelyn McCloughan, 'A History of the Development of Physical Education in the Public School System of NSW, 1788-1954', MA Thesis, Ohio State University 1956; Lilith Norman, *The Brown and the Yellow: Sydney Girls' High School 1883–1983*, Oxford University Press, Melbourne 1983; Coral Chambers, *Lessons for Ladies: A Social History of Girls' Education in Australasia 1870–1900*, Hale & Iremonger, Sydney 1986; Sheena Coupe and R. Coupe, *Walk in the Light: MLC School Burwood, a Centenary History*, MLC School Burwood, Burwood 1986; Jean Lang, *A Living Tradition: A History of Methodist Ladies' College Claremont*, Western Australia, Methodist Ladies' College Old Girls' Association, Perth 1980; Alanna Nobbs, *Kambala. The First Hundred Years 1887–1987*, Kambala Centenary History Committee, 1987; Leila Barlow, *Living Stones: Convent of the Sacred Heart, Rose Bay 1882–1982*, Kincoppal-Rose Bay School, Sydney 1982; Roslyn Otzen 'Recovering the Past for the Present: the History of Victorian Calisthenics', *Lilith*, No 5, Spring 1988; Ailsa G. Thomson Zainu'ddin, *They Dreamt of a School: A Centenary History of Methodist Ladies' College Kew 1882–1982*, Hyland House, Melbourne 1982; Helen Jones, *Nothing Seemed Impossible, Women's Education and Social Change in South Australia 1875–1915*, University of Queensland Press, St Lucia 1985; R. Crawford, 'English Influence on Victorian Physical Education', *Proceedings of the VII Commonwealth & International Conference on Sport etc*, Vol 9; Barbara W. Milne & Doris W. McKellar, *Cromarty School for Girls 1897–1923*, Melbourne 1972; Mollie Eichholzer, *Our Girls: Maitland Girls' High School 1884–1984*, Maitland 1985; Kathleen Fitzpatrick, *Solid Bluestone Foundations and Other Memories of a Melbourne Girlhood 1908–1928*, Macmillan, Melbourne 1983. Noeline Kyle, *Her Natural Destiny: The Education of Women in New South Wales*, NSW University Press, Kensington 1986; *The Story of Ascham School*, Council of Governors, Sydney 1952; R. Crawford, 'Sport for Young Ladies', *Sporting Traditions*, Vol 1, No 1, November 1984.

The 1901 speech day quotation is from *Merton Hall Jubilee History*, p. 68–9. The NSW Inspector of Schools is quoted in McCloughan, 'A History', p. 25. The sergeant is from Norman, *The Brown and the Yellow*, p. 25. Dick's advertisement is quoted in Otzen 'Recovering the Past', p. 100. McMillan is from Zainu'ddin, *They Dreamt of a School*, p 131. For Wearne see Coupe, *Walk in the Light*, p. 22. The MLC Adelaide v MLC Kew tennis match is from Zainu'ddin, *They Dreamt of a School*, p. 142. For rowing at SCEGGS Redlands see *SMH*, 5 April 1990, p. 1. The Argus hockey letters are from 27 & 28 May 1910. For shinty and hockey see *SMH*, 26 April 1934, 27 September 1934, 28 April 1936, 2 November 1937, and Age, 14 May 1953. Morris is from *Merton Hall Jubilee History*, p. 73. Sydney Girls' High playing grounds are from Norman, *The Brown and the Yellow*, p. 25. Heuston is quoted in Eichholzer, *Our Girls*, p. 20. Quotes comparing Catholic and Protestant schools are from Fitzpatrick, *Solid Bluestone Foundations*, p, 141, 143—4. The high jump record and costume is from *Merton Hall Jubilee History*, p. 107, 113.

CHAPTER 3: UNIVERSITY WOMEN GET THE BLUES

The Adelaide Observer, 1 August 1896 is quoted in Alison Mackinnon, *The New Women: Adelaide's Early Women Graduate*s, Wakefield Press, Adelaide 1986, p. 15. Macdonald is quoted in W. Vere Hole and Anne H. Treweeke, *The History of the Women's College Within the University of Sydney*, Sydney 1953, p. 77; the Vaka is from p. 96. Adelaide law students boat club is quoted in Mackinnon, *The New Women*, p. 136. For English universities as the nurseries of rowing see *SMH*, 29 March 1938. Mayo and Cilento are from Mackinnon, *The New Women*, p. 61 & 84. Street is from Jessie Street, *Truth or Repose*, Australasian Book Society, Sydney 1966, p. 23 and Sonja Lilienthal and Ursula Bygott, 'Sports, School and University', in Heather Radi (ed), *Jessie Street Documents and Essays*, Women's Redress Press Inc, Marrickville, 1990, p. 45–50. For Newton tarts and establishment of sports union see Street, *Truth or Repose*, p. 27–8. The Adelaide University hockey costume is from *Woman's Budget*, 29 March 1933. For Bage see *Australian Dictionary of Biography (ADB)*, vol 7, p. 131–2. For Buchanan see *ADB*, vol 7, p. 471–2. Cilento is quoted in Mackinnon, *The New Women*, p. 131. For Melbourne University see Farley Kelly, *Degrees of Liberation: A Short History of Women in the University of Melbourne*, University of Melbourne 1985, p. 66. For Dickinson see Hole and Treweeke, *The History*, p. 98. For Proud see Mackinnon, *The New Women*, p. 127. For Stone see Kelly, *Degrees of Liberation*, p. 46. For Street and Sydney University see Street, *Truth or Repose*, and Lilienthal and Bygott, 'Sports, School and University'. For Peden see *ADB*, vol 11, p. 192–3. The University of Melbourne quotation is from Kelly, *Degrees of Liberation*, p. 84. For Hattersley see *SMH*, 14 December 1933. On university sport in general see also Kathleen E. McCrone, *Sport and the Physical Emancipation of English Women 1870–1914*, Routledge, London 1988.

CHAPTER 4: A SPORTS ASSOCIATION OF ONE'S OWN, 1901–1939

The Mulgrave Rifle Club is from Susan Priestley, *Cattlemen to Commuters: A History of the Mulgrave District — Now the City of Waverley 1839–1961*, John Ferguson, Sydney 1979, p. 130. The estimate of over one million amateur sportswomen is taken from articles by Ruth Preddey in *Australian Women's Weekly (AWW)*, 17 February 1934, and April 1934.

For cricket see Betty Butcher, *The Sport of Grace: Women's Cricket in Victoria, the Beginning*, Melbourne 1984; Rachel Heyhoe Flint and Netta Rheinberg, *Fair Play: The Story of Women's Cricket*, London 1976. For hockey see Lena Hodges, *NSW Women's Hockey 1908–1983*, NSW Women's Hockey Association, Sydney 1984; 'Winifred West' in Heather Radi (ed), *200 Australian Women*, Women's Redress Press, Sydney 1988, p. 129–31; *SMH*, 27 September 1934, 28 April 1936; *Age*, 14 May 1953. For Bryant see *SMH*, 8 October 1930. For Pollard and McRae see *SMH*, 24 April 1939. For overseas tours in cricket and hockey see Mary-Lou Johnston and Marion K. Stell, *A Guide to the Australian Women's Cricket Collection 1934–1937*, National Museum of Australia, 1990; *SMH*, 4 July 1935, 3 November 1936, 13 September 1938, 30 August 1939.

For basketball see *People*, 11 February 1985, *National Times*, 9–15 December 1983. For night basketball see *SMH*, 11 January 1934. For vigoro see 'Latest Amended Laws, Definitions and Rulings of Vigoro' and 'History of Vigoro', National Library of Australia; and oral history interview with Ruby Monaghan, Johnston and Stell, *Australian Women's Cricket Collection*, National Museum of Australia. For baseball and lacrosse see *SMH* 18, 19 and 26 April, 10 and 31 May 1934.

For Kellermann and football see G. Lester, *Australian Rugby League*, 1988, p. 114. For Messenger see *SMH*, 20 October 1930. For Sydney competition see *Adelaide Advertise*r, 11 June 1921. For rowing controversy see *The Sportswoman*, 15 March 1937, p. 38. 'Strong but Dainty' is from *AWW*, 25 April 1936. For 1939 cancellation of rowing see *SMH*, 5 August 1939. For Gwendolen Game and Amateur Sports Councils see *AWW*, 2 December 1933. For 1934 sports see *West Australian*, 2 & 19 November 1934, *SMH*, 1 March 1934. For Maroubra and other playing areas see *SMH*, 27 October 1928, 20 September 1929, 8 June 1933, 17 & 24 May 1934, 18 August 1936 and 14 June 1938. For Annandale see oral history interview with Amy Hudson, Johnston and Stell, *Australian Women's Cricket Collection 1934–1937*, National Museum of Australia, 1990.

For golf see Pollard, *Australian Golf*. For Didrikson see *Argus*, 6 & 7 June 1939 and *Home*, 1 July 1939, p. 31. For NZ tennis visits see *SMH*, 24 October 1935. For withholding touring sanction see *Argus*, 27 February 1937. Nell Hopman is from *Sydney Sun*, 11 January 1968, *Age*, 6 January 1965, *Australian*, 11 January 1968, 'Nell Hopman' in Marilyn Lake and Farley Kelly (eds), *Double Time: Women in Victoria — 150 Years*, Penguin 1985. For Molesworth see *SMH*, 20 February 1939. Swimming is from *SMH*, 23 September 1954. For Kellermann see *People*, 23 May 1951. For Olympic swimming see R. & M. Howell, *Aussie Gold*, Brisbane 1988. For athletics see *Women's Athletics in Australia: Official History of the Australian Women's Amateur Athletic Union*. Kennedy is from 1938 Oral History Project interview, National Library of Australia.

The illogical shooting ban is from *AWW*, 18 August 1934. For the 1938 ban see *SMH*, 17 October 1938. Newcastle Life Saving is from *Newcastle Herald*, 18 January 1908. The South Australian clubs are from *Adelaide Advertiser*, 18 November 1932. For the two Brightons see *AWW*, 11 November 1933. Price's cycling record is from *Adelaide Advertiser*, 27 June 1932. For Barbour and Samuels see *Adelaide Advertiser*, 12 November 1932, *SMH*, 26 May 1934. For Thorpe see *Adelaide Advertiser*, 5 September 1932. For Unthank see *Argus*, 27, 28 & 29 November 1939. Squash is from *AWW*, 19 May 1934, and *SMH*, 19 May 1936. Croquet is from *AWW*, 2 February 1935. Polo is from *Adelaide Advertiser*, 17 December 1932, and *SMH*, 22 March 1934. The October 1938 comment is from *SMH*.

Hinder is from Heather Radi (ed), *200 Australian Women*, Women's Redress Press, Sydney 1988, p. 184-5 and Frances Wheelhouse, *Eleanor Mary Hinder*, Wentworth Books, Sydney 1978. For the City Girls' Sports Association see the *Home*, 1 June 1926, p. 38. Information on the Canberra YWCA is from YWCA scrapbooks held by YWCA Canberra office. The Adelaide YWCA is from *Adelaide Advertiser*, 15 July 1932. The rower's profiles are from *AWW*, 25 April 1936. The cricketer's profiles are from *1937 Official Programme*, England Women's Cricket Association. See *Principal Women of the Empire: Australia and New Zealand*, Vol 1, London, The Mitre Press, 1940. Hiking is from *SMH*, 1 August 1932. For YWCA camps see *SMH*, 29 March 1934. For *Sydney Morning Herald* editorial see 23 June 1927. For *Everylady's Journal* see 1 April 1929.

Chapter 5: The Cult of the Physical

The notion of physical culture as empowering for women is from a paper given by Roslyn Otzen at the Feminist History Conference at the University of Melbourne in 1988 later published as 'Recovering the Past for the Present: The History of Victorian Calisthenics', *Lilith*, No. 5, Spring 1988. Numerous physical culture advertisements appeared in the issues of the *Home* 1920-1921. For Edwards see Eileen Edwards, *Modern Physical Culture for Women and Girls*, Lothian Book Company, Melbourne 1916; quotations are from p. 1, 2, 7, 64, 80 and 82. The demonstration at the Conservatorium is from *SMH*, 13 June 1927. The Bjelke-Petersen demonstration is from *SMH*, 30 October 1935. For the ignited clubs see Otzen, 'Recovering the Past', p. 110. For Gore see Jacqueline Gore, *Good Looks and Long Life: A Guide to*

Beauty and Health in Australasia, Vol III, Melbourne 1913. For Kellermann see *People*, 23 May 1951.

The Women's League of Health is from *SMH*, 12 & 19 December 1935. For Dupain see George Dupain, *Diet and Physical Fitness*, Briton Publications, Sydney 1934, p. 8. For National Fitness see *SMH*, 1 July 1939, 11 June 1942, 18 January 1943. The politician at Bendigo is from *Argus*, 1 November 1937. For exercising with a broomstick and fencing see *Pix*, 11 March 1939. Information on Clarice Kennedy is from the 1938 Oral History Project Interview, National Library of Australia. The Swords club advertisement is from *SMH*, 12 December 1935. For Duras see *Argus*, 25 March 1937. For Le Maistre see the *Home*, 2 December 1940 and *SMH*, 1 April 1941. Beattie is from *Pix*, 10 August 1940. For sport in government schools see *SMH*, 22 April 1939. Gell is from *SMH*, 11 October 1951, 25 November 1954. The 1962 Conference is the *3rd British Empire and Commonwealth Conference on Physical Education*, WA 1962.

CHAPTER 6: KHAKI SPORTSWOMEN, 1939-1945

For 'Our Sportswomen are Ready' see *SMH*, 18 September 1939. Money raised by golfers is from *SMH*, 31 July 1943; by bowlers, *SMH*, 10 June 1944, 15 May 1945, 8 June 1945, 24 August 1944; by cricketers, *Argus*, 25 February 1941; by Amateur Sports Council, *SMH*, 25 February 1943. For the WAAAFs see Patsy Adam-Smith, *Australian Women at War*, Melbourne 1984, p. 234. Carter is from Clare Stevenson and Honor Darling (eds), *The WAAAF Book*, Hale & Iremonger, 1984. Kennedy is from 1938 Oral History Project Interview, National Library of Australia. Clements is from Oral History Interview, Mary-Lou Johnston and Marion K. Stell, *Australian Women's Cricket Collections 1934–1937*, National Museum of Australia, 1990. WAAAF sports carnival is from *Newcastle Herald*, 22 March 1943 and *SMH*, 13 April 1945. For Gordon see *SMH*, 1 March 1943 and 25 April 1944.

For factory and munition workers see *Pix*, 5 July 1941 and 10 March 1945. For rationalised exercises see *Pix*, 30 January 1943. For the cavalry corps see *Pix*, 14 December 1940. For cyclists see *Pix*, 14 February 1942. Target shooters are from *Pix*, 11 January 1941. Training on Water Board roof is from *SMH*, 3 June 1941. For American nurses see the *Home*, 1 September 1942. For softball see *Pix*, 30 September 1944. For polocrosse see *AWW*, 20 July 1946. For life saving see *Argus*, 4 October 1940 and 4 January 1944. For Fowler see Sue Hardisty, *Thanks Girls & Goodbye*, Viking O'Neil, Melbourne 1991. For sportswomen see: Brewer, *Pix*, 15 March 1941; McQuade, *Pix*, 23 December 1944; Talbot, *Pix*, 16 August 1941; McGibbon, *Pix*, 7 March 1942 and 27 September 1947; Cavill, *Pix*, 18 January 1941; Williams, *Pix*, 29 March 1941 Harney, *Pix*, 20 December 1941; Walsh, *Pix*, 15 June 1940. For Hawkins see *SMH*, 2 & 13 February 1942.

CHAPTER 7: GOLDEN WOMEN AT THE OLYMPIC, EMPIRE AND COMMONWEALTH GAMES, 1912–1990

Durack's race from *The Referee* quoted in R. & M. Howell, *Aussie Gold: The Story of Australia at the Olympics*, Brooks Waterloo, Brisbane 1988, p. 54. For Durack see *Aussie Gold*, p. 52–6, Australian, 27 March 1990, Heather Radi (ed), *200 Australian Women*, Women's Redress Press, Sydney 1988, p. 168–9, *AWW*, 3 November 1982. For Wylie see *SMH*, 11 July 1984, 13 May 1975, 20 February 1973, 14 May 1975, *Australian*, 28 June 1983, *Melbourne Herald*, 28 February 1973, *Daily Telegraph*, 15 May 1975. For 1928 Games see *SMH*, 9 August 1928, 2 November 1928. For 1930 Games see *SMH*, 21 August 1930. 1932: For Dennis see *West Australian*, 3 July 1981, *Sydney Sun*, 6 June 1984, *Aussie Gold*, p. 95–7; for Bult see *Argus*, 17 May 1949. Wearne report is quoted in *Aussie Gold*, p. 94. Italian doctors are from *SMH*, 31

January 1931. The Count is from *SMH*, 11 October 1932. 1934: For this and other Empire and Commonwealth Games see J. Blanch and P. Jones, *Australia's Complete History at the Commonwealth Games*, John Blanch Publishing, Sydney 1982. For selection see *SMH*, 6 January 1934, *AWW*, 17 February 1934. Dennis is from *SMH*, 29 March 1934. 1936: Selection is from *AWW*, 25 April 1936. For Carter see *Argus*, 30 July 1936. For the move to debar women see *SMH*, 17 August 1937, 13 April 1937. Nurmi is quoted in *Argus*, 10 December 1936. 1938: Doubt on participation is from *SMH*, 9 November 1935. For Norman see Radi (ed), *200 Australian Women*, p. 226–7, *Melbourne Herald*, 14 November 1974, 2 September 1983, *West Australian*, 10 June 1983, *SMH*, 15 February 1938. For Norton see *SMH*, 11 January 1938. For Dovey see *SMH*, 2 February 1937.

1948: For change to selection procedure see *SMH*, 17 April 1939, 2 February 1948, *AWW*, 28 February 1948. For Strickland see *Argus*, 6 March 1948, *SMH*, 6 March 1948. For Canty and McKinnon see *SMH*, 13 March 1948, *AWW*, 24 July 1948.

1950: For Jackson and Blankers-Koen see *AWW*, 25 February 1950. For Davis see *SMH*, 24 November 1949. 1952: For Jackson see *Aussie Gold*, p. 121–5; *Australian*, 18 July 1990, *Canberra Times*, 11 June 1990, *Woman's Day*, 25 March 1985, *SMH*, 24 July 1952, *Sunday Territorian*, 3 February 1985, *Sunday Telegraph*, 16 March 1980, *Daily Mirror*, 5 August 1977. For Strickland see *Aussie Gold*, p. 129–34. 1954: For *Australian Women's Weekly* fund see 19 May 1954, p. 29. Year round fitness is from *Sunday Herald*, 9 August 1953. 1956: For Fraser see Dawn Fraser, *Gold Medal Girl: The Confessions of an Olympic Champion*, Lansdowne Press 1965; the quotation on swimming officials is from p. 101 and the final from p. 73. For Cuthbert see Betty Cuthbert, *Golden Girl*, Pelham Books, London 1966; the quotations are from p. 55 and 58–9. The C.E.W. Bean letter is from *SMH*, 4 December 1956.

1960: For 'full Olympics' see *SMH*, 31 March 1958. For Fraser and Crapp see 'The two grand old ladies of swimming', *AWW*, 9 March 1960. 1962: For Strickland see *AWW*, 14 March 1962; for Norman see *AWW*, 24 October 1962. 1964: For Fraser as granny see Fraser, *Gold Medal Girl*, p. 109; for Tokyo controversy see Fraser, *Gold Medal Girl*, p. 173-86, *Daily Telegraph*, 23 January 1988, the *Bulletin*, 24 October 1964. For Cuthbert see Cuthbert, *Golden Girl*, p. 130–45. 1968: For Caird see *Aussie Gold*, p. 253–5, *Daily Mirror*, 25 March 1985, 12 March 1976, 26 July 1972, *People*, 7 December 1982. For McClements see *Aussie Gold*, p. 259-61, *Walkabout*, December 1969, p. 48. For Boyle see Raelene Boyle, *Rage Raelene, Run*, Caribou Publications, Melbourne 1983, p. 32.

1970: For Moras see *Sydney Sun*, 20 July 1970, *Canberra Times*, 9 May 1973, *Daily Mirror*, 29 July 1985. 1972: For Gould see *Aussie Gold*, p. 275–7, *Australasian Post*, 23 January 1986, *Daily Mirror*, 3 June 1985, *SMH*, 1 April 1985, *Sunday Telegraph*, 25 March 1984, *Daily Telegraph*, 24 November 1982, *Australian*, 14 June 1981. For Neall see *Aussie Gold*, p. 280–2. For Whitfield see *Aussie Gold* , p. 283–5. For Boyle see her *Rage*, p. 84–101. 1974: For Robertson see *SMH*, 17 January 1975. For Turrall see *Daily Mirror*, 3 December 1976, *Northern Territory News*, 28 June 1986, *Adelaide Advertiser*, 13 July 1982. 1976: For scholarships see *Newcastle Herald*, 29 June 1977. 1978: For Ford see *Woman's Day*, 11 June 1984, 25 July 1989, *SMH*, 30 January 1978, 20 February 1981, 4 May 1984, *Daily Telegraph*, 25 October 1979. For Wickham see *Brisbane Courier Mail*, 18 August 1990, *Canberra Times*, 29 August 1987, *Australian*, 22 December 1987, *AWW*, 24 November 1982, *Brisbane Sunday Mail*, 28 November 1982.

1980: For Boyle and Moscow see Boyle, *Rage*, p. 176–83. For Wickham and Moscow see *Bulletin*, 18 August 1987. For Ford see *Aussie Gold*, p. 307–10. 1982: For Boyle and Wickham see *AWW*, 14 October 1981, 16 June 1982. For Boyle see *Age*, 10 March 1990, *Melbourne Herald*, 17 June 1986, *Daily Mirror*, 11 April 1983, *Australian*, 13 November 1977. For Rivers see *Australasian Post*, 17 June 1982. 1984: For Nunn see *Aussie Gold*, p. 336–40. 1986: Information from A. Tunstall, *Australia at the Commonwealth Games 1911–1986*, 10th ed, Commonwealth Games Association, 1987. 1988: See 'Seoul Sisters', *Portfolio*,

September 1988. For rowing controversy see *Age*, 15 April 1988, *SMH*, 15 April 1988, 31 May 1988. For the decision not to allocate a women's crew coach see 'Minutes of the Mid-Year Meeting of the Australian Rowing Council Held on Saturday 21 November 1987', p. 13. For Martin see *Runner's World*, March 1990. 1990: See *Age*, 9 February 1990, 11 February 1990. For Lewis see *Australian Magazine*, 3–4 March 1990.

Chapter 8: Outdoors in the Outback

The Married Ladies Race is from Patsy Adam-Smith, *Hear the Train Blow*, Nelson Melbourne 1987, p. 16; Shepparton in the 1920s is from p. 38. Wallace's ponies are from Judith Wallace, *Memories of a Country Childhood*, UQP, 1977, p. 52 and her tomboy games from p. 93. Bullock riding at Adelong is from *SMH*, 10 June 1931. For rodeo cowgirls see advertisement in the *Home*, 1 March 1939, p. 86. For Skuthorpe see *Pix*, 12 December 1942. For New England rough riders see Wallace, *Memories*, p. 94. For Kitty Gill see *SMH*, 30 October 1951. For Bossley Park see *Daily Mirror*, 9 July 1982. For real horsewomen see Adam-Smith, *Hear the Train Blow*, p. 38.

For riding schools see 'Riding as a Sport and as a Profession', *SMH*, 20 June 1935. For fair riders see *SMH*, 22 September 1936. For world record side saddle jumping see *AWW*, 29 July 1981. Stead is from *SMH*, 7 January 1955. Macintyre is from *AWW*, 10 June 1964. *Gentlemen of the Australian Turf* is by David Hickie, Angus & Robertson, 1986. Murrell is from *Everylady's Journal*, 1 April 1929, p. 296-7. Bill Smith is from Heather Radi (ed), *200 Australian Women*, Women's Redress Press, 1988, p. 154.

Sydney's racing women are from *SMH*, 28 September 1937. Their 1935 success is from *SMH*, 26 September 1935; 1953 success, *SMH*, 1 October 1953; and 1950 success, *SMH*, 5 November 1950. For O'Mara see *SMH*, 16 August 1933, *Sun Herald*, 16 July 1961. For Leichney see *Brisbane Courier Mail*, 3 January 1935. For Forster see *Australian*, 19–20 July 1986.

For homestead tennis see Adam-Smith, *Hear the Train Blow*, p. 86. For Court see Margaret Smith, *The Margaret Smith Story*, Stanley Paul, London. For Goolagong see Evonne Cawley, *Evonne*, Hart-Davis, London 1975, p. 39 and 115. For Waaia see Adam-Smith, *Hear the Train Blow*, p. 30. Cricket at Hall is from L. Smith, *Memories of Hall*, Canberra 1975. For Peden see *AWW*, 24 June 1933. Thornton is from *Newcastle Herald*, 24 October 1931. Croquet country week is from *AWW*, 26 May 1934. For Ebert see *AWW*, 29 July 1933. For swimming at Bassendean see Jennie Carter, *Bassendean: A Social History 1829–1979*, Perth 1986, p. 201. Fishing at Yass is from *AWW*, 9 December 1933. For Street see Jessie Street, *Truth or Repose*, Australasian Book Society, Sydney 1966, p. 16. The Goulburn race is from R.Wyatt, *The History of Goulburn*, Goulburn 1941, p. 447. The rural survey is from Kerry James (ed), *Women in Rural Australia*, UQP 1989, p. 78–9. *The Rural Women's Guide* is from *Active*, Autumn 1990, p. 3.

Chapter 9: Sportswear

For clothes in the nineteenth century see Marion Fletcher, *Costume in Australia 1788–1901*, Oxford University Press, Melbourne 1984 and C. Flower, *Duck and Cabbage Tree: A Pictorial History of Clothes in Australia 1788–1914*, Angus & Roberston, Sydney 1968.

For Miller's swimming costume see Connie Miller, *After Summer Merrily*, Fremantle Arts Centre Press, 1980, p. 141. For skill and accomplishment see *SMH*, 25 July 1935. The old timers' hockey match is from *SMH*, 3 May 1934. Hockey uniform measuring is from *AWW*, 1 September 1934. Information on pioneer cricketers is from a conversation with Ann Mitchell, President Australian Women's Cricket Council, 1990. The nurses are from *Melbourne Punch*, 23 December 1915. For cricket uniforms 1934-1937 see Mary-Lou Johnston and Marion K. Stell, *A Guide to the Australian Women's Cricket Collection 1934–1937*, National Museum of Australia, 1990.

Tennis fashions are from *SMH*, 25 July 1935. For lifting of shorts ban see *SMH*, 7 December 1933. For the Baptist reaction see *SMH*, 22 July 1935. Kennedy is from 1938 Oral History Project interview, National Library of Australia. For Edith Robinson and the sewing machine see *Women's Athletics in Australia: Official History of the Australian Women's Amateur Athletic Union*, p. 14. For sweat suits see *Argus*, 30 July 1936. The YWCA wrap is quoted in *AWW*, 16 December 1933. Opperman is from *Sportswoman*, 1 August 1936, p. 22. For bathing costumes and councillors see *AWW*, 14 October 1933, p. 1 and 13. For 1936 Olympians see *Argus*, 30 July 1936.

Tasmanian badminton players are from *AWW*, 1 September 1934. The fencing regulations are from *SMH*, 1 October 1935. Baseballers are from *AWW*, 9 June 1934. For English golfers see *AWW*, 11 May 1935. For bowls regulations and the low-backed dress see *SMH*, 15 January 1934. Ryan is from Cawley, *Evonne*, p. 151. For sportswear fashions see *Home*, 1 December 1921 p. 52 and 1 December 1923, p. 44. See advertisements for Dunlop, *AWW*, 20 November 1937; Parker, *Home*, 1 April 1932; Prestige, *Home*, 1 July 1934; Kestos, *Home*, 1 March 1934. For accessories see *SMH*, 21 July 1936. For gifts see *SMH*, 1 December 1936.

See 1940s advertisements, Jantzen, *AWW*, 20 November 1948, p. 38; La Mode, *AWW*, 18 December 1948, p. 38. The cricket association's ruling is from *Argus*, 17 December 1947. For Magee see *Sunday Herald*, 8 February 1953. For Margaret Court see *Margaret Smith Story*, p. 163–4. For Blundell see *AWW*, 14 March 1962. Froud's letter is from *SMH*, 21 September 1953. For sunshine yellow see *Sunday Herald*, 16 March 1952. For 1974 Games uniform and McGill see *Age*, 18 September 1973. For *Australian* comment see 22 September 1973.

CHAPTER 10: MEDICAL AND SOCIAL HURDLES

For the 1928 Olympics and reintroduction of the 800 metres see Adrianne Blue, *Faster, Higher, Further: Women's Triumphs and Disasters at the Olympics*, London, Virago 1988. *The London Morning Post* is quoted in the *SMH*, 1 February 1928. Mussolini is from *SMH*, 12 January 1934. The WAAA medical inquiry is from *SMH*, 8 March 1934, results from *SMH*, 19 January 1938. For Abrahams see *SMH*, 1 February 1935. For CWA proposal see *SMH*, 12 April 1929. Dr Anderson is from *AWW*, 5 January 1935, p. 21. The Victorian ruling is from *Argus*, 5 October 1937. Rowing examinations are from *The Sportswoman*, 15 March 1937, p. 38. For cricketers see *AWW*, 14 September 1935. For military rejections see W. Vamplew (ed), *Australians: Historical Statistics, Sydney 1987*, p. 414. Restoration of broad jump is from *Argus*, 23 November 1938. For athletes heart see *AWW*, 7 March 1936. For Kellermann see *Daily Mirror*, 24 January 1983, *People*, 23 May 1951; for Fraser see Dawn Fraser, *Gold Medal Girl: The Confessions of an Olympic Champion*, Lansdowne Press, Melbourne 1965, p. 15; for McClements see *Walkabout*, December 1969, p. 48; for Bult see *Argus*, 17 May 1949 p. 8; for Hammond see *SMH*, 28 November 1935; for Cottee see Kay Cottee, *First Lady*, Pan Books Sydney 1989, p. 29-30. Norman is quoted in *SMH*, 8 February 1939. For Life Saving see *SMH*, 11 March 1953. For Land Army see Sue Hardisty, *Thanks Girls & Goodbye*, Viking O'Neil, Melbourne 1991. For the Qld ban see *Daily Mirror*, 1 September 1988. Boyle quotation is from Boyle, *Rage*, p. 34.

For Kellermann see Annette Kellermann, *Physical Beauty How to Keep It*, New York 1918, p. 241. Dawn Fraser's recollections are from *Winning Women*, Wide World of Sports video, Channel 9, 1990. *Handbook to Health* was in the 19 March 1958 edition of the *AWW*. For Fraser see *Gold Medal Girl*, p.

62–3. For Goolagong see Cawley, *Evonne*, p. 108. For Cottee see Cottee, *First Lady*, p. 210—20.

For Jackson see *AWW*, 25 August 1954, p. 21 and *Australian*, 26 September 1973. Blankers-Koen is from *SMH*, 10 January 1949. Mason is from *Newcastle Herald*, 16 October 1964. For the rumours surrounding Fraser see Fraser, *Gold Medal Girl*, p. 117.

See booklet, *Healthy Motherhood*, NSW Department of Public Health, 1943. For Goolagong see *Woman's Day*, 23 September 1981, p. 4. For De Lacy see *Pix*, 22 November 1941, p. 3–5. The *SMH* article on Curry is 5 April 1990. Stephenson is from *Newcastle Herald*, 21 November 1975. Goolagong is from *Woman's Day*, 23 September 1981.

For Strickland's career see *West Australian*, 5 October 1987, *Daily Mirror*, 11 March 1985, *People* , 15 February 1984, *Portfolio*, May 1988 and L. Hunt (ed), *Westralian Portraits*, University of Western Australia Press 1979, p. 247–52. See also 'Kids a Bonus for Mums in the Fast Lane', *SMH*, 12 July 1988. For Goolagong see Cawley, *Evonne*, p. 98.

For older women's sporting achievements see *SMH*, 3 August 1933, 28 August 1939, *Pix*, 15 June 1940, *SMH*, 21 April 1940, *Sun Herald*, 11 December 1955, 24 June 1956, *AWW*, 14 December 1960, *Canberra Chronicle*, 20 February 1990. For Marjorie Jackson see *Canberra Times*, 21 July 1990.

Mrs Thompson is from *Sydney Sun*, 10 April 1985. *The Australian Women's Mirror* is quoted in Rhonda Bushby, 'Decades of Sport and the Shape of Australian Womanhood', *Fit To Play*, Sydney 1985, p. 74. The quotation from Cades is from p. 33–4. For advertisements see: Veet, *Home*, 1 February 1929, *SMH*, 11 January 1938; Ven-Yusa, *Home*, 1 May 1926. Sportsgirls hints are from *Everylady's Journal*, 1 April 1926. Odorono is from *Home*, 2 January 1928. See 'In Defence of Women Athletes', *SMH*, 10 October 1938. Goolagong is from Cawley, *Evonne*, p. 141. Reducing theory is from Katie Holmes, 'Women's Diaries', *Talking History*, ABC Radio, 1990/11. For advertisements see soap, *Everylady's Journal*, 1 April 1926; tonic, *Everylady's Journal* , 1 May 1933. For Newman see *SMH*, 7 April 1936. Arnott's ad is from *Home*, 1 December 1936. Reducing suit is from *SMH*, 18 September 1949. Malvern Star is from *Pix*, 24 September and 22 October 1938. For diving see *SMH*, 20 November 1939. Billiards is from *AWW*, 25 August 1934. Badminton is from *SMH*, 16 July 1953. For cosmetics in cricket see *Adelaide Advertiser*, 23 December 1932. The Medical Journal survey is quoted in *SMH*, 20 December 1957. For *Sun Herald* see 30 September 1956. For Fraser's statistics see Fraser, *Gold Medal Girl*, p. 46.

CHAPTER 11: APPROPRIATE ARENAS, 1945–1970

For migrants and introduction of new sports see *Sun Herald*, 3 January 1960. For Berger see *SMH*, 10 June 1950. For Zaminko and Snarskye see *SMH*, 9 September 1953. For fencers see *SMH*, 12 September and 1 October 1950. For Winter see *Teenagers' Weekly*, supplement to *AWW*, 10 June 1968. For Jui Jitsu see *Argus*, 28 May 1949. Women at boxing is from P. Corris, *Lords of the Ring*, Cassell Australia 1980, p. 102. Fellows is from C. Stannage, *The People of Perth*, Perth City Council, 1979, p. 315. Sparring is from *SMH*, 21 March 1949. Lindrum is from *Argus*, 19 November 1947 and *Sunday Herald*, 25 January 1953. Jol is from *Teenagers' Weekly*, 15 August 1962. Strickland is from *SMH*, 9 May 1949. The invitation to Moscow is from *Sun Herald*, 5 May 1957.

 For Farrington and fishing see *AWW*, 12 March 1949, *SMH*, 29 January 1949, *Sun Herald*, 13 February 1949. Watkins is from *AWW*, 1 May 1948. NSW Amateur fishing is from *AWW*, 17 December 1952. For Vic yacht club see *Pix*, 16 February 1946, p. 28–9. NZ sailors are from *SMH*, 8 February 1951. Skiing is from *SMH*, 10 December 1948, NZ coach from *SMH*, 2 July 1953. Water skiing is from *Pix*, 1 May 1948, p. 23–4; Leighton is from *AWW*, 14 April 1954.

For Walker see *Sun Herald*, 9 November 1952, 24 November 1957. For motor cycles see *SMH*, 7

January 1951. For Taylour and Wells see *SMH*, 4 December 1952. For Cooper see *AWW*, 29 July 1964. For Redex trial see *AWW*, 7 July 1954. For polocrosse see *Sunday Herald*, 2 August 1953. For Barden see *SMH*, 31 December 1950. For Edwards see *Newcastle Herald*, 8 February 1951. For shooters and Fergusson see *SMH*, 8 October 1950 and 7 October 1951. Life Savers are from *SMH*, 5 February, 11 October 1947, 15 March, 8 April, 27 September 1953, *Newcastle Herald*, 21 October 1947 and 24 March 1949. Marching is from *Newcastle Herald*, 31 August, 20 September, 1 October 1951, 10 October 1953, and 28 September 1954. For bowls see *Argus*, 3 September 1947 and *Sun News Pictorial*, 23 August 1973.

Bush walkers are from *SMH*, 21 September 1945. For Moore see *Daily Mirror*, 11 July 1980. AWAS cycling is from *SMH*, 23 January 1947. For marathon canoe races see *SMH*, 28 October 1954, *Sunday Herald*, 19 October 1952. For McGill see *Sunday Mail*, 6 July 1986, *Newcastle Herald*, 30 September 1967 and *SMH*, 25 June 1986.

For softball see *SMH*, 4 April 1949 and *AWW*, 5 March 1949. For sex and hockey see *Sunday Herald*, 4 October 1953. For Hamilton see *Medical Journal of Australia*, 31 December 1955. For McLarty and cricket see Mary-Lou Johnston and Marion K. Stell, *A Guide to the Australian Women's Cricket Collection 1934–1937*, National Museum of Australia, 1990. For Dive see *SMH*, 17 August 1950. For netball see *SMH*, 3 May 1945. For football see *Pix*, 22 November 1947, *Argus*, 7 July, 22 July and 12 August 1947. For rowing see *SMH*, 28 January 1947, 30 October 1952. For water polo and volleyball see *Pix*, 15 February 1941. For athletics see *Women's Athletics in Australia: Official History of the Australian Women's Amateur Athletic Union*. For Cuthbert at SCG see Cuthbert, *Golden Girl*, p. 70. For Hopman and Smith see *Newcastle Herald*, 28 June 1962, *AWW*, 11 July 1962. For golf see *AWW*, 4 March 1950 and Pollard, *Australian Golf*. For McKay see *Woman's Day*, 24 February 1986, *Canberra Times*, 11 August 1990 and *Daily Mirror*, 6 January 1986.

CHAPTER 12: SHOESTRING SPORTS AND THE ADVERTISING DOLLAR

The chocolate factory survey is from *SMH*, 2 June 1936. For Arnott's sponsorship see *AWW*, 12 August 1933. The *Home* examination is from 1 June 1926. McLarty is from Oral History Interview, Johnston and Stell, *Australian Women's Cricket Collection 1934–1937*, National Museum of Australia, 1990.

For Cottee see Kay Cottee, *First Lady*, Pan Books Sydney 1989, p. 26. The Ford advertisement is from *Home*, 1 October 1925, p. 59. Hay and golf is from *Home*, 1 March 1921, p. 81. The 1937 women's cricket contract is in the Amy Hudson Collection, National Museum of Australia. For Horderns see *Home*, 2 November 1931. For Barry see *AWW*, 6 November 1937 and *Newcastle Herald*, 27 July 1937. For Vincents see *AWW*, 10 April 1948. For Aspro and Bent see *AWW*, 1 May 1948, p. 40. For the Milk Board see *SMH*, 7 July 1936. For Horlicks see *SMH*, 19 May 1936. For Dawn Fraser see *AWW*, 13 April 1946. For All-Bran see *AWW*, 13 April 1935. For Byrd see *AWW*, 2 September 1950, p. 56. Rinso ads are from *AWW*, 1946. Malvern Star is from *AWW*, 14 September 1946. Botha, Ruckle and Martin are quoted in *SMH*, 24 November 1990.

CHAPTER 13: PLAYING WITH THE PRESS

The survey is from *Women, Sport and the Media: A Report to the Federal Government from the Working Group on Women in Sport*, AGPS, Canberra 1985. For Preddey see *Mosman Daily*, 11 January 1983. For Commins see Oral History Interview, Mary-Lou Johnston and Marion K. Stell, *A Guide to the Australian Women's Cricket Collection 1934–1937*, National Museum of Australia, 1990. For radio golf clubs see *Argus*, 23 April 1936.

For Spillane see Margot Hilton, *Women on Men*, McPhee Gribble/Penguin 1987, p.116–33. For other sports journalists see 'In Sport, Women are Second-Class Citizens', *Wel-Informed*, No 181, August 1988, p. 17–23; 'The Last Male Bastion', *Look & Listen*, August 1985. On media coverage of women's sport see for example: 'Puerile Coverage of Women's Sport Blasted', *Australian*, 29 January 1985; 'Striking a Blow', *Hobart Mercury*, 25 July 1984; and 'Sportswomen Battle on in Silence', *Brisbane Courier Mail*, 17 August 1983. Statistics are from Women's Sport Promotion Unit, *Fact Sheet*, No 1. *Woman Golfer* is from No 1, 1990 edition.

CHAPTER 14: DOUBLE DISCRIMINATION: ABORIGINAL SPORTSWOMEN

For May and Marion Chalker see Pollard, *Australian Golf*, p. 1–2. For Evonne Goolagong-Cawley see *Woman's Day*, 15 July 1985, 6 October 1986, 30 May 1989, *SMH*, 5 July 1990, *Sunday Tasmanian*, 15 January 1989, *Sydney Sun*, 24 November 1977, *Melbourne Herald*, 21 November 1977, *Brisbane Courier Mail*, 5 October 1987, *Hobart Mercury*, 12 July 1980, *Sunday Telegraph*, 13 July 1980, *AWW*, 31 October 1979, and Cawley, *Evonne*. For Khan see *Sunday Telegraph*, 5 May 1985. For Freeman see *Active*, Winter 1990. For other Aboriginal sportswomen see C. Tatz, *Aborigines in Sport*, Australian Society for Sports History, No. 3, 1987 and B. Harris, *The Proud Champions*, Sydney 1989.

CHAPTER 15: EQUAL OR DIFFERENT

'Too Good at Games' from *AWW*, 24 November 1934, p. 5. For bowls and cricket during Second World War see *SMH*, 15 May, 8 June 1945, *Argus*, 25 February 1941. For Walker and Rutherford see *Sun Herald*, 24 November 1957, 9 November 1952. For motor cyclists see *SMH*, 7 January 1951. For Wells and Taylour see *SMH*, 4 December 1952 and *Sunday Herald*, 12 October 1955. 'How Strong is Our Weaker Sex?' is from *Sun Herald*, 2 December 1956. For McGill see *Newcastle Herald*, 4 January 1968, *Daily Mirror*, 27 August 1984. For Stephenson see *Daily Telegraph*, 30 September 1976. For 'scientific' comparisons see for example 'Woman v Man in the Sporting Field', *Good Weekend, SMH*, 7 June 1980; 'Yes Virginia, There is a Difference', *Age*, 28 May 1980.

For Kellermann see Annette Kellermann, *Physical Beauty How to Keep It*, New York 1918, p. 85. For Inwood see *Argus*, 24 January 1938; for Sams see *Walkabout*, June 1938; for Geerts see *Sydney Sun*, 5 April 1988; for Kennedy see *Melbourne Herald*, 27 August 1979; for Kearney see *Sunday Telegraph*, 4 June 1978. Hawke is from *Woman Golfer*, No 1, 1990, p. 21.

CHAPTER 16: THE IMPACT OF FEMINISM, 1970–1990

Vida Goldstein is from Flint and Rheinberg, *Fair Play*, p. 93. For powerlifting see *Active*, Winter 1990. For Sommerville see *SMH*, 25 June 1983. For VFL see *Age*, 4 January 1986 and *Ms Muffet*, June 1981. For soccer see *SMH*, 8 June 1973, 13 May 1978, *Australasian Post*, 10 September 1981. For Murray see *Active*, Winter 1989. For touch see *National Times*, 27 July–2 August 1984. For hang gliding see *Australian*, 9 December 1982. For parachuting see *AWW*, May 1986, *Canberra Times*, 9 December 1971. For surfing see *Australian Magazine*, 3–4 December 1988. For triathlons see *Australian*, 16 March 1984. For Spiers see *Australian*, 29 December 1987. For Cottee see Kay Cottee, *First Lady*, Pan Books Sydney 1989. For motor racing see *AWW*, 16 April, 8 October 1980, *Australian*, 23 April 1984, *Woman's Day*, 30 March 1981, *Daily Telegraph*, 3 March 1978.

For 'Problems of Being a Woman and a Winner' see *SMH*, 21 June 1973. For Nunn see *Melbourne*

Herald, 2 October 1984. For Goolagong and Court see Cawley, *Evonne*, p. 69 & 156. For golf and Stephenson see *Australasian Post*, 25 December 1986, *Woman's Day*, 24 May 1988, *Sydney Sun*, 2 March 1978, *AWW*, April 1983, *People*, 16 December 1985. For Lock see *Melbourne Herald*, 6 October 1981. For Kennedy see *Australian*, 22 June 1978.

For netball see Anne Sargeant, *Grace and Glory*, Hutchinson Sydney 1989. See also *National Times*, 9–15 December 1983, *New Idea*, 23 July 1988, *Age*, 8 June 1988, *Australian*, 11–12 April 1981. For hockey see *Age*, 13 April 1988, *Adelaide Advertiser*, 11 June 1988, *SMH*, 3 February 1990. For basketball see *Australian*, 27 September 1988. For volleyball see *Daily Telegraph*, 14 June 1981. For lacrosse see *Hobart Mercury*, 11 August 1978, *Canberra Times*, 18 February 1990. For waterpolo see *Australian Fitness and Training*, v. 4, 1989, *National Times*, 12–18 October 1984. For rowing see *Age*, 18 July 1988 and *Canberra Times*, 23 July 1988. For squash see *SMH*, 9 June 1990. For skating see *Melbourne Herald*, 27 April 1979, *AWW*, 19 September 1979.

For Newport bowlers see *SMH*, 1 September 1990. For Pam O'Neill see *Newcastle Herald*, 1 March 1974. For sport and the law see Deborah Healey, *Sport and the Law*, NSWUP, 1989 and G. Kelly, *Sport and the Law: An Australian Perspective*, Law Book Company 1987. See 'Girls Who Don't Play Sport Low Achievers', *Australian*, 27–28 October 1984; 'Women or Wimps', *SMH*, 13 September 1988. For Sportswomen of Excellence Committee see *SMH*, 11 September 1990.

For other views on women and sport in the last ten years see for example: Dot Browne, 'Women in Sport: Why Are So Few Participating?', *Fun Runner*, February–March 1983; Lois Bryson, 'Engendering Competition: Perspectives on Sport', *Scarlet Woman*, Summer 1988–89; Margaret Pewtress, 'Women's Sport in Australia — Now is the Time!', *ACHPER Journal*, June 1987; Carol Natsis, 'Women in Sport: Winners or Losers?', *Reader's Digest*, March 1986; Lois Bryson, 'Sport and the Oppression of Women', *ANZJS*, November 1983; Libby Darlison, 'If We Don't Who Will', *Women in Action Conference Report*, 1985.

INDEX

PICTORIAL SOURCES

Frontis: Percy Spence, *Women Lifesavers, Manly Beach*, 1910. Watercolour on paper, 18.4 x 27.2; page 5: 7127; page 7: Bicentennial Copying Project (BCP) 06066; page 10: 06839; page 19: from A.D. Ellis, *History of the Royal Melbourne Golf Club*, Melbourne 1941; page 20: BCP 06064; page 28: Media Production Unit, Resources Services, NSW Department of Education; page 32: BCP 00751; page 36: BCP 06166; page 38: 01849; page 39: BCP 01023; page 40: 00815; page 46: BCP 02941; page 50: BCP 02104; page 51: BCP 00518; page 61: BCP 00947; page 63: BCP 02743; page 69: BCP 01901; page 70: BCP 06669; page 76: BCP 05844; 05612; page 77: Fine Arts Press; page 79: Margaret Preston, *Women's Sport No. 1: Yo-Yo*, woodblock print, 8.7 x 4.6cm, 1934; *Women's Sport No. 2: The hiker*, woodblock print, 8.0 x 6.9cm, 1934; *Women's Sport No. 3: The cricketer*, woodblock print, 5.0 x 5.0 cm, 1934. Reproduced by permission of Permanent Trustee Company Limited, Sydney — Trustee of the Estate Late Margaret Preston; page 81: courtesy National Union of Rail Workers of Australia; page 84: Hicks Collection. Photograph by A.W. Emmerton; page 87: 44083; page 89: photograph by W.A. Munz, BCP 06972; page 94: Neg 6676; page 97: 44081; page 99: 39716; page 110: from *Australians: A Historical Library*; page 116: Australian Consolidated Press (ACP); page 120: ACP; page 123: ACP; page 143: BCP 03942; page 145: BCP 03940; page 146: ACP; page 148: BCP 03395; page 151: photograph by A. Costelow, BCP 04134; page 152: BCP 03690; page 156: BCP 00838; page 157: BCP 06062; page 163: BCP 05213; page 176: BCP 01802; page 181: ACP; page 185: ACP; page 200: ACP; page 201: ACP; page 204: ACP; page 206: photograph by L. Jenkin; page 208: ACP; page 211: ACP; page 237: ACP; page 249 and 250 from *Australians: A Historical Library*; page 252: courtesy Sally Penson.